The Complete Book of Personal Letter-Writing and Modern Correspondence

The Complete Book of Personal Letter-Writing and Modern Correspondence

Lassor A. Blumenthal

DOUBLEDAY & COMPANY, INC.
GARDEN CITY, NEW YORK

Library of Congress Catalog Card Number 68-18080

Printed in the United States of America

TO SUSAN

Acknowledgments

I am grateful to the many people who contributed their time and their knowledge to this book.

The chapter on business letters owes much to:

John P. Brion, Director of Communications, and Mrs. Marjane Cloke, The Mutual Life Insurance Company of New York; John Hilgert, Credit Manager, Lord & Taylor; Neil R. Gahagan, Manager, Public Relations, American Machine and Foundry Co.; Henry Lloyd, Manager, Press Relations, Institute of Life Insurance; Charles C. Clarke, Assistant General Manager, Insurance Information Institute; C. L. Christiernin, Public Relations Department, Metropolitan Life Insurance Co.; Gene Jagust, General Electric Co.; Richard Cannon, Royal McBee Corp.; L. D. Stone, Customer Relations Department, and George Mainardi, Manager, Customer Relations, Trans World Airlines; C. M. Rigsbee, Manager, Product Performance, RCA Sales Corp.; Daniel V. Duff, Manager, Policy Service Department, The Equitable Life Assurance Society of the United States; Pat Cody, Pan American World Airways; Theodore O. Cron, Washington, D. C.; Joseph D. Blumenthal, Scituate, Mass.

For his help in the chapter on classified advertising, I'm indebted to Paul Schulz, of the Indianapolis *Star and News.* And to the *New York Times,* which provided a wealth of information for this chapter, I'm particularly grateful.

The chapter dealing with the communications media represents the help of many people, including John Illo, Avon, N. J.; Martin Isaacs, New York, N. Y.; Dr. H. H. Gold, American Cyanamid Co.; Ellen M. MacKinnon, American Broadcasting Company; the *New York Times;* Mrs. Ray E. Lee, Jr., Forest Hills, N. Y.; Kay Cole, National Broadcasting

Company; Leonard Spinrad, Columbia Broadcasting System; Marylois P. Vega, *Time* magazine; *Good Housekeeping* magazine; *True* magazine; Patricia Johnson, New York *Daily News;* Charles S. Steinberg, CBS Television Network; Lever Brothers Co.; Colgate Palmolive Co.

Many officials supplied helpful information for the material in the chapter on government agencies. I am grateful to Harold R. Lewis, Director of Information, U. S. Department of Agriculture; Henry Scharer, Director, Office of Public Information, Department of Commerce; William E. Odom, Director, Information Services, Office of the Assistant Secretary of Defense; Robert M. Ball, Commissioner, Department of Health, Education, and Welfare, Social Security Administration; Wallace F. Janssen, Director, Office of Public Information, Department of Health, Education, and Welfare, Food and Drug Administration; Harvey A. Bush, Director of Public Information, Department of Health, Education, and Welfare; George E. Robinson, Deputy Administrative Assistant Secretary, Department of the Interior; Jack Rosenthal, Assistant Director, Public Information, Department of Justice; John W. Leslie, Director, Office of Information, Publications, and Reports, Department of Labor; Donald A. Campbell, Assistant Special Assistant to the Postmaster General, Post Office Department; James T. Rush, Office of Public Services, Department of State; Dixon Donnelley, Assistant to the Secretary of the Treasury; Howard Bingham, Chief, News Division, Office of Information Services, Federal Aviation Agency; George O. Gillingham, Chief, Office of Reports and Information, Federal Communications Commission; Gale P. Gotschall, Consumer Relations Representative, Federal Trade Commission; and F. R. Hood, Director, Information Service, Veterans Administration.

My special thanks also go to Irving Wallace, the author of *The Chapman Report, The Prize, The Man,* and *The Plot;* and to Peter Detmold, of New York City's East 49th Street Association.

The chapter dealing with letters to congressmen and senators could not have been written without the help of Congressmen Leslie C. Arends, of Illinois; Robert W. Kastenmeier, of Wisconsin; and John V. Lindsay (currently Mayor Lindsay) of New York; and Senators Thomas H. Kuchel, of California, and Carl T. Curtis, of Nebraska.

Help of many kinds for the chapter on landlord-tenant letters came from Julius Elkin, Chief, Administration Division, and Irving Scavron, Management Coordinator, both of the Management Department, New York City Housing Authority; Mr. Frank Lowe, formerly head of real-estate–tenant relations for the Metropolitan Life Insurance Co., and from the Mutual Redevelopment Housing Association of New York.

Mrs. Muriel Glazer, of Henri Bendel, and Miss Susan C. Callender, of Cartier, Inc., supplied information that I found most helpful for the chapter on social correspondence.

The chapter on organization publicity owes much to Don Dilworth, of the YMCA of Greater New York; to the League of Women Voters, and to the Bureau of Newspaper Advertising.

For providing information for the chapter on schools and colleges, I'm indebted to Harry Colman, Director of College Admissions, Columbia University; and Arnold Goren, the effervescent Dean of Admissions, New York University. James Stern, Headmaster, Columbia Grammar School, was especially generous in permitting me to draw extensively from the guide to college admissions which his school provides to its students.

To Harold Kuebler, my editor, I owe enormous gratitude for the enormous patience which he has exhibited. Editors so intuitively understanding are rare.

Finally, I'm delighted to acknowledge the help of Miss Elaine Fox, whose intelligence and secretarial skills are exceeded only by her unfailing good nature.

Many others have contributed valuable ideas and suggestions to the book. If I have not mentioned them, it is not because their contributions are small, but because neither my memory nor my records are perfect.

Table of Contents

The
Complete Book of
Personal Letter-Writing
and
Modern Correspondence

Chapter One

THE ABC'S OF GOOD LETTER-WRITING

If you're a typical American, you're in trouble. At least, you're in trouble when it comes to writing a large percentage of your letters. For, the chances are that a good share of them are going to people who know nothing–and care less–about you.

Consider how it was in our parents' and grandparents' time. Most of their letters were written to their families and to friends. Occasionally, to be sure, the head of the household might sit down and dash off a stern letter to the local newspaper stating in no uncertain terms that the condition of the streets, or the nation, was disgraceful. But for the most part, personal correspondence consisted of letters to people whom our forebears knew reasonably well.

Now, think about your own correspondence. Undoubtedly, some of it is still personal. But the chances are that a great deal is written to strangers. Here are a few typical situations; undoubtedly, you'll find several of them reflected in your own life.

The Smiths have a sixteen-year-old son with a fine scholastic record. They write to a college inquiring about scholarship possibilities. If they know the right things to say, they may receive a letter and a number of forms, one of which will request them to have friends send in character references.

Question: What should the Smiths say in their original letter in order to make a favorable impression on the school officials? How should they fill in the forms? Which of their friends should they ask to write references, if they expect to impress the school? And what should the references say?

A year ago, Mr. Smith bought a power mower from a local retailer. Two days after his warranty expired, the engine housing broke. The retailer says he can't do anything about it.

Question: Can Mr. Smith get a free repair by writing a letter to the manufacturer? He may be able to if he knows the right things to say.

The Smiths' daughter is graduating from college, and would like to work in Washington for the government.

Question: Should she write to her congressman or her senator or to some federal office? What should she say?

Mrs. Smith's brother recently died and left his small business to her. She'd like to find someone to manage it or buy it.

Question: If she puts a classified ad in the newspaper, what's the best thing to say?

Mr. Smith has just received a letter from the Internal Revenue Service, saying that he owes $153 in back taxes. Mr. Smith is sure they're wrong, but he doesn't want to waste a day arguing with an agent at the local IRS office.

Question: How can he straighten it out by mail?

In each of these cases, the Smiths are writing not to an individual, but to an institution. And that is the foundation of this book. For today, much of our life is influenced by, and depends upon, impersonal institutions. What this book will do, chapter by chapter, is suggest how to influence those institutions by mail—how to get them to answer your questions, or persuade them to do whatever it is that you want done.

MAKING YOUR LETTER EASY TO UNDERSTAND

Writing successfully to virtually any institution, or any public figure, requires an understanding of one fact: the person you're writing to is harried. He doesn't have time to do his job as well as he'd like; his boss is on his back; his peers are wondering if he really knows his business; and his subordinates, he is sure, are either incompetent or angling for his desk.

As a result, anything you can say in your letter that will make his job easier will be of enormous help in getting a satisfactory answer.

What *can* you do to make things easier for him? There are three things, and they can be called the ABC's of good letter writing. ABC stands for Accuracy, Brevity, and Clarity. Let's take a close look at each.

ACCURACY

Accuracy is very important because the person you're writing to does not, in all probability, know you, nor is he likely to be familiar with the circumstances which caused you to write. Therefore, be as specific as possible, giving all the pertinent information as accurately as you can.

For example, if you're complaining about a product you've bought that has become defective, include all the pertinent facts–where you bought it, the date you bought it, the model number of the product, if it has one. (For a more detailed discussion, see Chapter Two.)

Remember, much of today's institutional business is run by the number. Computers shape the activities of a surprisingly large number of institutions, from setting up college classroom schedules to renewing your magazine subscription.

I recently ran across an excellent example of just how firmly we are all locked into this situation. Mrs. Carmela P. Lare, a friend of mine, received a renewal form for her driver's license. A clerk in the license bureau had apparently made an error, and the computer-produced form listed her middle name as her last name.

When she notified the bureau of the mistake and asked them to correct it, they sent her a computer-produced change-of-name form, along with a computer-produced form letter saying that since she had changed her name, she should now send them her correct name, along with proof that she *had* changed her name legally. She had not, of course, changed her name since her marriage some twenty years before. But, as far as the license bureau was concerned, she must have changed it, since the computer said so.

She finally managed to straighten out the matter by sending them an old library card with her correct name on it, as proof that she did exist. Her license still shows the incorrect name, but she is fairly certain that in three years, when she's due for another renewal, they may admit that she has a right to her own name.

Once we're in a nightmare like this, we can do little but slog on to the end. But, forewarned, we can take steps to avoid it.

Accuracy is a major rock of salvation here. Give the important facts and the pertinent figures correctly, and you may be able to save considerable time and annoyance.

BREVITY

You can take it for granted that the person you're writing to hasn't time to wade through a long letter. If he receives a piece of correspondence that runs more than a page, or at most, two, he'll probably slip it at the bottom of his pile of incoming mail, with the thought that he'll look at it when he has more time.

Don't blame him. You'd probably do the same. So, pare your letter down to essentials, eliminating every sentence that will not help the letter's recipient to help you.

As a general rule, you can probably organize your letter into three parts:

1 Tell why you're writing.
2 Give the important facts.
3 Describe what you'd like the recipient to do.

1 Telling the recipient why you're writing immediately lets him know what's on your mind. It gives him, so to speak, a framework in which to read your letter, or a signpost telling him where he's to focus his attention.

For example, suppose you were writing to a television station to complain about the contents of a certain show. A good way to begin would be a simple declaration of that fact; for example, "I object strongly to the slurring remarks you made about civil service workers on the program 'Dr. Kildare' which was shown last night on Channel 4."

Or, suppose you're writing to urge a congressman to vote "Yes" on a certain measure. You might start: "Your support of HR 347, the immigration bill, will help strengthen the traditions on which this country was founded."

Contrast this with less direct methods. The recipient will wonder what it's all about if you write, in the case of the television station: "I feel there is too much joking about the civil service in your programs," or, in the case of the congressman, "We need to strengthen our constitutional heritage."

2 Giving the important facts to support your first sentence will show that you're businesslike and thoughtful. Limit the facts to the one or two or three which are most important. If you give a long string of reasons why, the letter becomes boring and irritating. *Remember: you don't want to irritate the reader, you want to get him on your side.* One excellent, subtle way of doing it is to keep the letter clear and simple.

A practice that I have found useful is to put each of my reasons or arguments in a separate paragraph, preceded by a number. Thus, a letter to the editor of a newspaper might read:

> I believe we should install street lights at the corner of 16th Avenue and A Street.
>
> There are several reasons why this is desirable:
>
> First: It is the only block in the area without overhead illumination.
>
> Second: There have been three nighttime accidents there in the past year.
>
> Third: The city has promised in the past that this would be done, but so far, there has been no action.

3 Finally, describing what you'd like the recipient to do gives him something to act upon. In preparing this book, I've spoken to scores of administrators in business, government, and education. They told me repeatedly that frequently a letter will confuse them because the writer doesn't say specifically what action he wants taken.

If you're complaining to a company, tell them what it is you want of them: "I believe you should refund my purchase price," or, "I want to exchange this for an undamaged model."

If you're writing to a government agency: "Please send me the correct forms," or "Can you tell me where I can find this information?"

The guidelines are worth repeating:

Why are you writing?
What facts support your reasons for writing?
What should the reader do?

CLARITY

It is difficult to tell somebody, "Go out and be clear." It is like saying, "Be funny." But, if you follow the suggestions given above for accuracy and brevity, you'll have gone a long way toward achieving clarity.

Here are a few additional suggestions which will make your letters—and any other writing you do—more easily understood.

1 Keep your paragraphs short. Frequent paragraphing breaks up the solid look of a letter, and even if it isn't easy to understand, the indentations make it *look* easier, and give the reader courage to go on. As a general rule, try to keep typewritten paragraphs under ten lines. Handwritten letters might well be paragraphed every five or six lines.

2 Keep your sentences short. Your harried reader simply does not have great powers of concentration, and even if he does, he'll probably be too busy to exercise them. If any sentence runs more than four lines, try to break it up into two shorter sentences.

3 Keep your words short. Don't try to impress the reader with long or unusual words or phrases. You may not be using them correctly, in the first place. In the second place, the reader will tend to be put off by them.

The General Services Administration of the Federal Government has published a booklet called "Plain Letters," to help Government employees improve their correspondence. One page lists common, roundabout phrases, and suggests shorter alternatives. I reprint it here because the disease is not limited to government correspondents. The words in parentheses are the ones to use.

In regard to (about, concerning)
With regard to (about, concerning, on)
In relation to (toward, to)
In connection with (of, in, on)
On the part of (for, among)
With reference to (on, about, concerning)
In view of (because, since)
In the event of (if)
In order to (to)
On behalf of (for)
In accordance with (with, by)
By means of (with, by)
In the case of (if, in)
In the matter of (in)
In the amount of (for)
For the purpose of (for)
In the majority of instances (usually)
In a number of cases (some)
On a few occasions (occasionally)
In the time of (during)

At the end of this chapter, you'll find another list, also taken from "Plain Letters," of hackneyed, overlong, and misused words. Familiarize yourself with them and you'll have taken another step on your journey to clarity.

LETTERHEAD STYLES

How important is a letterhead? It depends. Usually, you probably won't need one to accomplish your goal. After all, the reader is more concerned with what you say than with how the stationery looks.

On the other hand, the overall appearance of the letter can be enhanced if there's a good-looking name-and-address at the top. It's a bit like the difference between an apprentice seaman and an admiral. You know they are both created equal. But you can't help being impressed by all that gold braid. Similarly, the man who reads your letter may be enough impressed by the letterhead to give it more attention.

A businessman recently told me a story that illustrates this point. On a trip from New York to Florida, one tire of a new set of four blew out. Upon returning home, he asked the dealer for a new tire. The dealer refused, but offered to give the man a partial refund of the money he'd paid for that tire. My acquaintance felt that this was unsatisfactory; he felt he'd been sold defective merchandise, and that he should not be penalized. Letters written on his company letterhead to the local sales manager, and then to the vice-president in charge of sales, elicited offers that were no more satisfactory than the dealer's offer.

Then, my friend became wily. From the tire company's annual report, he obtained the names of the board of directors. He looked up each one in *Who's Who,* and found that one belonged to a club of which he was a member. Marching off to the club, he dashed off a handwritten letter to this man, on the *club's* stationery. He did not mention that he was a member of the club—he simply let the letterhead speak for itself.

Within a week, he received a telephone call from the vice-president in charge of sales, suggesting that if he now went to his local dealer, the company would be pleased to give him—not just a replacement—but a whole set of new tires.

Obviously, this gambit will not work in every similar situation, but it does show that there are cases where the appropriate letterhead will work wonders.

Therefore, as a general rule, I would suggest that a good-looking letterhead on good-quality paper is an asset in almost any institutional correspondence.

Now, how do you go about obtaining a good-looking letterhead? The simplest method is to visit a stationery store, or the stationery department of a department store, and browse through their sample books. You'll find a wealth of letterhead designs, and most of them will be satisfactory for your purposes. I would suggest that you keep the following points in mind when making your selection:

1 Unless you have an excellent sense of design, choose a letterhead that is simple and clear, and devoid of embellishments.

2 Select an ink that is dark, and contrasts well with the paper. Black ink on white paper probably offers the best contrast.

3 Choose a legible type. Either block letters or a manuscript type are satisfactory, as long as the reader can take them in at a glance.

You will probably find, when you go to make your selection, that for almost the same price as a printed letterhead, you can buy one with raised printing, which resembles engraved print. This process, known as thermography, has become so popular that I shall probably sound like a crank if I enter an objection to it. But let me enter the objection, anyway.

I object to it because it is often poorly printed. Unless the printer exercises great care, the type may not come out as clearly as does engraving. There is a tendency for the fine lines of the print to become blurred, and the overall effect of the stationery is not as impressive as either true engraving or as crisp as a simple, well-executed print job.

My suggestion is that if you can afford an engraved letterhead, by all means, buy it. It looks wonderful and, perhaps just as important, it gives you, the purchaser, a feeling of great prestige at very low cost.

On the other hand, if you feel that engraving is too expensive, then stay with a regular, printed letterhead. As long as your printer is competent, it will be almost impossible from him to do a poor job.

STATIONERY

SIZES

As you know, most business correspondence is conducted on stationery measuring 8½ by 11 inches. Whether you select this size or something a bit smaller is irrelevant insofar as the effectiveness of the correspondence is concerned. In fact, you might find that the next smaller size is much more useful for general purposes. This measures 7¼ by 10½ inches.

Stationery is available not only in single sheets, but also in folded sheets, called double letter. Select the one most appropriate to your own habits. If you tend to write longer letters, the double-letter size is appropriate and practical.

In recent years, smaller sizes have become increasingly popular for personal correspondence, particularly for short notes. One size measures about 7 inches wide by about 4¼ inches high. Even smaller sheets, measuring about 4½ inches wide by 3½ inches, are also widely used. These may be single or double sheets, the single sheets often being of a heavier paper stock, approaching thin cardboard in weight.

Customarily, this smaller stationery carries a monogram or the writer's initials. Double sheets usually bear these in the middle of the front sheet. The message is written on the inside sheets. Single sheets usually have the monogram or initials centered at the upper edge.

It is also appropriate here to make a distinction between formal and informal cards. Informal cards, used for correspondence, may be of almost any color that a good stationer provides. Formal cards, usually used for invitations, expressions of sympathy, announcements, etc., are customarily restricted both in color and weight.

Traditionally, formal cards are white, although ecru may be used on slightly less formal occasions. Two weights are common: parchment, or lightweight cards; and satin, which is somewhat heavier.

A representative of Cartier, Inc., the dizzyingly prestigious purveyor of elegancies to the wealthy, offers these two sensible opinions:

There is no regimented size for cards. The longer the message, the larger the card should be.

Many people choose heavier stock for the larger cards; lighter stock is considered more appropriate for smaller cards.

My last word on stationery size brings us back to the problem of writing to institutions. I suggest that you avoid, if possible, sending a letter on stationery smaller than 4 by 5 inches. While the smaller-dimensioned paper is perfectly satisfactory for short notes to personal friends, it is not suitable for business correspondence. It bespeaks a certain amateurishness which the bureaucrat is likely to disdain. And perhaps more important, it may get lost in his piles of paper.

TYPES OF PAPER

The types of writing paper available to the average American are vast beyond belief. Ranging as they do from inexpensive pads at the drugstore or five-and-dime, to costly sheets that radiate an aura of wealth, one is safest, in offering suggestions, to confine himself to general statements.

First, in paper as in life, you get what you pay for. Inexpensive pads or sets are adequate for social correspondence and for most business correspondence. However, if you hope to make an authoritative first impression, you would be wise to think about a more costly grade of stationery.

Let's consider two broad categories: plain white paper, and fancier, personal stationery.

Plain white paper (or any other color, for that matter) may be categorized by its weight. Excluding airmail stationery, the heavier the weight, the better the paper's quality. As a minimum, I'd suggest that you go no lower than paper designated "16 pound." Anything less tends to feel flimsy and cheap.

Better than 16 pound is 20 pound, which is more opaque, and feels crisper and heavier. Still heavier weights are available at heavier prices.

If you type your letters, you may be especially interested in the so-called "erasable" papers, which several companies manufacture. These papers (they come in several weights) permit you to cleanly erase typewritten errors with a soft pencil eraser. More expensive than non-erasable papers, they almost guarantee that your finished letters will look error-free—assuming that you take the trouble to erase your mistakes.

For social correspondence, wide varieties of paper are available that fit almost any type of personality. Women have the edge on men: one expert told me, "There is no 'proper' any more." This is perhaps stretching it a bit. But the fact is that we are in an era when stationery styles for women have virtually no limits.

Suitable personal stationery of the more costly sort for women ranges from the traditional white, off-white, and pale, almost-white blue, to striking, bold, bright colors. One of America's finest stationery stores provided me with samples of two popular colors. One is bright yellow, with a narrow white border. The other has a narrow forest-green border, with a slightly wider border inside of it (both borders together measuring about one-quarter of an inch in width) and the rest of the paper being a strong, moss green. Both styles are quite attractive.

So far, men have had to eschew such sprightliness. Masculine stationery is usually plain white or ecru. One store that I know of has had some small success selling khaki-colored paper to men. As for borders, they're inappropriate on men's stationery.

ENVELOPES

When you buy stationery, you will also do well to buy envelopes that match the sheets, both in width and texture. Here is another situation where, if you purchase from a reputable stationer, you won't go wrong.

A word may be appropriate about lined envelopes. They certainly add elegance to stationery, and if you can afford this frivolity, enjoy yourself. However, don't be taken in.

Muriel Glazer, a knowedgeable lady who works at Henri Bendel, which is to department stores what Rolls-Royce is to automobiles, tells me that all envelopes have to be lined by hand. So, if a store tries to charge you a higher price for an envelope because it's hand-lined (implying that others are lined by machine), don't you believe it.

FOLDING YOUR STATIONERY

The fewer the folds in your stationery, the better its appearance. Ideally, the width of your sheet will be just slightly less than the width of the envelope. This will enable you to avoid making a bulky little fold at one end of the sheet, which, when it's opened, causes the page to look like a rumpled bed. The following suggestions should take care of your paper-folding problems.

If the paper fits without folding, don't fold it.

If it won't fit without at least one fold, fold it halfway down from the top to the bottom.

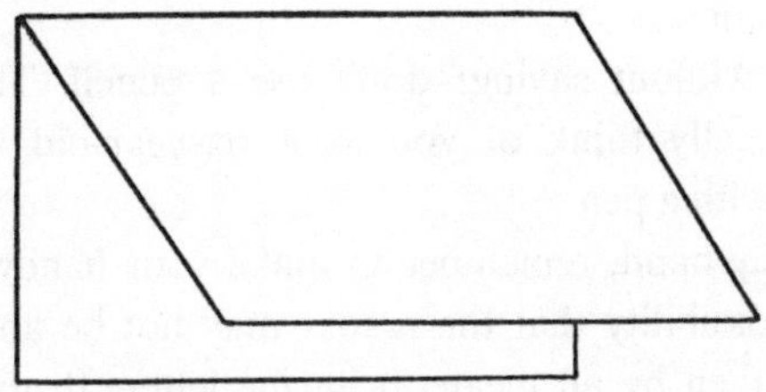

If a single fold won't do the trick, two folds, dividing the paper into equal thirds, are perfectly suitable.

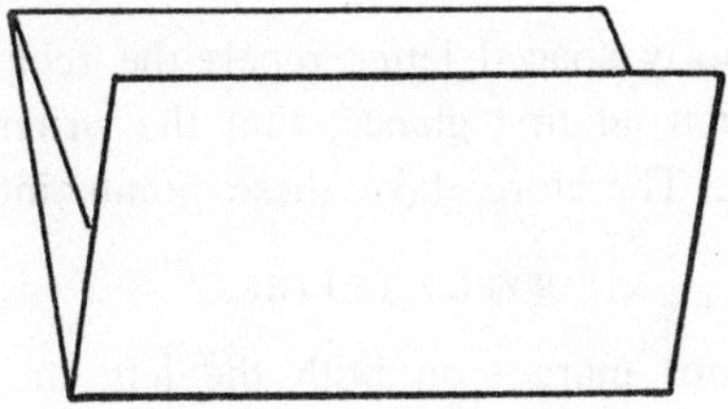

WHAT TO WRITE WITH

In your correspondence with institutions, a major goal is to make the letter as legible as possible, so that the person reading it can get straight to the meat of your problem, without having to first decipher your handwriting.

Obviously, the best way to ensure that this will happen is to type your letter. If a typewriter isn't available, use a pen with black or blue ink. Brighter colors, such as red or green, will call attention, but on the other hand, they set you apart as someone a bit out of the ordinary. The average bureaucrat is likely to think that the person who uses unusual colors doesn't deserve quite the serious consideration that is due to a more somber letter writer.

This is a subtle psychological point, and it is perhaps unwise to try to generalize about what goes on in the mind of any official. But I suspect that by playing it safe with a dark-colored ink, and leaving the contents of your letter to call attention to the importance of your message, you will stand a better chance of securing the kind of attention you want.

It should go without saying: don't use a pencil. The reader will almost automatically think of you as a six-year-old whose mother won't trust him with a pen.

If you write by hand, remember to make your handwriting legible. If there's any possibility that the reader may not be able to decipher your scratches, then by all means print the letter. It may not look as sophisticated as a manuscript hand, but at least it will be readable.

SPACING, LAYOUT, PAGINATION

A crowded, poorly spaced letter repels the recipient; one which gives the impression, at first glance, that the writer is businesslike, compels attention. Therefore, take these points into consideration.

TYPED LETTERS

Leave a generous margin on both the left and right sides. By generous, I mean at least an inch. One and a half inches will be even better.

Single-space your letters, unless, because of their extreme brevity, they'll leave too much white space on the page.

Paragraphs can follow either of two formats: double-spacing between paragraphs, as in the following example:

> I am unable to complete the forms which you sent me because of the following reasons.
>
> First, I have not lived at the above address for three years. I moved from that location in 1962, and since then, have been living in California.

Second, I have not yet received the information which I requested about my income tax payments.

or indenting, as in the following example:

> I am unable to complete the forms which you sent me because of the following reasons.
>
> First, I have not lived at the above address for three years. I moved from that location in 1962, and since then, have been living in California.
>
> Second, I have not yet received the information which I requested about my income tax payments.

I prefer the first format for typewritten letters. Indenting on a typewriter takes time; you have to press the space key three or four times to reach your beginning point. Also, breaking up the masses of black type with a white line between paragraphs makes the page more attractive, and easier to read.

Some letter writers combine both methods, leaving a space between paragraphs *and* indenting. This seems to me to be wholly unnecessary, and I encourage you to avoid this rococo affectation.

HANDWRITTEN LETTERS

Leave a generous margin—about an inch on the left and right.

Leave enough space above and below each line so that the letter does not seem crowded. If your handwriting is not exceptionally large, a good rule of thumb is to imagine that you're writing on standard, lined paper. Lines are usually about three-eighths of an inch apart.

Make a generous indentation at the beginning of your paragraphs.

GENERAL SUGGESTIONS FOR FORMATS OF HANDWRITTEN AND TYPEWRITTEN LETTERS

Avoid crowding at the bottom of the page. Rather than squeeze everything in, run on to a second page; in writing to institutions, the custom is to use a second sheet of paper, rather than write on the back of the first page. As a general rule, leave the last inch of the page clear.

If your stationery consists of a folded sheet of paper, you are faced with the question of whether to make page two the inside left or the inside right page. Genteel tradition dictates the right, so that, if you were writing a letter that covered all four pages, the front sheet would be page one, the back of that would be page three, the inside right would be page two, and the other side of two would be four. Whatever the origin of this system, it is confusing. However, this does not change the fact that it is a very widespread custom.

Therefore, if you're going to write a letter that will cover more than two pages of a folded sheet, I suggest that you number all sheets after the first one at the top of the page, so that the reader will know where to cast his eye next.

MODEL 1:
A STANDARD TYPEWRITTEN LETTER ON LETTERHEAD STATIONERY

RICHARD ROE
321 MAIN STREET
CENTERVILLE, CONN. 06000

January 1, 1999

Mr. John Doe
123 Maiden Lane
New York, N. Y. 10000

Dear Mr. Doe:

I enjoyed meeting you last week, and look forward to our next appointment on Monday, January 23.

In the meantime, I am preparing the material you requested, and shall mail it tomorrow.

Sincerely,

This sample will provide you with a model to follow if you are typing a letter on stationery which is imprinted with your name and address. Note these points:

All lines begin at the left margin.

Double space between:

the date and the recipient's name and address;

the recipient's name and address and the salutation;

the salutation and the first paragraph;

all paragraphs;

the last line of the last paragraph and the complimentary closing—if you use one (see pages 22–24 for comments on complimentary closings).

An acceptable alternative location for the complimentary closing is slightly to the right of center, thus:

```
In the meantime, I am preparing the material you
requested, and shall mail it tomorrow.

                        Sincerely,
```

See page 15 for comments on paragraph indentation.

It is unnecessary to type your name below your signature if it is the same as the name imprinted on the stationery. If you sign your name differently, see pages 24–27 for further comments.

MODEL 2: ALTERNATIVE FORMAT FOR A STANDARD TYPEWRITTEN LETTER ON LETTERHEAD STATIONERY

RICHARD ROE
321 MAIN STREET
CENTERVILLE, CONN. 06000

January 1, 1999

Dear Mr. Doe:

I enjoyed meeting you last week, and look forward to our next appointment on Monday, January 23.

In the meantime, I am preparing the material you requested, and shall mail it tomorrow.

Sincerely,

Mr. John Doe
123 Maiden Lane
New York, N. Y. 10000

Model 2 is identical with Model 1, except that the recipient's name and address appear *below* the signature. This has the virtue of putting first things first: the most important reason for writing the letter is to convey the message. Since the recipient's name and address are primarily for record-keeping purposes, they are relegated to the bottom of the page.

Some highly respectable individuals, including the President of the

United States, prefer this format. If you like it, have no doubts about its propriety.

In this type of letter, the complimentary closing may start at the left margin or slightly to the right of center.

The recipient's name and address should appear about six or seven spaces below the complimentary closing–far enough away so that it doesn't crowd the signature, but not so far that it appears disconnected from the letter. It *always* lines up with the left margin.

MODEL 3:
A STANDARD TYPEWRITTEN LETTER
ON PLAIN STATIONERY

```
January 1, 1999

Mr. John Doe
123 Maiden Lane
New York, N. Y.  10000

Dear Mr. Doe:

I enjoyed meeting you last week, and look forward
to our next appointment on Monday, January 23.

In the meantime, I am preparing the material you
requested, and shall mail it tomorrow.

Sincerely,




Richard Roe
321 Main Street
Centerville, Conn.  06000
```

Model 3 is identical with Model 1, except that the writer's name and address appear below the complimentary closing and a space for the signature. Usually, six lines are ample.

The complimentary closing and the sender's name and address may start at the left margin, as shown here, or they may begin slightly to the right of the center, thus:

```
In the meantime, I am preparing the material you
requested, and shall mail it tomorrow.

                         Sincerely,






                         Richard Roe
                         321 Main Street
                         Centerville, Conn. 06000
```

If you prefer this format, your letter will look neater if the name and address line up with the closing, as shown.

MODEL 4: STANDARD FORMAT FOR A HANDWRITTEN LETTER ON LETTERHEAD STATIONERY

RICHARD ROE
321 MAIN STREET
CENTERVILLE, CONN. 06000

January 1, 1999

Mr. John Doe
123 Maiden Lane
New York, N.Y. 11111

Dear Mr. Doe:

I enjoyed meeting you last week and look forward to our next appointment on Monday, January 23.

In the meantime, I am preparing the material you requested, and shall mail it tomorrow.

Sincerely,

Richard Roe

This is an acceptable format for a handwritten letter on letterhead stationery. Note that the date customarily starts slightly to the right of center, as do the complimentary closing and the signature.

The recipient's name and address and the salutation are at the left margin.

Paragraphs are indented.

If you write on plain stationery, do not forget to put your address directly below your signature, especially if you are writing to someone who may not know you.

TITLES AND SALUTATIONS

Let us move with the times and recognize that ours is an age of democratic informality, a time when even our highest elected officials are known as often by their initials as by their names.

Recognizing this, we can dispense with some of the pomp that has traditionally accompanied the salutations of letters sent to the high and the pretty-high. We will, of course, recognize that a few institutions, such as the church and the military, still retain a certain symbolic majesty, and we will feel uncomfortable if we do not address their functionaries with the traditional salutations of respect.

The Appendix presents a simple set of titles for most of the high functionaries to whom you may have occasion to write.

COMPLIMENTARY CLOSINGS

Complimentary closings should be banned. At one time, in an age that was more elaborate than ours, they reflected the formality of the era. Today, the use of such frivolities as "Very truly yours," "Truly yours," "Yours," "Sincerely yours," is an anomaly and a time-wasting nuisance. To the contention that this is simply one of the amenities of correspondence, indicating a certain sense of courtesy, I answer, "Nonsense." If a letter is courteous in content, it needs no complimentary closing to make it courteous. If it is not courteous, no complimentary closing will make it so.

Perhaps the first man who recognized the silliness of the complimentary closing was the sagacious Benjamin Franklin. I do not have a copy of his delightful letter at hand, but if memory serves me correctly, it was sent to someone who had gravely offended him. The letter went more or less like this:

Sir,
You are my enemy, and
I am
Yours,
Benj. Franklin

Now, some two centuries later, isn't it time we took his hint and recognized that the complimentary closing is long since due a quiet interment?

You will find it difficult to drop the complimentary closing in your letters—bad habits are always difficult to root out. Nevertheless, I urge you to try. It will take courage, but I think you will be surprised at how marvelously, indeed, how almost breathtakingly, courageous you will feel.

And your letters will be better. At first, they may look peculiar. But very soon, you will feel about them the way Detroit automobile designers must have felt when they finally decided, a few decades back, to eliminate running boards. It took courage, but it made sense—and it made for a better-looking car.

I bow, however, to the weight of tradition. Recognizing that only a few of the more iconoclastic will adopt my suggested amputation, I have retained the complimentary closing in many of the sample letters in this book. I have included them because I want the book to be as useful as possible, and I know that the majority will be hesitant to change the old traditions, and will question the whole if just one part seems radical.

One more word on the subject, for the traditionalists. Practically speaking, it makes no difference to any reader whether you sign off with "Sincerely," "Very truly," "Yours sincerely," or any of the other common varieties of ending. They all mean the same thing, and one will do as well as the next. There are a few ultraconservatives who still insist on—or are afraid to forego the use of—

I am,
Yours sincerely (or truly, etc.)

For heaven's sake, at least give this up, unless you wish to be marked as a very old fogy.

SIGNATURES

The way you sign your name is important because unless it leaves the recipient with a clear idea of who and what you are, he may be puzzled about how to answer you. Keep the following points in mind:

1 Make your signature legible, especially if you're not writing on stationery which contains your name printed on the letterhead. If there's any doubt in your mind—*and there probably should be*—that the recipient will be able to read every letter of your name, then type or print it under your written signature.

2 If your sex is not immediately discernible from your first name (for example, if you're a man whose first name is Shirley, or a woman whose first name is Sidney) or from the subject of the letter, put in the appropriate "Mr.," "Miss," or "Mrs." next to your signature. (If you're a man with an immediately recognizable man's name, "Mr." is not necessary.) If your signature stands alone, with no printed name beneath it, put the appropriate label in parentheses before your name:

(Mr.) Shirley Smith

or without parentheses.

If you print your name below your signature, put the label there:

(Mr.) Shirley Smith

Ladies can get away without the parentheses:

Miss Sidney Smith

3 If you're a single woman, *always* precede your signature with "Miss"–it looks better in parentheses–or your printed name below your signature with "Miss." In the latter case, parentheses are superfluous. It is true that one eminent secretarial guide says, "If no title is included, the implication is that it should be *Miss.*" It takes little skill to know that this sentence could have been written only by a woman. While the woman may *make* such an implication, few men would be brash enough to make the inference. Countless numbers of men have suffered countless hours of anxiety because they did not know whether to address the writer who signed herself "Mary Smith," as "Dear Miss" or "Dear Mrs."

4 If you're married, a widow, or a divorcee, you're pretty much on your own, as far as your signature goes. We can talk about this under two categories: what is traditional usage, and what makes sense.

Traditional usage dictates that a married woman (perhaps as punishment, perhaps as reward, depending upon how you look at it) sign her name in two ways. Her written signature consists of her own first name, the initial letter of her own last name, and her husband's last name. Beneath that goes her printed or typed signature, usually in parentheses, which consists of her husband's name preceded by "Mrs." Thus, when Miss Mary Jane Smith marries Roy Jones, she signs her letters:

Mary S. Jones

(Mrs. Roy Jones)

This is the form to use if you want to stick with tradition. Hopefully, the person to whom you're writing will know that, according to tradition, he's supposed to write to the name in parentheses.

A more sensible method is to take yourself firmly in hand and decide which of the two names you want to be known by, and use that for both the written signature and the name typed under it. Thus:

Mary S. Jones Mrs. Roy Jones

Mrs. Mary S. Jones Mrs. Roy Jones

If you're widowed or divorced, tradition is a little less clear-cut. For widows, there is a tradition that they continue signing their names as they did before their husbands' death. But some ladies are not happy with this arrangement and drift into an ambivalent state, halfway, as it were, between heaven and earth. My own mother, one of the best-bred ladies I know, has still been unable to decide, after nearly four decades of widowhood, whether she is Mrs. Dora Blumenthal or Mrs. Abraham Blumenthal in her letters to strangers.

I suggest simply that if you're a traditionalist, stick with the traditional usage described in the paragraph above about traditional usage for married women. If you're not, and you want to simplify your life, select a single name and stick with it in your correspondence.

If you're divorced, the world, insofar as traditional signatures are concerned, is your oyster. You can go back to your maiden name, and to being a "Miss."

Or, again in accord with tradition, you can sign your own first name and middle initial and your ex-husband's last name. However, again according to tradition, the name you print under it should be just the same. In giving up the husband, you give up the right to use his first name. So, your signature would appear as follows:

Mary S. Jones Mary S. Jones

(Mrs.) Mary S. Jones or (Mrs. Mary S. Jones)

Another acceptable tradition is for the printed signature to combine the last names of both parties, thus:

Mary S. Jones

(Mrs. Smith Jones)

If you like any of these three quite socially acceptable versions, take it and cherish it. My own advice is to do whatever you feel most comfortable doing. Divorce has become so commonplace, and women today are so frequently in a different position than they were when the traditional forms were becoming crystallized, that now almost anything goes. I would urge only that you consider the proposal which I put forth a few paragraphs ago, namely, that your written signature match your typed signature as closely as possible.

ADDRESSING ENVELOPES

Of course, the way in which you address your envelopes is important. An improper or unclear address may cause your letter to become lost or be returned. Therefore, be sure that the name and address are correct and complete.

ZIP CODES

The Zip Code is here to stay, and despite the loathing that many people feel toward it, we might as well accept it with the same resignation with which we accept traffic jams and all-digit dialing.

As you probably know, the Post Office invented the Zip Code as a means of speeding up the handling of bulk mailings—newspapers, magazines, and all the junk mail that you wish could be slowed down instead of speeded up. The idea is that eventually computers will "read" the numbers and send the mail to its proper destination.

The Zip Code consists of five digits. The first identifies one of ten large areas in the nation. The next two pinpoint a major city or distribution point. The last two identify an individual post office, a zone of a city, or some other delivery unit.

According to the Post Office, the Zip Code should appear on the last line of both the address and the return address, following the city and state. Not less than two, or more than six, spaces should be left between the last letter of the state and the first digit of the code.

Right: Mr. Harold Jones
3025 Theresa Street
Arlington, Virginia 22207

Wrong: Mr. Harold Jones
3025 Theresa Street
Arlington 22207, Virginia

THE ADDRESS

The address on the envelope should duplicate the one on the inside of your letter. As long as the format is clear and readable, it's satisfactory. Here are two standard formats:

Mr. James S. Smith, President
Midville Manufacturing Co.
42 Main Street
Midville, New York 10000

Midville Manufacturing Co.
42 Main Street
Midville, N. Y. 10000
Attention: Mr. James S. Smith

HACKNEYED WORDS AND PHRASES

By avoiding overworked and exhausted words and phrases, you can add considerable liveliness to your letters. And there are a number of other words that don't mean exactly what you think they mean. Read this list (which is based on a similar list in "Plain Letters," published by the General Services Administration) and improve, thereby, your writing.

About "He will arrive at about nine o'clock" is incorrect. Use "at" or "about," but not both.

Accompanied by The preposition *with* is usually better. "I am enclosing a form with this letter," rather than "This letter is accompanied by a form."

Acquaint Use "tell" or "inform"; "acquaint" is terribly stiff and a bit dated. "Advise" is another word that you can eliminate; use "tell" or "inform" here, too.

Affect, Effect "Affect" is always a verb meaning to modify or influence. "Effect" may be noun or verb. As verb, it means to accomplish or bring about; as a noun, it means outcome or result. Thus, correct examples would be: affect: "The accident affected my health"; effect as noun: "The program has a bad effect on my children"; effect as verb: "I cannot effect a solution to this problem."

All-around is incorrect. Use "all-round."

All of Say "all the people," not "all of the people."

All ready, Already The first is an adjectival phrase, and is correctly used in the following example: "When the hour came, they were all ready." The second is an adverb that oftener than not should be omitted: "We have (already) written a letter."

Alternative Don't say, "the only other alternative"; say "the alternative."

Anxious is proper only when anxiety exists. Do you really mean eager? If so, use it.

Appreciate your informing me is a clumsy phrase. Use something simple, such as "Please write me" or "Please tell me."

Apt Don't use this word when you mean likely. Apt suggests a predisposition, as in, "A tactless person is apt to write a blunt letter," "Likely" suggests the idea of possibility, as in "Delayed replies are likely (not apt) to damage your chances."

At *all times* Say "always."
this time Say "now."
the present time Say "now."
an early date Say "soon."
your earliest convenience Do you mean this? A convenient time may never come.
the earliest possible moment Say "soon" or "immediately."

Attached *please find*
herewith
hereto
These are all unnecessary. "Attached" is enough.

Between, Among "Between" refers to two only. "Among" refers to more than two.

Biannual is the same as semiannual. Both mean "twice a year."

Biennial means "every two years."

Bimonthly means "every two months." Semimonthly means "twice a month."

Commence "Begin" and "start" are less pompous; why not use them?

Communicate, Communication Avoid these long words by being specific. Instead of communicate, use "write," "wire," or "telephone." Instead of communication, use "letter," "telegram," "memorandum."

Conclude It is better to close a letter than to conclude it.

Continuously, Continually The first word means "without interruption"; the second, "intermittently," "at frequent intervals."

Demonstrates "Shows" is a good simple word to use instead of this long one.

Desire "If you wish" or "if you want" is usually better than "if you desire."

Determine is overworked. "Decide" or "find out" are better.

Different is often unnecessary, as in this typical sentence: "Six different plans were discussed at the meeting."

Due to the fact that is a roundabout way of saying "because."

Earliest practicable date What is a "practicable" date?

Effectuate A word mothered by bureaucrats, nourished by journalists, and beloved by all who cherish hollow pomposity. "Effect" means exactly the same thing and is shorter.

Enclosed	*herewith*	
	please find	"Enclosed" is sufficient.
	with this letter	

Equivalent is seldom better than "equal."

Farther, Further "Farther" indicates distance; "further" denotes quantity or degree. You go farther away; you hear nothing further.

Few, Less "Few" is for numbers; "less" for quantities or amounts. Write fewer letters and say less.

Finalize, Finalization These are manufactured words. Why not use such natural words as "end," "conclude," "complete?"

For	*your information*	Superfluous.
	the month of July	Say "For July."
	the reason that	Use "since," "because," "as."

Fullest possible extent Meaningless padding. Say "full extent," or just "fully."

Furnish Use "give" as a preferable, shorter and more direct, substitute.

Further See *Farther.*

Implement Say "carry out."

In compliance with your request Say "as you requested."
- *addition to* Say "besides."
- *a satisfactory manner* Say "satisfactorily."
- *the near future* Say "soon."
- *the event that* Say "if."
- *the amount of* Say "for."
- *the meantime* Say "meantime" or "meanwhile."
- *order to* Say "to."
- *regard to* Say "about."
- *view of the fact that* Say "as."

Inasmuch as "As," "since," and "because" are a lot shorter.

Indicate "Show" is a better word, not nearly so overworked.

Kindly should not be used for "please." "Please reply," not "kindly reply."

Liquidate Say "pay off" if you use the word in that sense.

None as a subject is usually plural unless a single subject is clearly indicated. "None of the jobs are open." "None of the work is done."

Notwithstanding the fact that is a long-winded way of saying "although" or "even though."

On is superfluous in stating days and dates. "He arrived Tuesday," not "He arrived on Tuesday."

Previous to, prior to Why not say "before"?

Principal, Principle The noun "principal" means head or chief, as well as capital sum. The adjective "principal" means highest or best in rank or importance. Principle means "truth," "belief," "policy," "conviction," or "general theory."

Quite means "really," "truly," "wholly," "positively." Avoid its use in phrases like "quite a few" and "quite some."

Rarely ever, seldom ever "Ever" is superfluous in these two cases.

Reside The conversational word "live" is preferable.

Submitted "Sent" is shorter, more direct.

Subsequent to "After" is shorter, more direct.

This is to inform you You can generally omit this phrase.

is to thank you Why not simply "Thank you"?

Utilization an inflated word for "use."

Wish to apologize, Wish to advise Instead of the first phrase, simply say, "We apologize." Instead of the second phrase, start off with what you want to say.

Chapter Two

WRITING TO BUSINESS FIRMS—AND GETTING RESULTS

Fortunately for you, American industry is hungry for your money. The company which expects to stay in business knows that it must keep you, the customer, happy.

For this reason, most reliable companies pay close attention to customer mail, particularly mail from dissatisfied customers. But, writing letters to a company is one thing: getting the company to do what you want is another. And it requires a certain amount of know-how to persuade a manufacturer to repair your broken toaster, or make an adjustment on your mishandled airplane reservation.

First, you must observe certain principles that have nothing to do with letter writing. The most important is that you must deal with a reliable company. Let's say that you've spent fifteen dollars on a gold-plated hand-warmer which won't work. If you bought it from a fly-by-night retailer who bought an odd lot from a fly-by-night wholesaler, who bought the hand-warmers from a fly-by-night manufacturer, you can resign yourself to having thrown away fifteen dollars.

Second, if the product carries a guaranty or warranty, be sure that you understand its terms. If there's a one-year warranty on the picture tube of your television set, the manufacturer will probably not make good if it breaks down after thirteen months. There's a legitimate reason for this. As one spokesman for a large company put it: "It costs us a certain amount to make a warranty, because we know that in a year's time, we're going to have to pay a certain amount on repairs. We figure this out before we sell the product, and it's included in the price. In other words, the warranty is an insurance policy, and the customer pays for that insurance when he pays for the product."

The same man did add, however: "If a product becomes defective a few weeks after the warranty has run out, we may make the adjustment for the sake of good will."

In other words, if you're dissatisfied with the product, it doesn't hurt to write a letter. If it's a good letter, the company may help you out, even if the warranty has expired.

Now, let's assume that you feel you have a legitimate grievance about a product you've bought. Let's also assume that the store from which you've bought it refuses to give you satisfaction. You're immediately faced with two problems:

1 Whom should you write to?
2 What should you say?

Unfortunately, there is no simple answer to the first question because almost every company is organized differently. In some large companies each major product is handled by a product manager, who's responsible for making all decisions concerning his products. In other cases, a central customer service bureau will handle all correspondence.

Perhaps the best way to handle the problem, then, is first, to look at the user's manual you received with the product—assuming that (a) you received one and (b) that you've held on to it. This will probably tell you where to write in case of trouble. (If you haven't held on to it, shame on you! In the future, remember to file these manuals away where you can get them quickly.) If the manual doesn't tell you, the store where you bought it may be able to give you the manufacturer's address. Another source is the item itself, which will invariably carry the manufacturer's name and usually the city where the company is located.

If the street address isn't given, however, and if the manufacturer isn't a large one, the post office is likely to return your letter for lack of sufficient address.

All is not lost, however. You can find out the address of almost any company in the country by using your telephone. Call your local operator and ask for the Information Operator of the city in question. When you reach her, ask for the telephone number of the company you want. When she gives it to you, ask in your most pleasant voice, for the address of the firm. Although operators are instructed not to give addresses, they will usually do so.

If the operator gives you a choice of several different addresses, for example, the executive office, the service office, or the sales office, ask for the executive office. The executive office will generally know where to forward any letter sent to it.

SHOULD YOU WRITE TO THE COMPANY PRESIDENT?

There is one school of letter writers which firmly believes that the way to get fast action from a company is to write directly to the president. This, however, is not always the best course. In many cases, the president will never see complaint letters addressed to him. His secretary will simply route them to the proper department. In this kind of company, absolutely nothing is gained by writing to the president; you've simply wasted a couple of days while the letter is in transit to the correct department.

In other cases, however, the president does take a close interest in complaint mail. The head of the correspondence department of one large public utility explained what happens in his company: "The quickest way to get a response is by writing to our president. Although usually he won't answer it himself, he insists that we file a report on the disposition of the case. You can be sure that we handle his letters more promptly than the routine ones. We even have a couple of expert correspondents who handle mail which he wants answered."

As a general rule, then, the following would seem to be sound practice: If you're not in a great hurry for an answer, write to the president of the company. He may not see the letter, and in that case, all you've lost is time. But he may take an interest in customer correspondence, and in that case, you may get a more satisfactory answer.

SHOULD YOU BE ANGRY?

Again, there are two schools of thought. Some effective letter writers feel that the only way to budge a company is to write an explosively angry letter, letting the company know in no uncertain terms that you're disgusted with its product or service. Undoubtedly, this tactic can sometimes achieve the desired end.

Unfortunately, people who write in anger sometimes forget to include important information that the company needs in order to correct the situation. If that information is lacking, all the anger in the world will get you nowhere. The company will simply write back asking you coolly for the information it needs.

A calm, reasoned letter that presents all the facts will, in all probability, get the same results, or better ones, than an irate one.

WHAT ABOUT THREATS?

With a few exceptions, threats do not frighten companies. Most of them want to keep their customers happy, but they will not be especially worried if you tell them you'll never buy their product again, or if you warn them that you'll tell your friends about your bad experience. They are used to these problems; they crop up in the mail regularly, and, threaten though you may, the company knows that your complaints will probably not make too much difference in its overall profit picture.

Perhaps the most significant exception is the public utility, which is hemmed in by state and federal regulations. Here's what the spokesman for one public utility admitted: "If a customer threatens that he'll complain to the state Public Service Commission, we'll generally pay closer attention to him. This is because when the PSC steps into a case, it usually wants a whole raft of information. It's a nuisance for us to collect, and it takes up a lot of our time. Therefore, we handle these letters with extra care so that we can avoid the headache."

By extension, when dealing with any company which is subject to extensive government regulation, it may help if you threaten to report the complaint to the authorities. Public utilities, railroads, truckers, and insurance companies fall into this group.

HOW LONG THE LETTER?

The single most-often-voiced complaint that companies have about customers' letters is that they're too long. "So often," said one company correspondent, "we have to wade through a couple of pages before we can find out the problem. And then we have to wade through a couple more before we can find out what they want us to do about it. In the end, we're irritated, and we're less inclined to be as helpful as we might otherwise be." In short, be short.

WHAT INFORMATION SHOULD YOU GIVE?

In order to take action on your complaint, the company has to know some simple factual data. When a product is involved, include the following information:

1 The model number, or a detailed description, of the product.
2 The name and address of the store from which you bought it.
3 The date of your purchase.
4 A copy of the bill of sale, plus a copy of paid invoices for any service that has been rendered on the product since you bought it.
5 A *brief* description of the problem.
6 An indication of whether you're writing for the first time. If not, give the dates of your previous correspondence—either the date of your last letter to the company, or the date of the last letter you received from the company, and the name of the person who wrote you.

(If you're writing in answer to a letter from the company, include the company's filing number, if there is one. This will usually appear near the top of the letterhead, and will be often preceded by some such notation as "Reference" or "Ref." or "Account No." Some companies even say quite clearly at the tops of their letters: "When replying, please refer to File No. 000." This enables the filing clerk—who may be dreadfully incompetent—to get your correspondence from the files with a minimum of trouble.)

SAMPLE COMPLAINT LETTERS

Angry Complaint Letters

The XYZ Bicycle Co. received this angry blast one morning:

Attention: Parts Division
Reference: 16″ Two-Wheel Bicycle
Model A32

Gentlemen:

I am angry, disgusted, and will never believe anyone who sells or represents the XYZ Company. I need not tell you that the best way to lose future sales is to misrepresent a product; and I'll also tell you that if I could get my hands on the salesman who sold this bike to me, I'd hit him.

When I bought the bike from the Anderson Department Store, Main Street, Jonesville, in March of this year, I was told that this was the best bike on the market, and also that replacement parts would be easily obtainable.

As you will note, there is a box along with this letter. Inside the box is the broken part, which is the cause of all the trouble. [Note: if you know the name of a broken part, mention it.] After having talked to seven repair shops in my city, I am furious at being told: "The company doesn't have replacement parts," and "The big stores sell this bike, and we repairmen get the gripes. It shouldn't be on the market."

I am asking that you either replace the enclosed part, or send me a replacement bike. I've never begged, borrowed, or cheated in my entire life, and I have absolutely no feeling of guilt in making this request.

Mrs. M. J. Warner

The company sent back a replacement part, along with a letter explaining that the model had been discontinued; that was the reason the customer had been unable to obtain a replacement locally. It is doubtful that Mrs. Warner's anger helped her get better service, but it certainly made her feel better—and this is one of the legitimate reasons for writing an angry letter.

Incidentally, Mrs. Warner did a very nice—and a very smart—

thing after receiving the replacement. She wrote a gracious thank-you note to the company. If she ever has trouble with the bicycle again, the company will probably go out of its way to help her. Here is what she wrote to the man who sent her the company's apologies:

Dear Mr. Johnson:

Thank you for your letter of June 5, and the new sprocket and rear wheel assembly. These parts have been a perfect replacement.

You people certainly restored my faith in your company, and have made us very happy. I do hope that you won't think me an old shrew for my letter of July 31, but sometimes people just won't take the time to help one another. Your company and you have proved me wrong, and I shall speak of your firm with pride.

Yours very truly,
Mrs. M. J. Warner

A Calm Complaint Letter to a Manufacturer

Dear Sirs:

In the fall of 1961 I bought a Jones Typewriter, Portable Special Model, at ABC Store in Jonesville. I had used it only a few days when the space bar broke.

We took it to a local repair shop; they told us that it was a factory defect and suggested that we take it back to ABC. ABC accepted the machine and sent the part in. We waited three months, and since your company did not send a replacement, they let us have the space bar from another typewriter.

Now, six months later, it has broken again. We took it back to ABC. They are no longer carrying your typewriter but they assured us that the guarantee is still good, and suggested that we write you for further instructions as to what steps to take.

The guarantee was registered in my name, at the address below.

I will appreciate anything you can do to help us on this matter.

Respectfully,
James Christopher
14 Way Street
Smithville, N. Y.

A Polite Complaint Letter and Its Sequel

Toy Co.
XYZville

Gentlemen:

I am aware of your reputation for quality products plus reliability, consequently I do not hesitate to write to you.

For the past two years, my two sons, ages eight and ten, have enjoyed your Electronic Hockey Game. The other day, a welded joint gave way and rendered the game absolutely useless. It was the joint that connects the side to the top of the game.

The purpose of this letter is to ask your permission to send you the set for rewelding.

Rainy days become quite dull for them without that game, so I trust I shall hear from you soon.

Very truly yours,
Howard Gerber

The company's parts-and-service manager, apparently charmed by Mr. Gerber's letter, answered that Mr. Gerber need not send back the game; the company would send a new frame if he could give the model number listed on the instruction sheet. Mr. Gerber replied:

Permit me to thank you for your prompt and considerate reply. My sons were delighted to know that you cared.

Since the instructions are long since gone, I am enclosing a snapshot of my sons playing the game. If possible, please send the picture back; it is the best one my wife has ever taken of the youngsters.

I regret that I can find no identifying numbers on the game itself, but perhaps this information will help you:

The frame is red. It measures 2′ by 4′ by 6″ high.

Again, my sincerest appreciation of your kind attention.

Sincerely,
Howard Gerber

Mr. Gerber got his frame.

A Firm, Impassioned Letter

My brother, Joe, a man with a methodical mind, sent the following letter to a nationally known firm after his method had been reduced nearly to madness. It is a good letter because it states the problem clearly and succinctly:

Mr. John Blank, President
Blank and Company
123 Main Street
Centerville, Calif.

Dear Mr. Blank:

Last October I signed a contract with your company for the installation of dry walls and the renovation of a bathroom in my home at the above address. I am now appealing to you to have this work completed in a satisfactory manner.

I have spoken to your Quincy, Mass., store manager on several occasions, to the plumbing department manager, to your maintenance people, and to anyone else who seemed to be in a position to assist in completing the work. I have received considerate responses followed by service people trying to do the necessary work.

Nevertheless, I have had expensive broadloom rugs badly stained; I have had water pour through my kitchen ceiling at least six times after your people left my home with everything supposedly in order; and I now again have leaks, grout falling out, and other defects.

I have experienced nothing but trouble with your workmanship and materials from the outset. I will illustrate with details—an incomplete list—which your records should confirm.

1. An expensive vanity was delivered with doors assembled upside down and door catches not functioning properly.

2. The dry wall work was left in such rough condition that your installers had to return several times. In some areas sanding was overlooked; in others, dry wall taping was not used, and molding was left incompleted.

[The next few paragraphs listed additional defects.]

Mr. Blank, I had your service people come to the house at least six times because of leaks from the bathroom to the floor below. There were denials of responsibility. Children were blamed, etc. And in each case, it was finally established that the installation was faulty. At this writing, water is again leaking to the floor below when the shower is used.

Frankly, I believe I have reached the point of no return in dealing with your local staff.

I now want to have my bathroom completed in a workmanlike manner, even if it means removing the entire installation. In the event that any removal is necessary, I will not accept a patched-up finish.

For a job that costs about $2500, your performance has been outrageously bad. I expect the courtesy of a prompt reply from you, and the necessary inspections and corrections from qualified personnel.

Sincerely yours,

The president did send various executives to view the shambles, and some corrective measures were taken. As I write this paragraph, some two years after the letter was written, the work has still not been completed satisfactorily, but it is considerably further along, and with one or two more letters, my brother may eventually achieve a completely satisfactory job.

SAMPLE REQUEST AND ADJUSTMENT LETTERS

Requesting Replacement Parts

When an item breaks or wears out, and you want a replacement, a simple, short letter will best serve your purpose. If you still have descriptive literature that came with the product, see if it contains information about reordering. If the literature includes a price list for parts, send along a check or money order. Otherwise, ask the company to bill you or to send the item C.O.D. If you don't know whom to write, send it to the Order Department.

Gentlemen:

Please send me Part No. 21—the heating rod—for your broiler unit, Model 23.

You may bill me or send it C.O.D.

Gentlemen:

I should like to order the following items of glassware from your Sven Hagstrom smoked crystal set:

Three old-fashioned glasses

One piece of stemware
Two snifters

Please bill my charge account, No. 20–321.

When you're not sure of the model, or the serial number, give any other details that might help to identify it:

Gentlemen:

Can you supply me with a cutting-blade unit for your Quik-Shear Lawn Mower?

The mower is about thirty years old. The cutting blades are thirty-six inches long, and are both welded and bolted to the frame.

If the part is available, please send it C.O.D.

Requesting Missing or Defective Parts

Gentlemen:

Can you send me Item No. 57, the lock-nut washer for your Tripod Model Mark II?

The item was left out of the carton in which the tripod came.

I purchased the tripod on March 3, at the Community Camera Store, 45 Main Street, Centerville, Oregon.

Dear Sirs:

Please send me a handle for your four-cup percolator.

I ordered the percolator from your factory, and it arrived with the handle broken.

May I suggest that you examine your shipping carton with an eye to providing more padding adjacent to the area of the handle. I suspect the skimpiness of the padding accounted for the breakage.

Sincerely,

Complaint about Nondelivery

If a store fails to deliver an item, you'll probably call first to find out why. If you get no satisfactory response, a letter to the store manager may help. Include any information that will enable the store to track the item down, including:

1 Your sales slip number.
2 A detailed description of the item.

3 The department from which you ordered it (this should appear on the sales slip).

4 Your charge-account number, if the item was charged to your account.

Dear Sir:

Your store failed to deliver the order described below, which was scheduled for delivery to our home on January 17.

Items ordered: 54″ mattress
54″ bed spring
Bed frame

All items ordered from Dept. 66
Sales Slip No. 325-45
Revolving Charge Account 101-12

Please take the following action:

1 Arrange to have your truck deliver the merchandise to our home on Friday, January 31.

2 Confirm, either by mail or phone, that you have received this letter and will take the action requested. You may call me at 617-3224, any day between 8:00 and 12:00 A.M.

Dear Sir:

On April 15, I ordered an oven rack (Part No. 587) and a broiler pan (Part No. 586) from you. I requested that you bill me for the items.

They have not yet arrived, although more than a month has passed.

Will you please send the items, or tell me why they have been delayed?

Sincerely,

Unjustifiable Overcharges

When you feel you have been overcharged, write to the top man at the store. Give him as many details as are needed to explain the situation, but try to be brief and factual.

The following letter is one which I sent to a store when I felt I had been unjustly overcharged. The important things to note are:

1 It reviews the problem.

2 It requests specific action, i.e., a request for a refund.
3 It provides relevant documentation.

Dear Mr. Jones:

I hope you will be able to correct a large overcharge.

On June 16, I spent $600 in your store on a range, a refrigerator, and a washing machine.

They were to be delivered to my home in Poughquag, N. Y.

Your salesman, Sam Casey, told me that shipping charges would come to about $17. He suggested that the order be sent express collect by truck. I agreed and paid immediately for the merchandise.

A couple of days later, he called to ask if it would be all right to ship by Railway Express. He assured me that the charges would be about the same. Again, I agreed.

You can imagine my feelings when the Railway Express agent called from Brewster, about twenty miles from Poughquag, to tell me that the items had arrived, and that shipping charges would be $22. Further, that if I wished them delivered to my house, I should have to get a trucker and pay *his* charges, also.

I obtained a trucker who charged me $38 more.

You will agree, I'm sure, that I should not be forced to pay for Mr. Casey's error, particularly since I permitted him to make precisely the arrangement he wanted.

I'm willing to pay the Railway Express charges of $22.93, although they are about $6 more than Mr. Casey estimated.

However, I feel that your store should reimburse me for the $38 extra I had to pay because of your salesman's miscalculation.

Sincerely,

P. S. For verification, I am enclosing photostatic copies of your invoice, and those of Railway Express and the trucker.

Interestingly enough, I received no answer. The next letter which I wrote explains why:

Dear Mr. Smith:

Several months ago, when I decided to write you about a serious overcharge, I asked the salesman with whom I dealt, Sam Casey, for the name of the president of the store. He gave me the name of Joseph Jones.

On June 29, I wrote to Mr. Jones. I have never received an answer.

Recently, I called your headquarters. The switchboard operator told me that you, rather than Mr. Jones, are the president. Mr. Jones, she told me, is responsible for out-of-town shipments.

Thus, I assume that Mr. Jones was probably responsible for the overcharge, which may account for the fact that I did not hear from him.

I am enclosing a copy of my letter to Mr. Jones. I trust that you will send me the $38 which I have requested.

This letter achieved the results. I got the refund. The moral? Don't give up until you've exhausted all the possibilities.

Establishing a Charge Account by Mail

In opening a charge account by mail, two courses are open: you can request a charge-account application form in a brief letter to the store's Credit Department:

Gentlemen:

Please send me the forms necessary for opening a charge account at your store.

Or, you can send in the information the store will probably require, and let the store fill out the form. This will probably be what you'll want to do when you're also ordering an item from the store. Include the following information in your letter:

1 The names of other stores where you have charge accounts, and the serial numbers of those accounts.

2 The name of at least one bank with which you do business.

3 It may be helpful to include one other credit reference, such as a Diner's Club or American Express Credit Card.

4 Give the names and addresses of your and your spouse's employers, and the length of time you've been employed.

5 Your telephone number.

Gentlemen:

I should like to order the plant holder–item 32G–advertised in your Spring Catalog.

I should also like to open a charge account with your store, and have this item billed to my account.

I have charge accounts with the following stores:

Smith Brothers
Centerville, N. J.
Account No. 317

Armand's Clothiers
Smithtown, Pa.
Account No. 628-43

For further credit references, you may check with the following:

First National Bank of Centerville
35 Main Street
Centerville, N. J.
Account No. 42,876

American Express Credit Card Division
770 Broadway
New York, N. Y.
Account No. 040 428 641 2

My husband, Martin Cline, has been an employee of Smith's Dry Cleaners, 32 Auburn St., Medford, N. J., for three years. I have worked for Dr. John Cleves, 83 Main Street, Medford, N. J., for eight years.

My telephone number is 323-6146.

Sincerely,

When a Store Fails to Record Payment

If a store's monthly statement fails to record a payment you've made, give the following information in your letter asking for a correction:

1 The date of your payment. This is quite important. If the store knows approximately when your payment arrived, it will be able to check its records more accurately and more quickly. (Giving your check number is of no use to the store. Don't bother to include it.)

2 The name under which you sent the payment. For example, if you're a married lady, your account may be under your husband's

name, but you may have paid by check, signing your own first name. Or, conceivably, you may have endorsed your paycheck over to the store. If the name on the check differs from that on your charge account, the store may not have given you proper credit.

3 The amount of the check.

4 Your charge-account number.

Gentlemen:

I believe your statement of March 3 is in error.

If you examine your records, I think you will find that I paid you $75 by check on April 25. I signed the check "Mrs. Mary Cline."

Please send me a corrected statement.

Sincerely,
Mrs. Mary Cline
Account No. 456 890

When a Store Fails to Credit Returned Merchandise

If the store has failed to record a credit for merchandise which you've returned, include:

1 The serial number on your credit slip.

2 The name or number of the department which granted the credit. (This usually appears on the credit slip.)

3 It may also help to include the date the credit was issued.

Dear Sirs:

I believe your statement of March 3 should include credit for a sweater which I returned on February 25.

The amount of the credit was $16.

The credit slip number is 567-23.

The Department Number is 43.

Please send me a corrected statement.

Sincerely,
Mrs. Mary Cline
Account No. 456 890

When a Store Fails to Credit Picked-Up Merchandise

If a statement fails to reflect a credit for merchandise which you've had the store's delivery service pick up, mention the number on the receipt given you by the driver.

Gentlemen:

Your bill of January 15 failed to credit my account for a pair of shoes which I returned to your store.

Your delivery man picked up the shoes on December 23. The number on the receipt which the driver gave me is 537-1.

Please correct this in your next statement.

Sincerely,
Mrs. Mary Cline
Account 678 901

When You Can't Pay a Bill

If the bill you've run up is so high that you've given up trying to pay it, then it's time to take yourself in hand. If your delinquency is due to a temporary inability to meet the payments, this is also a good time to send a letter of explanation.

Perhaps the best way to handle this situation is to make a firm resolution to pay back a certain amount each week or month—no matter how small. Then you might send a letter in which you:

1 Apologize for your delinquency. A sincere apology will make the credit manager feel that you're as worried as he is, and that you're just as determined that you do the right thing as he is.

2 State that you expect to pay *regularly*. This is terribly important to credit managers. If they're receiving regular payments, they can handle your account with no additional work. If the payments are irregular, the manager will have to set the card aside in a special file, or flag it with a special tab, or otherwise treat it in a manner designed to remind him—and his boss—that he hasn't done a very good job of screening credit risks.

3 Enclose your first payment.

Note: In an effort to encourage regular repayment by delinquent customers, some stores will send them a form which states that the signer agrees to repay a certain amount regularly, plus a small interest charge. Unless you need this club over your head in order to force yourself to repay the bill, don't sign it—at least, not without the advice of a competent lawyer. You have nothing to gain by signing, and of course, you'll be losing the interest.

The following letter will serve as a model:

Dear Mr. Smith:

Your records will show that I have been in arrears on my account for five months.

I am sorry about this delinquency. Certain personal affairs have until now made it impossible for me to pay what I owe.

However, I now want to pay this debt as soon as possible. Therefore, I plan to send you $3.00 a week regularly until the debt is cleared.

I enclose the first payment. And I again apologize for my tardiness. It will not be repeated.

Sincerely,
Mrs. Mary Cline
Account No. 23456

OTHER LETTERS: INQUIRY AND COMMENT

You may want to write to a company for reasons having nothing to do with a business transaction. For example, you may want a copy of the firm's annual report, or you may want a catalog, or you may want to comment on their advertising, or you may want to do any one of a number of other things.

These suggestions will help you write a better letter:

1 Keep your message short: one or two paragraphs is usually sufficient.

2 If you want printed literature which the company might be expected to have on hand, and you don't know whom to send the letter to, address it to the Public Relations Department.

3 Make sure that you've included your return address.

Mr. John Smith
President
John Smith & Co.

Dear Mr. Smith:

I congratulate you on the advertisement your company placed in *Time,* concerning our government's foreign policy in Asia.

Your statement that we must fulfill our overseas commitments is in the finest tradition of patriotism.

Keep up the good work.

Mr. John Smith
President
John Smith & Co.

Dear Mr. Smith:

I am appalled by the advertisement your company placed in *Time* magazine concerning our government's foreign policy in Asia.

It has been said that patriotism is the last refuge of the scoundrel. I trust you are no scoundrel, and I hope you are no fool. But your defense of our military adventures leaves me in doubt about both your morality and your acumen.

I suggest that in the future, you plough your company's revenues back into the company, rather than vaporizing them in inanities like those expressed in your advertisement.

LETTERS OF INQUIRY

One form of correspondence that bulks large in company files consists of letters from students, requesting information for class projects. With one exception, these letters pose no problem. The exception is the letter which requests the company, in effect, to write the student's paper. Virtually no firm will do it; most companies have neither the time nor the personnel to handle this type of request.

Here are some samples of good inquiry letters from high school and college students. Note that all of them identify the writer, and explain the reason for the request: This is important because (a) companies are sometimes reluctant to release information about themselves unless they know how it's going to be used, and (b) knowing the age-level of the writer helps guide them in sending the appropriate type of literature.

Gentlemen:

I am a college student making a study of new office filing equipment.

I will appreciate it if you will send me any free literature you have which describes your filing cabinets and other office supplies. If they are available, I should also like to have prices of these items.

Sincerely,

Gentlemen:

I am a student in the Retail Merchandising class of Newtown High School. Our teacher has suggested that each of us write to a company and find out how the firm conducts its business. Can you tell me:

1. How long you have been in business?
2. How many branches do you have?
3. Approximately how many machines do you sell each year?
4. What kinds of machines do you sell?
5. How many people do you employ?

If you can send any other information that would give me a more complete understanding of your company, I would appreciate it.

Truly yours,

Gentlemen:

I am the managing editor of the *Clarion,* North College's student newspaper.

In a forthcoming issue, we are planning an article on electronic translating machines. The article will stress recent developments in the field, particularly in its applications in colleges.

Can you send black-and-white photographs to illustrate the article? We plan to use three to six pictures. We will, of course, be happy to return the pictures, if you wish, along with a complimentary copy of the issue. Naturally, we will credit your company as the source of any pictures we use.

Since the deadline for the article is August 20, we would appreciate receiving the pictures by August 12.

Very truly yours,

SPECIAL SITUATIONS: MAIL-ORDER CLUBS, AIRLINES, INSURANCE COMPANIES

In more and more industries, the computers are taking over routine clerical jobs. This often has a direct effect on the letter writer, for he may literally find himself corresponding with a machine. (For some years now, many companies have been using automatic typewriters which will, at the push of a button or two, type out any desired combination of paragraphs.)

Three industries with which the public has frequent contact have become highly automated. They are: book clubs, airlines, and insurance companies. In writing to each of them, it's worthwhile to keep certain points in mind.

MAIL-ORDER CLUBS

It is impossible to estimate how many millions of Americans are now members of the scores of book, record, and other speciality-item clubs that now clutter our mailboxes with their subscription solicitations. But the number is great and is growing.

Clubs present a special problem to the consumer because they are (1) so large, (2) so automated, and (3) so impersonal. They are able to sell products at a discount because, first, they buy from the producers in large quantities, and second, because they are geared to the pace of machines which can handle a large number of orders at a very low cost.

For you, this almost-complete mechanization spells trouble. If the machines get out of order, it may take a long time for the humans who tend them to move them back to health. In the meantime, there is almost nothing you can do about it.

Notice, I said *almost* nothing. You can, with persistence and good humor, eventually straighten out most problems. But you must be willing to approach them in the spirit of a multimillionaire gambling on a speculative stock. You must be willing to recognize that the whole venture may result in nothing more than money down the drain—*and you must not let it bother you.*

With this attitude, you have a better than even chance of coming out, if not ahead of the game, at least still in your right mind. To take these matters seriously is the sure road to an evil temper and a loss of sanity. If you cannot bring a sense of humor to your mail-order club correspondence, stay away from the club and buy from your friendly, starving, neighborhood retailer.

A friend of mine by the name of Theodore O. Cron has provided me with a delightful illustration of these principles, and has permitted me to quote at length from his correspondence with a book club.

Ted approached the club with precisely the right attitude. He went in blithely, and came out blithely, with only a few scars which are now hardly visible.

I have chosen to use his letters not only because they are models of good writing but also because they demonstrate the attitude of benevolent superiority which is fundamental to this type of correspondence.

Incidentally, these letters are not intended as a slur upon book clubs. The same thing might have happened—and does happen, daily —to hundreds of other citizens with scores of other types of organizations.

Ted's first membership application was automatically rejected by the club because he asked that the books be sent to his office. The club said that it needed his home address. Ted replied to the Membership Director:

Dear Mr. Anderson:

I have received your careful letter of the 21st, in which you explained that I cannot be admitted to your Club because I will not list my home address.

My hesitation is based on past experience. I refer specifically to your practice of selling mailing lists to whoever can pay for them. As a magazine editor, this practice is not unknown to me; every publisher realizes sizable revenue from such a sale.

However, I also believe that a person's residence is—or can be—a private matter which he is entitled to give only when he deems it to *his* advantage, not the advantage (especially the profitable advantage) of another.

I am re-submitting the enclosed form as an act of good faith on my part. I am not a crank; I would really like to join your Club. I hope your group will respond in good faith and accept me on these terms.

Cordially,

The club did accept Ted this time, and after several months, during which several books were sent in error, and others which Ted had ordered were not sent at all, the club sent a bill. Ted responded:

Gentlemen:

I have received the enclosed bill for $13.03.

This bill includes, I imagine, the $5.50 cost of "Ship of Fools," which I ordered, and which you sent me.

I imagine it also includes a book called "George: An Early Autobiography" ($4.95), which I did not order, but which I received and have since returned to you.

I imagine it also includes the cost of "Vanity Fair," by Thackeray, which you sent me, which I did not order, and which I returned.

It could also include "The Coming of the New Deal," by Arthur Schlesinger, Jr. ($4.75), a book I did not order but which you sent and which I sent back to you.

And it may also include $1.00 I still owe you as part of my original entrance fee to the Club. At that time, I ordered the three books from your Club for which I was liable for payment of $3.00 to you. I received only two of those books. The third one I have yet to receive; it is "The Best of Vanity Fair," edited by Cleveland Amory and Frederick Bradley.

If this book should ever be sent to me, I will gladly send you the $1.00.

In the meantime, I owe you only $5.50 for "Ship of Fools," so I am returning your bill for $13.03, with regret.

Cordially,

A couple of months later, Ted received a notice from the club's Collection Division, that his bill was "LONG OVERDUE" and that if he did not pay, he would be stigmatized by the club as a "BAD CREDIT RISK." Ted answered:

Gentlemen:

I have in hand your "Final Notice" that I owe you $13.03. Of course, I do not owe you $13.03 as a review of our correspondence will quickly reveal.

The fact is that you still have not completed your part of the contract under which I joined your Club; to wit, the sending to me of three books of my choice for the sum of $3.00.

I have received only two of those books—for which I duly paid—and a variety of other books which I have duly returned. I am now in receipt of a book which I did not order.

According to my records, I owe you only for "Ship of Fools." I am quite aware of that bill to you, and will certainly pay it when I have a mind to. From all I can gather of our correspondence, this is how business between us should be carried on, anyway.

But, I will strike a bargain with you. I will pay you for "Ship of Fools" if you will just take me off your mailing list. From all the direct mail I have received from other organizations, it would appear that the sale of my name and address on your mailing list has netted you sufficient profit to make this arrangement acceptable to you.

I hope this letter spares you the unpleasantness of having to call me "a bad credit risk." Certainly, your defaulting on the original terms of the membership contract has not made you the best risk to me.

Cordially,

This letter brought out the humans, at last. About a month later, a Miss Mary Ryan, a correspondent, sent a very polite letter to Ted, adjusting the charges, and asking him to pay $12.00, which would cover "Ship of Fools," the club's latest selection, "The Reivers," and $.55 for handling charges and sales taxes. Wrote Ted:

Dear Miss Ryan:

I have received your letter of August 30th, and am pleased to report that the amusement with which I have viewed our relationship thus far was not abated by your letter.

Since I did not ask for it, I am returning "The Reivers," unopened, which, with the check I have enclosed with this letter, should bring our association to a pleasant end.

You will note that my check is for $6.01 for payment of "Ship of Fools." It does not include the $.55 mentioned in your letter because

I have borne mailing and handling charges certainly equal to yours, and according to my records, I've already paid the sales tax on the two books of my original membership contract.

I am delighted to learn that my account will be closed; this leaves me free to contribute to my local public library and to avail myself of their services which, by comparison with your esteemed club, are impeccably organized and eminently helpful.

Cordially,

Unfortunately, the machines took over again. Ted received a bill for $5.44 and a polite, mechanically-reproduced form letter from the Credit Manager asking him for payment, or at least for an explanation of "where the trouble lies." Ted responded:

Dear Mr. Mason:

I have received your bill, and your letter in which you multigraphically ask me "where the trouble lies" in satisfying the books on my account.

Where does the trouble lie? Usually, I expect an unreasonable fee when an organization asks me such a question. However, as our correspondence has frequently brightened an otherwise tedious routine, I will do my best to consult with you.

For one thing, I would look about for a Miss Mary Ryan, who has struck me as being a reasonable person. In fact, she accepted my check for $6.00 and some odd cents a while back in a discreetly silent fashion. And I also believe she good-naturedly wrote me right out of your Club at the same time, so I would recommend her very highly as someone aware of your "trouble."

I twinkled inwardly on reading your bill, because there seems to be some naughty discrepancy between what you think I owe the Club and what I was billed by Miss Ryan. In my haste to preserve Miss Ryan's good humor, I apparently over-paid the Club something on the order of $.59.

Rather than put the matter into the hands of a collection agency, I would prefer that you spread this modest sum among your industrious mailroom staff to whom, I'm sure you will admit, we both owe a great debt.

Please accept my best wishes for the Thanksgiving holiday when you sit down to carve up your next turkey.

Cordially,

Upon receiving that letter, the club apparently closed its files on Ted. At least, he has not heard from them since, and unless the machines resurrect him, he is safe.

THE AIRLINES

Another area where the computers have largely taken over is in the airlines. Without computers, it would be virtually impossible for a company to give efficient reservations service. They must be given credit for the fantastically good job they perform. But the machines occasionally fail. A small piece of dirt gets into a switch, or a relay wears out, and dozens of passengers may, as a result, find themselves waiting in Peoria when they should have arrived in Dallas.

In the matter of mixed-up reservations, there is not much that you can do. The company has robbed you of the thing you paid for—time—and there is no way you can get your money back.

Nevertheless, it does help sometimes to blow off steam. That, for example, is what a friend of mine did when he encountered a series of mishaps with one airline. He wrote the president of the company, explaining the fiasco. As a result of the letter, he was taken out to lunch by the public relations director of the airline.

The letter, which was picked up by the magazine *Printers' Ink,* is reprinted here, slightly condensed, because it's an excellent example of a clear, calm letter which expresses the writer's irritation with the company.

Mr. C. R. Smith, President
American Airlines, Inc.
633 Third Avenue
New York 17, N. Y.

Dear Mr. Smith:

You have just lost a customer, and I have decided to take the trouble to tell you why.

On June 14, I called your reservations department and spoke with a Miss Cruz. I asked her to figure out a routing for me leaving New York for Detroit on Monday morning, June 18, then from Detroit to Dallas on June 28, and from Dallas to New York on July 1—all coach.

While I waited, she figured this out. She quoted me a price of $197 and some odd cents. Miss Cruz insisted on mailing me the tickets, as I was using an air travel card. I told her I would much rather have the tickets picked up since the time was short. However, she assured me that I would get the tickets on time.

At my request she also checked the service on the Chicago-Dallas flight, and told me it would be possible for coach passengers to purchase cocktails and that they would be served a complimentary dinner.

As of Sunday, the eve of departure, I had not received the tickets. I called the night supervisor of your New York reservations department and explained my predicament. He assured me that my tickets would be made up and waiting for me at Idlewild at 8:30 A.M. Monday, a half-hour prior to departure.

I arrived at Idlewild at 8:30, waited for 20 minutes in line while the young lady laboriously went through schedules figuring out a round-the-world trip for a prospective passenger. When I finally got waited on, there were no tickets in the file.

The young lady called reservations and was told that they planned to have my tickets there at 9:00 A.M., the time of departure. She quickly made up a new set, overcharging me by $8. Although I was aware of this, there wasn't time to complain, so I boarded, strapped myself in, and waited.

At 9:15, the captain advised us that there was a delay. At 9:30 he suggested that we get off the plane since there were fueling problems. We finally took off at 10:45. The explanation was that someone had put in 1,000 extra gallons of fuel, and it had taken that long to locate the problem, drain it out, and rebalance the plane. We were one hour and 45 minutes late in Detroit.

The next incident occurred shortly after I boarded flight 59 in Chicago. I rang for the hostess and ordered a martini. I was informed that coach passengers were not permitted any liquor on the flight, contrary to what Miss Cruz had told me. There is no excuse for misinforming passengers on such matters.

I realize that there are many factors over which airline management has no control. However, it seems to me that you could do a much better job of eliminating stupid mistakes such as these.

Very sincerely,

If you find yourself similarly disaccommodated, there *are* certain things that you can do by mail—if you write promptly. For example, if you make reservations on an economy flight, and when you go to pick up your ticket, you find yourself charged for a first-class flight, you're entitled to a refund. You can get it, if not on the spot, then later on, when you complain by mail. But, what does the airline need in order to take care of you quickly? According to several different airline executives, this is the information you should include:

1 Your flight number.
2 The date of the flight.
3 The points of origin and termination.
4 If the incident occurred between the origin and destination, tell where.
5 Tell the company what you'd like them to do. (As one man said, "Many people complain and sign their letters without telling us what they expect. It leaves us completely–no joke intended–up in the air.")

Timing is important in writing letters. Airlines maintain reservations records for sixty days. If you delay writing until after that date, there's almost no hope of getting satisfaction.

If you're writing about a matter having to do with the flight, such as lost baggage, or an item you left behind, write to the station where it occurred–if you can, write inside of a week after the event occurred. If your letter goes out more than a week later, write to headquarters, which by this time will have records of all mishaps.

Whatever the reason for your letter, address it to a specific department. This will prevent the letter's drifting around the offices until it lands on the right desk. Therefore, address claims letters to: Manager, Claims Department; address complaint and commendation letters to: Manager, Customer Services Department.

Complaints and Commendations about Service

Nobody can please everybody, and this is particularly true of airline clerks, who work under constant pressure. If you feel like complaining about–or commending–a clerk, or any other airline personnel, by all means write the company a letter. It can do nothing but help the man.

You're being needlessly softhearted if you hesitate to complain about a clerk who has treated you rudely. Said one TWA official: "All airlines constantly receive complaints from customers who feel they've been overcharged on excess baggage. Invariably, they describe the clerk with whom they dealt as 'rude.' We read and answer these letters, but they don't hurt the man's job. It's a part of the cost of doing business."

On the other hand, if an airline employee is consistently rude, and his manager receives complaints about him with some regularity, he will be told to mend his ways, or else.

Where an employee has been especially kind or helpful, a letter of commendation can help his career. When the Customer Services Department receives such a letter, copies will usually go to his supervisor and his regional manager. If the letter is from a well-known person, or someone in an important position, or if it's a really emphatic commendation, it will go into his personnel file, and it may help him when he's up for his next raise or promotion.

Lost Baggage

The perennial problem of lost baggage is best handled when it can be handled fast, in person or by telephone. Sometimes, however, you have to resort to mail to track down that missing luggage. How can you do it most effectively?

First: most airlines observe a seventy-two-hour rule on lost luggage. After seventy-two hours, unclaimed bags are forwarded to the airline's central depot. (The companies are, as of this writing, working out plans for a single, central depot for all lost luggage. It should improve matters somewhat.) So, if your letter will arrive more than seventy-two hours after your flight, don't bother writing to the place where it was misplaced. Write to the central office.

Second: Giving a description of the luggage is not sufficient. One executive said: "There are thousands of suitcases, and most of them are plaid cloth." Airlines could never track down lost luggage if they had to depend upon a description of the outside. After the bag reaches the depot, it's opened and the contents are inventoried. This information is placed on an "On Hand Report" and is circulated to all other airlines. Therefore, when you write a letter inquiring about your luggage, or a claim for lost luggage, include the following information:

1 Proof that you made the trip. Ideally, this will be a photostat of your ticket.

2 A photostat of the claim check. A photostat is better than a description because sometimes the check's appearance, or numbers or letters written on it and crossed out, will give a clue as to where it might be.

3 A complete description of the contents. This should include the minor things, such as a deck of cards, or a pipe, as well as the more expensive items. The reason: the contents of most bags are similar. Nearly everyone carries the same items: shoes, clothing, etc., and it's difficult to identify a bag on the basis of these contents alone. It's the small, personal item that may set it apart from the countless others piled next to it.

4 An estimate of what you think the company should pay you in case the baggage cannot be found.

INSURANCE COMPANIES

While computers have taken over much of the tedious handwork of caring for policyholders, insurance companies still maintain vast staffs of clerks and correspondents in vast and endless halls, writing, writing, writing, in response to letters from their customers. There's a good chance that if you have trouble in getting fast, efficient service from your insurance company, it's your own fault: either you neglected to give the right information, or you gave the wrong information.

The important things to remember in writing to insurance companies are these:

- Identify yourself fully. If your name isn't printed on your letterhead, print it clearly beneath your signature.
- Make sure that your present address is included. This is especially important if you've moved to a new address, and the company doesn't know it. Of course, if you're writing about a change of

address, you'll give both the new and the old address. If you're writing about some other matter, and the company hasn't been told of your change of address, you'll include both your current and previous address.

- Indicate your policy number, preferably at the top of the letter, where it can easily be seen.
- As an extra means of identifying yourself, you can include your birthday.

These points are important because so many policyholders' names are quite similar. One insurance executive estimated that 25 per cent of the names in his company's files are duplicates of one other.

Whom to Write

Again, the question arises: should you write the company's president if you have a problem? As a general rule, no. Astonishing as it may seem, he may not know too much about specific insurance problems. Being president, he's much more involved with high policy than insurance policy, and while he may be able to quote you down to the last decimal the rate of return on the company's stock portfolio, he may not have the foggiest notion of what premiums you should be paying. One insurance administrator told me: "Our president has a very soft heart. This is fine, except that he may tell a policyholder that the company will do something very nice, when the company rules absolutely forbid it. Then, we underlings have to figure out a way to renege." So, as a general rule, it's best to stay away from the president, unless you've reached a point of total exasperation.

Whom, then, should you contact? Your first contact should be by telephone to the agent or the broker who sold you the policy. If this isn't possible, then write to the insurance company's headquarters. Check the literature that came with your policy; it may tell you exactly where to address your letter. If it doesn't, then write to the Policy Service Department. Most companies have a department with this name, or with a name similar to it, which handles policyholders' correspondence.

An additional suggestion: if you have a question about the status of your policy, or about a claim of the surrender or loan value of your policy, write to the local field office. If your question is of a more general nature, dealing with such matters as policy benefits and options, write to the home office, which can usually give more precise information.

There are two major exceptions to this rule. Exception one: if you're replying to a letter sent to you by the company, reply to the person who signed the letter, in care of his department. Otherwise, the letter may float around the office for days, looking for the right man.

Exception two: if you're writing about a group insurance policy, check first with the organization through which you got the policy. Many large companies and organizations which offer group policies to their employees or members maintain a full set of records on each policyholder. It's a good idea, therefore, to approach that office first. If they can't help you, or if there isn't such an office, then address your letter to the insurance company's headquarters, to the attention of the Group Service Department. In your correspondence, include, in addition to your name, address, policy number, and birth date, the name of your employer, or the organization through which you bought the policy.

Making Yourself Clear

Few languages are more specialized than that of the insurance world. If you're not a specialist in the field, avoid, as far as possible, the use of technical insurance terms. Instead, state your problem in simple everyday language. If you must use a technical word, refer to the Glossary of Life Insurance Terms on page 68, which lists most of the special words and phrases.

When asking a question, it's a good idea to explain why you want the answer. Take the case of poor Joe Doaks. Joe didn't know that his life insurance policies had both a "cash value" and a "loan value." The cash value was the amount he'd get from the company if he turned in his policy. The loan value was the amount that he could borrow on the policy. The loan value was less than the cash value. Joe wanted to borrow money from a bank, using his insurance policy as collateral. He wrote the insurance company, and not knowing any better, asked for the cash value of his policy. Then, armed with this reply, he went to the bank and requested that amount. He was a very unhappy man when the banker told him that he couldn't lend that much. The banker explained that he needed the loan value and Joe had to write another letter, and wait another couple of weeks for an answer.

On the other hand, if Joe had explained to the insurance company that he wanted the information in order to borrow money from a bank, the company would have understood that he'd meant to ask for loan value rather than cash value, and would have been able to give him the required answer.

This rule of giving the "reason why" holds true in all cases. For example, if you can't pay the premium, but you'd like to hold on to the policy, don't simply decide all by yourself that you'll have to surrender the policy. Remember, the insurance company wants to keep your policy in force. So, write and explain your situation, and ask if they can make some suggestions as to how you can maintain the insurance.

Signing the Insurance Letter

One final point may be important: If you're writing to request information about a policy held by someone else, say a spouse or a relative, get their signatures on the letter. Often, companies hesitate to give out certain information to anyone other than the insured. One insurance man told me: "We never know when a couple has been separated or divorced, and we want to stay out of trouble." Therefore, the insured person should always sign, or countersign, the letter.

SAMPLE INSURANCE LETTERS

I—and you—have been most fortunate in securing the help of John Brion, Communications Director of the Mutual Life Insurance Co. of New York. John went to some trouble to collect well-written letters from policyholders, and, with the names changed, here they are. You will notice that they cover a wide range of insurance problems and should prove a helpful guide to your own letter writing.

Incidentally, if you haven't the name of a specific person or department to write to, address your letter to: Director of Policyholder Services.

Status Request

Gentlemen:

Would you please bring me up to date on insurance policy No. 123456789, issued on the life of the undersigned, John Smith.

I should like to know:

1. How much I now owe in premiums;
2. The amount of dividends now accumulated;
3. What the policy will be worth at death or maturity.

John Smith
654 Center Street
Centerville, Mass.

Premium Payment

Reference: Your File No. 3456

Gentlemen:

Your letter of January 5th says that my policy—No. 98765—will expire unless I pay the premium by February 10th.

I paid this premium to your Centerville agency on January 1st, since your letter implied that I should pay the premium to them, rather than to you.

Please check with the Centerville agency before enforcing termination.

You might also want to know that I am married, and that my name is Mrs., not Miss, Judith Grivage.

Sincerely,

Refund Request

Re: Policy No. 23480

Dear Sir:

I am writing to you for clarification regarding the above policy, which I allowed to lapse on June 12, 1966.

This policy was obtained through James Hardy, Hardy Insurance Agency, 234 Main St., Centerville, Arizona.

I discussed this matter personally with Mr. Hardy before the lapse of the policy. He told me that I would receive a refund if I dropped the policy. So far, no refund has been forthcoming.

Please tell me the status of the refund, and whether I may expect to receive it.

Sincerely,
Bertram Foley

Dividend Request

Gentlemen:

Would it be possible for me, as the mother of Joseph Jones, to withdraw the dividends that have accumulated on his policy No. 08642?

As your records will show, I am a widow, and the sole support of Joseph. At the present time, we need additional cash, and I should like to withdraw the dividends, if it is possible.

Sincerely,
Myra Jones

Tax Information

Re: Policy No. 35790
Howard S. Johnson

Dear Sirs:

Please tell me the amount of dividend earned on the above policy during the year 1966 which is taxable by the Internal Revenue Service.

Yours truly,
Howard S. Johnson

Loan on Policy

Re: Policy No. 53970

Gentlemen:

1. I wish to obtain a loan on this policy. Please send me the proper forms.

2. Am I correct in believing that the maximum I may borrow is $120?

3. Please change the policy mailing address from 123 Main Street, Centerville, Maine, to 345 Grove Street, Ashway, N. H.

4. Please remove the present beneficiary, Mrs. Howard Eversham, and replace her with: Mrs. Marilyn Forster Minos, my wife.

Sincerely,

GLOSSARY OF LIFE INSURANCE TERMS

Insurance terms are often hard to understand, and they may mean something quite different from what you think they mean.

This glossary of life insurance terms will explain most of the jargon you're likely to encounter. It will help you to ensure that when you're corresponding with an insurance company, you're using the terms you mean to use.

Accidental Death Benefit A provision added to a life insurance policy for payment of an additional death benefit in case of death as a result of accidental means. It is often called "Double Indemnity."

Actuary A technical expert on insurance and related fields, particularly on the mathematics of insurance.

Agent A sales and service representative of an insurance company.

Annuitant The person during whose life an annuity is payable, usually the person to receive the annuity.

Annuity A contract that provides an income for a specified period of time, such as a number of years or for life.

Annuity Certain A contract that provides an income for a specified number of years, regardless of life or death.

Application A statement, signed by the applicant, requesting insurance.

Automatic Premium Loan A provision in an insurance policy that any premium not paid by the end of the grace period (usually thirty-one days) be automatically paid by a policy loan if there is sufficient cash value.

Beneficiary The person named in the policy, to whom the insurance money is to be paid at the death of the insured.

Cash Surrender Value The amount available in cash upon surrender of a policy before it becomes payable by death or maturity.

Convertible Term Insurance Term insurance which can be exchanged, at the option of the policyholder, and without evidence of insurability, for a permanent plan of insurance.

Credit Life Insurance Term life insurance sold through a lender or lending agency to cover payment of a loan, installment purchase, or other obligation, in case of death.

Deferred Annuity An annuity providing for the income payments to begin at some future date, such as in a specified number of years or at a specified age.

Deferred Annuity Group Annuity A type of group annuity providing for the purchase each year of a paid-up deferred annuity for each member of the group, the total amount received by the member at retirement being the sum of these deferred annuities.

Deposit Administration Group Annuity A type of group annuity providing for the accumulation of contributions in an undivided fund out of which annuities are purchased as the individual members of the group retire.

Disability Benefit A provision added to an insurance policy for waiver of premium, and sometimes payment of monthly income, if the insured becomes totally and permanently disabled.

Dividend Addition An amount of paid-up insurance purchased with a policy dividend and added to the face amount of the policy.

Double Indemnity An accidental death benefit providing for payment of double the face amount of the policy in case of death as a result of accidental means.

Endowment Insurance A plan of insurance payable after a specified number of years if the insured is then living. If the insured dies during the endowment period, payment is made to a beneficiary.

Expectation of Life The average number of years of life remaining for persons of a particular age according to a particular mortality table.

Extended Term Insurance A form of insurance available as a nonforfeiture option. It provides the original amount of insurance for a limited period of time.

Face Amount The amount stated on the face of the policy that will be paid in case of death or at maturity. It does not include dividend additions or additional amounts payable under accidental death or other special provisions.

Grace Period A period (usually thirty-one days) following the premium due date, during which a premium may be paid. The policy remains in force throughout this period.

Group Annuity A pension plan providing annuities at retirement to a group of persons under a master contract, with the individual members of the group holding certificates as evidence of their coverage. It is usually issued to an employer for the benefit of employees. The two basic types are deferred annuity and deposit administration group annuity.

Group Life Insurance Life insurance issued, usually without medical examination, on a group of persons under a master policy. It is usually issued to an employer for the benefit of employees. The individual members of the group hold certificates as evidence of their insurance.

Individual Policy Pension Trust A type of pension plan, frequently used for small groups, administered by trustees who are authorized to purchase individual level premium policies or annuity contracts for each member of the plan. The policies usually provide both life insurance and retirement benefits.

Industrial Life Insurance Life insurance issued in small amounts, usually not over five hundred dollars, with premiums payable on a weekly or monthly basis. The premiums are generally collected at the home by an agent of the company.

Insured The person on whose life an insurance policy is issued.

Lapsed Policy A policy terminated because of nonpayment of premiums. For accounting purposes, the term is sometimes limited to a termination occurring before the policy has a cash or other surrender value.

Legal Reserve Life Insurance Company A life insurance company operating under insurance laws specifying the minimum bases for the reserves the company must maintain on its policies.

Level Premium Insurance Insurance for which the cost is distributed evenly over the period during which premiums are paid. The premium remains the same from year to year, and is more than the actual cost of protection in the earlier years of the policy and less than the actual cost in the later years. The excess paid in the early years builds up the reserve.

Life Annuity A contract that provides an income for life.

Life Insurance in Force The sum of the face amounts, plus dividend additions, of life insurance policies outstanding at a given time. Additional amounts payable under accidental death or other special provisions are not included.

Limited Payment Life Insurance A plan of whole life insurance with premiums payable for a specified number of years or until death if death occurs before the end of the specified period.

Mortality Table A statistical table showing the death rate at each age, usually expressed as so many per thousand.

Mutual Insurance Company An insurance company owned and controlled by its policyholders. Mutual companies, in general, issue participating insurance.

Nonforfeiture Option The value, if any, either in cash or in another form of insurance, available to the policyholder upon failure to continue the required premium payments. The other forms of insurance available are extended term insurance and reduced paid-up insurance.

Nonparticipating Insurance Insurance on which no dividends are payable. The premium is calculated to cover as closely as possible the anticipated cost of the insurance protection.

Ordinary Life Insurance Life insurance is usually issued in amounts of one thousand dollars or more with premiums payable on an annual, semiannual, quarterly, or monthly basis. The term is also used to mean the straight life plan of insurance.

Paid-up Insurance Insurance on which all required premiums have been paid. The term is frequently used to mean the reduced paid-up insurance available as a nonforfeiture option.

Participating Insurance Insurance on which the policyholder is entitled to share in the surplus earnings of the company through dividends which reflect the difference between the premium charged and actual experience. The premium is calculated to provide some margin over the anticipated cost of the insurance protection.

Policy The printed document issued to the insured by the company stating the terms of the insurance contract.

Policy Dividend A refund of part of the premium on a participating life insurance policy representing its share of the surplus earnings apportioned for distribution. It reflects the difference between the premium charged and actual experience.

Policy Loan A loan made by an insurance company to a policyholder on the security of the cash value of his policy.

Policy Reserves The amounts that an insurance company allocates specifically for the fulfillment of its policy obligations. Reserves are so calculated that, together with future premiums and interest earnings, they will enable the company to pay all future claims.

Premium The payment, or one of the regular payments, a policyholder is required to make for an insurance policy.

Premium Loan A policy loan made for the purpose of paying premiums.

Reduced Paid-up Insurance A form of insurance available as a nonforfeiture option. It provides for continuation of the original insurance plan, but for a reduced amount.

Renewable Term Insurance Term insurance which can be renewed at the end of the term, at the option of the policyholder and without evidence of insurability, for a limited number of successive terms. The rates increase at each renewal as the age of the insured increases.

Revival The reinstatement of a lapsed policy by the company upon receipt of evidence of insurability and payment of past due premiums.

Settlement Option One of the several ways, other than immediate payment in a lump sum, in which the insured or beneficiary may choose to have the money from a policy paid.

Stock Life Insurance Company A life insurance company owned and controlled by stockholders who share in the surplus earnings. Stock companies, in general, issue nonparticipating insurance, but may also issue participating insurance.

Straight Life Insurance A plan of whole life insurance with premiums payable until death.

Supplementary Contract An agreement by the company to retain the lump sum payable under an insurance policy and to make payments in accordance with the settlement option chosen.

Term Insurance A plan of insurance payable at death provided death occurs within a specified period.

Waiver of Premium A provision that under certain conditions an insurance policy will be kept in full force by the company without the payment of premiums. It is used most often as a disability benefit.

Whole Life Insurance A plan of insurance for the whole of life payable at death. It may be either straight life or limited payment life.

Chapter Three

SOCIAL CORRESPONDENCE

A good deal has been written about social correspondence. You will find on the shelves of your public library probably half a dozen books providing you with model letters for every conceivable situation under the sun.

Why then, has this book a chapter on social correspondence? Because there *are* formal occasions that call for correspondence. There are also other situations which can be handled equally well either by voice or by letter, such as party invitations, bon voyage messages, and congratulations of one sort or another. In this chapter, then, we'll deal with both sorts—the formal correspondence dictated by tradition, and informal correspondence, which might be handled, alternatively, on the phone or in person.

Our guiding principle is to follow the forms that you, personally, are most comfortable with.

ANNOUNCEMENTS AND INVITATIONS

BIRTH ANNOUNCEMENTS

The overriding rule to observe in birth announcements is to keep them simple and tasteful. I cannot urge you strongly enough to avoid those atrocious, five-and-dime-store cards which drip gaudy sentiments about the new baby, and leave blank spaces for you to tell everything about the infant including the diameter of its fanny. Your relatives and friends will be delighted to know that you've become a parent. They will also want to know the name of the child. But beyond that, who really cares how much the infant weighs, or what color its eyes are, or how long it is?

My own feeling is that a formal, engraved card is best. Your local printer or stationery store will have several good samples. In making your selection, keep these principles in mind:

Let the card be white or a close relative of white.

Let the shape be rectangular.

Let the edges be smooth.

Let the border, if any, be simple.

Let the style of type be simple; if you prefer script, let it be easily readable.

As for the commercial cards which leave blank spaces for you to fill in the essential information, pick the simplest one you can find—preferably sticking with black ink, or as few colors as you can bring yourself to accept, and with as little information as possible outside of the name and birth date.

PARTY INVITATIONS: COCKTAILS, LUNCH, DINNER, AND TEA

These invitations, unless you live a fairly formal life where almost every invitation is committed to print, are in that gray area that I spoke of at the beginning of the chapter. Some people like to telephone invitations; some like to write them. We will now address ourselves to the problem of the written invitation. Let us go by degrees from the most formal to the most informal.

If you do a considerable amount of entertaining of a rather formal nature, you may want to have engraved cards made up for each special occasion or a supply which can serve for all functions equally well. The traditional card looks like this:

Mr. and Mrs. James Smith
request the pleasure of

company at
on
at o'clock
25 Cherry Lane

Equally acceptable is a handwritten version which line by line follows the format of the engraved invitation. It would look like this:

Mr. and Mrs. James Smith
request the pleasure of
Mr. and Mrs. Jones'
Company at Crest Country Club
on March the fourth
at one o'clock
25 Cherry Lane

When you send handwritten formal invitations, it's customary to use letterhead stationery.

Remember also, whether you're sending an engraved or a handwritten formal invitation, to print out your first name fully.

RESPONDING TO A FORMAL INVITATION

The response to a formal invitation is as formal as the invitation. This is the way it's written, if you accept:

Mr. and Mrs. Howard Johnson
accept with pleasure
Mr. and Mrs. Smith's
kind invitation for dinner
on Saturday, the 12th of August
at nine o'clock

And if you can't go, you write:

Mr. and Mrs. Howard Johnson
regret that they are unable to accept
Mr. and Mrs. Smith's
kind invitation for the 12th of August

And if one of you can go, and the other can't:

Mr. Howard Johnson
accepts with pleasure
Mr. and Mrs. Smith's
kind invitation for
Saturday, the 12th of August
but regrets that
Mrs. Johnson
will be absent at that time

Less formal invitations are usually written, either on your letterhead or on a card, which may be folded or unfolded.

Dear Mrs. Cribbs,

Will you and Mr. Cribbs dine with us on Saturday, the fifteenth of December, at eight thirty?

We shall hope to see you then.

Sincerely,
Jane Mason Brown

and the answer can read:

Dear Mrs. Brown,

We will be very pleased to dine with you on Saturday, the fifteenth, at eight thirty.

Thank you for your invitation.

Sincerely,
Charlotte Cribbs

or, if you're unable to go:

Dear Mrs. Brown,

We are sorry that another engagement prevents us from accepting your kind invitation for Saturday.

Thank you for thinking of us. We hope to see you soon.

Sincerely,
Charlotte Cribbs

Always write these notes by hand; typing is traditionally taboo.

Completely informal notes are increasingly popular. Just a line or two will do:

Dear Mary,
Will you have lunch with us next Tuesday at 2:00?

Marian

And the reply is equally informal:

Dear Marian,
Lunch at 2:00 Tuesday will be lovely.

Mary

CHRISTENING ANNOUNCEMENTS AND INVITATIONS

You may want to telephone your invitations to the christening, but if you prefer to write, a brief note giving the time and place is appropriate:

Dear Mary and Jim:
The christening for Nancy Elizabeth will be at Saint Barnabas Church, Third Avenue and Main Street, July 15, at one o'clock. There will be a small gathering at our house afterward.
We do hope you can come.

Sincerely,
Jane Wisdom

You may use your regular stationery, or a calling card, if it's sufficiently large.

JEWISH NEWBORN RITUALS

The Jews traditionally have two ceremonies for newborn boys which may call for invitational correspondence, although in both cases, the invitation is usually extended by telephone.

The first is the circumcision, called the *Berith Milah,* and it traditionally takes place on the eighth day after birth, usually in the hospital. A short note is all that's called for:

Dear Helen,

On Wednesday, August 15th, at 2:00, we will be having a *Berith* for our son, Harold, at Centerville Hospital.

We hope you and Joe can be there.

Sincerely,
Gladys

The second is the *Pidyon Ha-Ben,* or the redemption of the first-born. The ceremony derives from Biblical tradition, which holds that the first-born, if he's a boy, must be dedicated to God's service. The redemption ceremony symbolically absolves him of the religious obligation. Again, a short invitation is all that's required:

Dear Helen,

On Tuesday, September 16th, at 3:00, we will hold a *Pidyon Ha-Ben* at our home for Carl.

We hope that you and Joe will be able to come.

Sincerely,
Gladys

ENGAGEMENTS—ANNOUNCEMENTS AND INVITATIONS

Engagement announcements in the newspapers usually follow a standard format. The following list covers the basic information usually included:

Girl's parents' names
Girl's parents' address (if they are living apart, give addresses of both parents)
Girl's name
Fiancé's parents' names
Address of fiancé's parents (if they are living apart, give address of both parents)
Fiancé's name
College which girl attended
Date of graduation
Degree obtained or being worked for
Fiancé's college

Date of graduation
Degree obtained or being worked for
Girl's position and employer, if she is working
Fiancé's position and employer, if he is working

The proper procedure is to send a note to the newspaper—address it to the society editor—adopting or adapting any one of the following formats:

> Dr. and Mrs. John Smith of 100 Main Street have made known the engagement of their daughter, Miss Mary Smith, to Steven Jay Jones. He is the son of Mr. and Mrs. Harvey Jones, of Centerville.
>
> The prospective bride attended Centerville College. [If the father is quite prominent, this might be mentioned in a sentence; for example, "Her father is headmaster of the Laurence School."]
>
> Mr. Jones, a graduate of Syracuse University, is with IBM as a computer engineer.

> Mr. William Haverstraw has announced the engagement of his daughter, Miss Amy Haverstraw, to Francis Stipple, son of Mrs. John Stipple of New York and the late Mr. Stipple.
>
> The bride-to-be, daughter also of the late Mrs. Haverstraw, was graduated from Middleburg Academy and in 1963 from Cornell University. She is a doctoral candidate at Columbia University and a lecturer in French at the City College.
>
> Her fiancé, an alumnus of the City College, class of '63, is also a doctoral candidate and an instructor in English.

> The engagement of Miss Ann Todd Merriwether, daughter of Mrs. James Merriwether and the late Mr. Merriwether of Andover, to Donald John Cook, son of Mr. and Mrs. Maxwell Cook, of Phoenix, Ariz., has been announced by the prospective bride's parents.
>
> Miss Merriwether made her debut at the Debutante Cotillion in Chicago. She was graduated from the Wylie School there, and in 1964 from Manhattanville College of the Sacred Heart in Purchase, N. Y.
>
> Her fiancé, who is in his final year at the University of Chicago Law School, was graduated from Dartmouth College.

It's appropriate, of course, to notify close friends and relatives of the engagement before the announcement, and there will be few prospective brides who will fail to do this promptly. The letter should be as exuberant or as quietly happy as the young lady is:

Dear Uncle Bob,

I wanted you to be one of the first to know that I'm engaged. His name is Jack Townsend and he is the most superb man in the world.

We're announcing the engagement formally next week, and we plan to be married on June 15th. You'll be receiving a very formal invitation to the wedding, so keep the date open.

Jack is a systems engineer at Lockheed. We met last year while we were skiing, and while it wasn't love at first sight, it was love very soon after.

I know that you'll like Jack enormously, and I'm looking forward to having the two of you meet at the wedding, if not before.

Love,
Susan

FORMAL WEDDING INVITATIONS

The written material involved in a wedding should correspond as far as possible to the tone of the wedding itself. An elaborate affair calls for elaborate announcements. A simple affair calls for simple announcements. Let us turn first to the elaborate wedding, which is girded heavily with the bright armor of nearly unalterable tradition.

Your stationer will have a book full of formal, model invitations. They will, of course be engraved, and may be folded or unfolded cards. This is a matter of personal preference, and my only advice is the suggestion I have repeated throughout this book: when in doubt choose the simpler style.

The models you'll see will be in either Roman or script lettering; either is suitable.

The invitation will be enclosed in two envelopes. The inner will have no mucilage, and on it will be handwritten the last names of the recipient or recipients, e.g.:

Mr. and Mrs. Smith

Or, if other members of the family are to be invited:

Mr. and Mrs. Smith
Miss Ann Smith
John Smith

If it's a close relative, the bride may write:

Aunt Mary and Uncle Joe
Ann and John

The outer envelope is addressed in standard fashion; the return address goes in the upper left corner.

Pew Cards

Those to whom money is no barrier may have the printer prepare special invitations for guests invited to reserved pews–invitations identical to the others except that they have "Pew No. —— or "Within the ribbon" printed in the lower left corner. It is more practical for the bride's and groom's mothers to write the information on their visiting cards, and tuck it into the inner envelope, along with the invitation.

Special Situations

Normally, of course, invitations will be made up by the bride's parents, and will follow the standard format of the stationer's sample book. But there are special situations which call for some changes in the wording. The following examples should take care of most of these.

Where the bride is a widow:

The invitation is identical to that of a first wedding, with the exception that the bride's married name is used. Thus:

Mr. and Mrs. Lothrop Hamilton
request the honor of your presence
at the marriage of their daughter
Alice Hamilton Armstrong
to
Mr. Tad Maypole
etc.

Where a grandparent, aunt, or uncle is issuing the invitation:

Mr. and Mrs. John Stonington
request the honor of your presence
at the marriage of their granddaughter [or niece]
Alice Hamilton

Where friends of the bride or relatives other than grandparent, aunt, or uncle are issuing the invitations:

Mrs. Howard Anderson
requests the honor of your presence
at the marriage of
Miss Alice Hamilton
etc.

Where the bride herself sends the invitations:

The honor of your presence
is requested at the marriage of
Miss Alice Hamilton
etc.

Where the bride is a divorcée:

Opinions differ on what is proper. Those who hold fast to tradition say that a divorcée's wedding should not be heralded by engraved invitations. Those of a less conservative bent say that it is perfectly all right to send out engraved invitations, the only difference between them and those of an unwed girl being in the use of the bride's maiden and married names, for example Harriet Smith Jones, as in the case of a widow.

If the bride is in service:

marriage of their daughter
Jane Doe
Ensign, Nurse Corps, United States Naval Reserve

If the groom is in service:

to
William Henry Taft
Captain, United States Navy

If he's a lieutenant, there's no need to indicate whether he's a first or second lieutenant. If the groom is a noncommissioned officer or an enlisted man, the military designation may either be omitted, or included in smaller type under the name; for example

William Henry Taft
Pvt. 1st Class, U. S. Army

If the wedding must be postponed or canceled, one of the three following examples will do the job. These may be engraved, or printed on paper similar to that used for the invitations.

Mr. and Mrs. Gregory Croft
announce that the marriage of their daughter
Ann Martha
to
Mr. William Declension
has been postponed from
Thursday, the fifteenth of February
until
Thursday, the twenty-second of February
at three o'clock
Madison Presbyterian Church
Centerville

Mr. and Mrs. Gregory Croft
announce that the marriage of their daughter
Ann Martha
to Mr. William Declension
will not take place

Mrs. Gregory Croft
regrets exceedingly
that owing to the recent death of
Mr. Gregory Croft
the invitations to the marriage of their daughter
Ann Martha
to Mr. William Declension
must be recalled

At-Home Cards

"At-Home" cards may be enclosed in the envelope with the wedding invitation or announcement. Two forms are in general use:

Mr. and Mrs. Howard Krasner
After the first of August 32 Main Street
Centerville

or

At Home
after January thirteenth
32 Main Street
Centerville

The card is usually plain white, about 2¾ by 4 inches.

Receptions

Combination of wedding and reception invitation:

Mr. and Mrs. Theodore Crown
request the honor of your presence
at the marriage of their daughter
Jacqueline May
to
Mr. Frederick Thomas Hinge
on Saturday, the fifteenth of January
at half after three o'clock
Church of the Transfiguration
and afterward at the reception
Marymount Country Club

R.s.v.p.

When more guests will come to the reception than to the wedding, include a small card, about 3 by 4 inches, the same stock as the invitation, reading:

Mr. and Mrs. Theodore Crown
request the pleasure of your company
on Saturday, the fifteenth of January
at five o'clock
Marymount Country Club

R.s.v.p.

or

The pleasure of your company
is requested at the reception
after the ceremony
at
Marymount Country Club

R.s.v.p.

When there are guests whom you want to invite to the reception, but not to the wedding:

Mr. and Mrs. Theodore Crown
request the pleasure of your company
at the wedding reception of their daughter
Jacqueline May
and
Mr. Frederick Thomas Hinge
on Saturday, the fifteenth of January
at five o'clock
Marymount Country Club

R.s.v.p.

WEDDING ANNOUNCEMENTS

A wedding announcement is often used after a small wedding when the family wishes to let its many friends know of the event. The form is standard:

Mr. and Mrs. Alfred Meisel
have the honor of announcing
the marriage of their daughter
Felicia Georgette
to
Mr. Crispin McGowan
on Friday, the twenty-third of June
One thousand nine hundred and sixty-seven
Baltimore, Maryland

An alternative form is "have the honor to announce." Announcements do not go to those who've attended the wedding.

INFORMAL WEDDING INVITATIONS

For small, informal weddings, engraved invitations are inappropriate. A short note is probably the best way to handle it, if you do not, in fact, merely use the telephone. The note can read:

> Dear Mrs. Smith,
>
> Howard and Elaine are being married here at the house, at 15 Gossard Street, next Wednesday afternoon. My husband and I, [or "Jim and I"] hope so much that you and Mr. Smith and all the children will be able to come. The ceremony will be at three o'clock, and we hope that you will have tea with us afterward.
>
> Sincerely,

ANSWERING WEDDING INVITATIONS

When replying to a formal invitation to a reception, follow the form of the invitation:

Mrs. Howard Freeman
accepts with pleasure
the kind invitation of
Mr. and Mrs. Maxwell
to the marriage of their daughter
Susan Ellen
to
Mr. Bernard Franks
on Thursday, the twelfth of February
at three o'clock
St. Croix Hotel
and afterward at
35 East Fifty-ninth Street

or, if the invitation is to the reception only:

Mrs. Howard Freeman
accepts with pleasure
the kind invitation of
Mr. and Mrs. Maxwell
to the wedding reception of their daughter
Susan Ellen
to
Mr. Bernard Franks
on Thursday, the twelfth of February
at five o'clock
35 East Fifty-ninth Street

These letters are written, not typed, on personal stationery. Normally, one does not write an acceptance for an invitation just to the wedding. The reason of course, is that it makes little difference how many come to the ceremony; but the bride's parents would like to know how many they can expect to feed afterward.

Declining Invitations

If you cannot attend a reception, use the same form as you would in accepting it, but change the second and third lines to read:

Mrs. Howard Freeman
regrets that she is unable to accept
the very kind invitation of
Mr. and Mrs. Maxwell
to the wedding reception of their daughter
Susan Ellen
to
Mr. Bernard Franks
on Thursday, the twelfth of February
at five o'clock

THANK-YOU NOTES FOR WEDDING GIFTS

This is one of those categories to which the rule applies: the simpler the better. Keep the letter short, and keep it personal. If the gift is anything other than a check or money, mention it in the letter:

Dear Mrs. Anderson:

Thank you so much for the lovely pitcher. It is not only one of the most useful presents we received, but it is certainly one of the most beautiful.

or

Dear Joan:

The blender was a perfect gift. I know that we'll be using it frequently.

Thank you so much.

or

Dear Mr. Henly:

The salad bowl is exquisite. Jim and I will cherish it as one of our favorite possessions. We'd both like to thank you for your thoughtfulness.

If the gift is in the form of money, the safest reply is to thank the person for his generosity:

Dear Aunt Martha,

Thank you for your generous present. We shall be able to put it to very good use. I do hope that as soon as we're settled you'll come to visit us.

Sincerely,

or

Dear Mary,

Jim and I are quite grateful for your gift. I can tell you that we've already planned on turning it into a very handsome sofa pillow that I've had my eye on for some time. Thank you so much.

NOTES FOR OTHER OCCASIONS

BROKEN APPOINTMENTS

Usually, of course, your apologies will be made by telephone. Occasionally, though, a letter will be called for. Keep it short and to the point:

Dear Mary,

Will you forgive me for not having met you for lunch while I was in Washington? I had planned to call you in the morning at the office, but an unexpected client conference tied me up until it was time to rush for the plane.

I expect to be in the city again next month, and will call you a couple of days in advance–and this time, I promise to make it.

Dear Jack,

You are entitled to give me thirty lashes. I did expect to visit you and Marcia, but the family was more demanding than I had expected, and it wasn't until we got back home that I realized I didn't even have a chance to call you and say hello.

BON VOYAGE NOTES

The spirit of these is one of lightness and good will. In the excitement of departure, the traveler probably won't be able to concentrate on more than a couple of sentences, so keep them brief:

Dear Jim and Mary,

Have a lovely trip. And when you return, you must come and visit and tell us all about it.

Dear Harvey,

I trust you'll have such an excellent trip that you won't have much time for reading. But if a quiet moment comes, I hope you'll enjoy this book.

Dear Mrs. Williston,

We know you're going to have a wonderful time. All of our best wishes go with you.

CONGRATULATIONS

Your friends and acquaintances will appreciate your thoughtfulness in congratulating them on a noteworthy event in their lives. The most effective and sincere note is a brief one. Such notes would cover a wide range of happenings from an appointment to a new job to the receipt of an award or citation.

For a Promotion

Dear Howard:

You deserve it. I don't know of anyone who knows his field as well as you, and I'm sure that you'll justify the company's faith in you.

I send my sincerest congratulations.

Dear Mary,

The only thing wrong with your promotion is that it didn't come sooner.

I know that you'll do an excellent job, and that the hospital will be a better place because of your abilities.

Dear Mr. Jansen:

Yesterday's paper carried the news of your elevation to the presidency of the company.

Frankly, none of us here have been very surprised. It's been obvious for quite some time that you were exactly the right man for the top spot.

We all wish you the very best of luck.

For a New Job

Dear Bill,

Mary told me of your appointment as an assistant professor.

I know that State College is exactly the kind of place you've been hoping to teach at, and I'm most happy for you.

Please send our very best wishes to May and the children. They must be very proud of their dad.

Dear Jack,

It was wonderful to learn that General Foundry has hired you as plant foreman.

Obviously, they must be a good company; they recognized an excellent man when they found one.

We're all rooting for you, and know that you'll do as great a job there as you did here.

Dear Mr. Mason,

Congratulations on your new job.

There's no doubt in my mind that the agency selected the finest man on the East Coast for the position.

I hope that I'll have a chance to see you soon, and wish you all the best in person.

BIRTHDAYS

The appropriate birthday letter, naturally, depends greatly on your relationship to the celebrant. Chances are, your greeting will consist of nothing more than a birthday card. If a letter is called for, the likelihood is that the birthday is merely an excuse for sending a longer letter. So, the best thing to do is get the congratulations out of the way quickly, and then go on to your news, which, of course, I wouldn't presume to tell you how to write. For introductory paragraphs, you might consider:

The congratulation simple:

Dear Mary,

Happy birthday!

I'd meant to write before this, but the pressure of keeping the family fed, washed, dressed, and so on, has consumed every waking minute, and too many of the sleeping ones.

Etc.

The congratulation indirect:

Dear Joe,

I'm never certain whether birthdays deserve congratulations because we have reached them, or sympathies–for precisely the same reason.

In your case, I think congratulations are in order, mainly because you've done such an excellent job so far in the years you've had.

Etc.

The congratulation flip:

Dear Phil,

What? Another birthday?

Don't be depressed. Remember, Michelangelo did his best work after sixty.

Etc.

The congratulation delayed:

Dear Harry,

I've just realized that your birthday was last week. Even though I'm late, I wish you many happy returns for the rest of the year.

Etc.

The congratulation pontifical (mainly for absent sons and daughters)

Dear Harold,

Happy birthday. Your mother and I miss you, and hope that you'll be able to use the small gift we're sending along.

Note: The foregoing letter can stand by itself if the parent has considerable self-control. It also serves as an introduction to a longer letter which may contain gossip, parental advice, or whatever thoughts the writer deems advisable to pass along on the occasion.

NOTES TO CONVALESCENTS AND INVALIDS

For the bedridden, few pleasures are greater than those of receiving a letter from a friend, unless it be a visit. Even if you send a letter to an invalid whom you visit occasionally, it can help lift his spirits enormously. A couple of general principles may be useful.

First, this is one of the rare occasions when I cannot counsel you, as I have so frequently elsewhere in this book, to be brief. The longer the letter, the better.

Second, make sure your letter is easy to read. The energy level of an invalid is likely to be low; don't make him work any harder than necessary. If you can type, by all means do so. If your handwriting isn't easily legible, print the letter.

Third, keep the letter reasonably cheerful, but not so much so that you run over into the trivial. Essentially, the letter should act as a proxy for you.

Fourth, if the invalid is going to be confined for quite some time, and you're worried because the routines of your life make poor material for an interesting series of letters, consider sending along clippings from newspapers and magazines that you think will interest the patient. Jokes, humorous columns, even serious articles that will help make him feel a part of the world will be morale-building.

Several years ago, I was confined to bed for nearly a year, and I remember that my greatest source of gloom was the feeling that the world was passing me by, that my acquaintances were all making their way in the world, while I was vegetating. Letters which cheered me most were those which generally followed the suggestions I've offered in the preceding paragraphs.

INTRODUCTIONS

Introductions may be written for a variety of reasons; basically, though, they all serve one function: to ease the path for someone you know. In this section, we'll consider a few of the more common types of introduction letters.

A Friend Moves to a New City

Dear Mary,

Good friends of mine, Harry and May Johnson, will be moving to Centerville in a couple of weeks. I think you'd enjoy knowing them as much as I have.

Harry is a computer programmer, and is to be in charge of a department at the ABC Computer Corp. He had been working for the company at their office here, and the promotion is a large feather in his cap.

Like you, May is an excellent cook, and has done quite a bit of volunteer work with retarded children, so I suspect you'll have a great deal in common.

I've given them your name and telephone number, and suggested that they call you after they're settled. If you can invite them over for an informal evening, I think you'll have made yourself a couple of very interesting friends.

A Child Goes Away to School

Dear Joe,

Our son, Bobby, will be starting as a freshman next month at Centerville University.

Although he's a fairly mature and independent boy, I shouldn't be surprised if he experienced a touch of the homesickness most youngsters feel the first time they leave home.

I know that Bobby would enjoy meeting you, for we've talked about you frequently. You can reach him by telephone through the main office of the college. He'll be living in Mason Hall.

My best wishes to you and your family.

An Employee Looks for Work

Dear Sir:

It is always difficult to lose a valued employee. It has been almost painful to lose James Madden.

He has been with this firm for seven years, five of them under my immediate supervision.

I have rarely met a man as dedicated and as loyal as Mr. Madden.

If circumstances had not forced him to move to a new city, he would have been assured of a secure position with this company.

I shall be happy to answer any detailed questions you may have about his abilities. In the meantime, I recommend him strongly to any prospective employer.

FUNERALS

Funeral announcements for the newspapers are discussed in Chapter Eleven, pages 257–58.

The newspaper notice is sufficient notification for all except those who've been told by telephone or telegram.

Letters of condolence are frequently difficult to write, because one cannot easily put into words the emotions one feels in such an occasion. In a sense, it is presumptuous to provide model condolence letters, for they should come from the heart. However, a few suggestions and a few models may be useful for those who are truly at a loss.

The major suggestion is to make the letter no longer than you feel absolutely necessary. A couple of sentences may be perfectly adequate to express your feelings:

Dear Mr. Hogarth:

The news of Mrs. Hogarth's passing has saddened all of us. We send you our sympathy in this most difficult time.

Sincerely,
Jane Anderson

If you've been a close friend of the deceased, you may feel a longer letter is appropriate. The customary practice is to mention something about the person who has died: think of why you liked him so well; what his best points were; why you will miss him.

Dear Mrs. Madison:

John's death came as a tragic shock to us.

We shall always remember him as we last saw him. It was at the beach, and he had driven over just to say hello, and let us know that he was home from school. He was full of fun, and he made our lives happier and richer.

For us, he will always be a reminder of what a fine young man should be.

We send you and Mr. Madison our sincere condolences.

Howard Quickly

Whichever member of the family is responsible for overseeing the funeral arrangements will undoubtedly have to engage in some correspondence.

First, there may be a letter to the clergyman who officiates at the funeral. Often, of course, he is simply thanked by a member of the family, and he may be given a small fee, usually $10 or more, depending on the family's circumstances. If this is done immediately after the funeral, no correspondence is necessary. However, a letter is a nice gesture, and it might go something like this:

Dear Mr. Berkey,

Your service was a comfort to the whole family. Thank you for the lovely way in which you described mother as you knew her. You understood her as few others have.

We are all most grateful.

Sincerely,

If you include a check, you may want to mention it in the last paragraph:

I hope you will use the enclosed check in any way that you deem proper.

Next, it will probably be necessary to answer letters of condolence. If there are many of them from acquaintances who were not particularly close to the deceased, you may want to have a printed or engraved card made up:

Mrs. John Gardner
wishes gratefully to acknowledge
your kind expression of sympathy

This card may or may not have a black border, as you prefer.

To anyone who's sent flowers, or to any reasonably close acquaintance who's sent a letter of condolence, it's appropriate to send a brief note of thanks:

> Thank you for your kind letter. I am very grateful for your sympathy.

or:

> You were very sweet to recall such pleasant memories of Dad. We shall all miss him, but your letter helped soften the pain.

or:

> The flowers and the letter which you sent were very thoughtful. Please do let us know when you will be visiting the city, for we should very much like to see you, and I know that will be an especial comfort for Mother.

A word about mourning stationery is in order. Mourning paper is used today by only a few. If you want to use it, it should be white and have a thin, black border, about one-sixteenth of an inch wide.

Otherwise, any standard stationery is suitable, if the color is white or a subdued gray.

Chapter Four

JOBS AND CAREERS

Probably nobody ever won a job solely through a letter of application, or a printed résumé of his experience. But a well-written presentation of your work history can help to point out your qualifications to an interested employer. What's more, when you're competing for a job opening, a good written presentation can create a strong impression that may prejudice the interviewer in your favor.

First, we'll discuss job résumés, since they're usually essential when you're applying for a job that calls for you to prepare written material about your working life.

In line with our stated principles of good communications, a résumé should be accurate, brief, and clear. It should put your best foot forward, tell the most important things about you that a prospective employer might want to know, and it should do these things fully, but with no padding.

There are two schools of thought about the résumé. One school says that it should be kept skeletally brief–that more than a page is too much. The other says that a page isn't enough; that at least two pages are needed: one page to present the highlights, and a second to fill in some of the details.

Because the second school is somewhat more flexible, I'd be inclined to go along with it. If you haven't had much working experience, and can fit everything on one page, then do so. But if you've had four or five years of work, and a considerable amount of experience behind you, it may be quite worthwhile to go on to a second sheet.

Let's take a look at a standard résumé.

James C. Cartwright
333 Centerville Street
Centerville, La.
Telephone: (914) 898-7274

RÉSUMÉ OF WORKING EXPERIENCE

1963–1966 Eastern Regional Sales Manager
ABC Electronic Corp.
Centerville, La.

Supervised sales force of 25 men selling radio and TV components. Responsible for recruitment, training, and the establishment and fulfillment of sales goals. During this period, region's sales rose an average of 30% annually, compared to previous rise of 18%.

Presently employed by the firm, but family ownership prevents rising any higher in the foreseeable future.

1958–1963 Field Salesman
DEF Sales & Service Co.
Waco, Texas

Sold hardware to stores and supermarket chains. Opened up new territory after six months on job and built it to second largest in company.

Left to assume better-paying job with ABC Electronic.

1956–1958 GHI Engineering Co.
Los Angeles, Calif.

Designed machine tools for the aircraft industry. In last six months of work, became a customer engineer. Left in order to become a full-time salesman.

EDUCATION

College:	Boston University, Boston, Mass.
	B.S. (Engineering), 1954
High School:	Boston High School, Boston, Mass.

PERSONAL

Age: 35
Married: 1956
Children: Three, ages 3, 5, 8
Health: Excellent
Height: 5′9″ Weight: 160
Affiliations: Sales Executives Club of Centerville; Kiwanis
Civic: Member, Centerville School Board; Chairman, Centerville Muscular Dystrophy Fund Drive

SERVICE

1954–1956 U. S. Army
Enlisted as Pfc, honorably discharged as Staff Sgt. Overseas duty in France, Germany

REFERENCES

Available

That résumé is by no means the only perfect type. It will, however, provide a good model, and will serve as a target for comments and criticism. Let's take it line by line.

Name, address, telephone: This information should always go at the top where it can immediately be seen. Whether you put it on the left or right side is immaterial. If you want to put your name on the left and your address on the right, that's all right, too. Personally, I think it's a good idea to keep all this data together.

Title: "Résumé of Working Experience" is one of several alternatives. "Résumé," alone, is satisfactory, too. (Incidentally, "résumé" is a French word, pronounced ray-suh-may, with all syllables equally accented.)

Some authorities suggest that this title be placed above the name, and that below the name, there should be inserted:

JOB OBJECTIVE

Regional Sales Manager
(or whatever job it is that you're seeking)

here's nothing wrong with this suggestion. In many cases, though, it's probably unnecessary, since the person to whom you're applying for a job will know quite well what position you're applying for. This will have been mentioned in a letter that you'll have sent along with the résumé, or, of course, in the interview.

Date listings: The usual format is to have the dates stand alone in the left margin. This makes a neat appearance.

Also, it's customary to list your most recent position first. The reason is that a prospective employer will be most interested in your latest experience.

Job data: List first your title, and then the name of the company. This helps the prospective employer place you in time and space.

Job description: This is the most difficult part of your résumé, and the most important. It is worth spending quite a bit of thought on before you write the final draft. Your goal is to present yourself in the best possible light, playing up your strong points and playing down your weak ones. (In the section, "Special Situations," starting on page 102, we'll discuss some deceptions that you may want to use, in case your best possible lights aren't very good.)

In preparing the job description, ask yourself: what did I do in this job that would impress a prospective employer? Or, you might ask: if I were hiring somebody for the job I want to get, what sort of experience would I look for? This is the kind of information you should try to get into your job description.

Here's a little checklist that may help you in composing your job description:

Can you indicate any unusual responsibility you've been given?

Can you give any examples of having helped the company grow?

Can you give any examples of how you saved money for the company?

Can you show that you were promoted rapidly?

Did you receive any other form of recognition that would show your ability? (For example, if your salary increased substantially within a year or two or three, you might give this in terms of percentage.)

When explaining why you're looking for a new job, or why you left your previous job, consider whether it's to your advantage to do so. If you left because of "personality clashes" don't say so. To a prospective employer, this indicates that you may be a troublemaker, and you'll have one strike, or possibly two, against you. Think hard and you'll probably be able to come up with some other reason, such as a company reorganization leaving your position uncertain.

In describing the jobs you held prior to your most recent one, try to avoid repeating duties that you've mentioned. An employer is likely to favor an applicant who's had some diversity of experience in related areas, rather than one who's been doing exactly the same thing in all of his jobs.

Education: Give the name and location of your college, the degrees you've earned, and the dates you earned them. If you didn't go to college, give the date of your high school graduation. Unless you're a relatively recent graduate, there's no need to go into detail about your college activities. (See "Special Situations," page 102.)

Personal: The information listed in the model is what's usually expected. If you've been divorced and have remarried, there's no need to tell the employer about it unless he asks. You might want to eliminate the "Married" entry, and insert instead: "Marital Status: Married, three children."

If you'd just as soon not mention that you have children, leave it out and don't mention it unless you're asked.

If you prefer to be discreet about the fact that you're divorced or widowed, you might write: "Marital Status: Unmarried."

Service: List the branch of service, and if you had substantial promotions, your beginning and leaving ranks. Mention any overseas duty. It will make you feel better, and may add a dash of color to the résumé.

References: There's not much point in listing references in the résumé, since the prospective employer won't use them until he's talked to you, and he may not want to talk to the references you put on your résumé. Come prepared, however, to give him the names of people he can call who will give you a good recommendation.

Salary Desired: Notice that no mention is made of this point.

The reason is, it's irrelevant. If you list a salary and it's less than the man is willing to pay, you're selling yourself short. If it's more than he's willing to pay, you're automatically disqualifying yourself before you have a chance to let him talk to you. If you're good enough, and he wants you strongly enough, he may be willing to come up in his salary. But let him talk to you, first.

A NOTE ON STYLE

There are three possible styles of language in writing a résumé.

There's the first-person style: "I did this, I worked as that, etc."

There's the third-person style: "He did this, he worked on that, etc."

There's the impersonal style: "Did this, worked on that, etc."

The first-person style is apt to sound a bit egotistical, because you'll find yourself putting "I" into almost every sentence, and if you've a sense of modesty, you'll feel uncomfortable with it after the first two or three sentences.

The third-person style tends to pomposity. The reader knows that you prepared it, and cannot avoid wondering, "Why does he pretend that somebody else prepared it?"

The impersonal style is, I think, the easiest to read, and is quite easy to write. I recommend it to you.

SPECIAL SITUATIONS

There are a number of "special situations" that require special résumés. Let's consider the most common ones.

YOUNG JOB-SEEKERS

If you're a young man or woman with little job experience, your problem will be to impress your employer with your potential, rather than with your past. To do this, you'll have to make the most of your scholastic and extracurricular activities. The first step is to list on a worksheet everything that might impress a prospective employer.

If you're fortunate, you'll have done some work—perhaps full-time during the summer, or part-time during the year, or both. Make a list of these jobs and give a brief description of them.

Next, if you've majored in any subjects at school which you think may help you in your work, put those down.

Third, if you've won any scholastic or athletic honors, or have achieved any meritorious recognition, put it down.

Fourth, list the extracurricular activities in which you've engaged. If you achieved any positions of prominence on teams or other organizations, list them.

Fifth, if you're a member of a college fraternity or sorority, put it down. You may be fortunate enough to hit an employer who belonged to the same organization.

When you've put down everything, you can arrange it in a résumé that follows the format below. This is a résumé for someone who's just graduated from college and is seeking her first job.

Résumé of
Marjorie B. Major
120 Main Street
Centerville, Mass.
Telephone: MA 1-2345

OBJECTIVE

Laboratory Technician

SCHOLASTIC RECORD—COLLEGE

1963–1967 University of Chicago
Chicago, Ill.
B.Sc., 1967
Majored in Chemistry
Scholastic Average: B plus
Minored in Mathematics
Scholastic Average: B plus
Scholarships:
1963–1964: Half-tuition scholarship
1964–1967: Full-tuition scholarships

Working Experience

1965–1966 Laboratory Assistant, Chicago Downtown Hospital. Work involved blood, urine analyses; record-keeping. Average

10 hours per week during the school year. Worked full-time during summers of 1965 and 1966.

1963–1965 Clerical Assistant, Chemistry Department, University of Chicago. Maintained records of Ford Foundation project on the body chemistry of twins.

Extracurricular activities

1963–1967 Chemistry Club; Treasurer 1965

1963–1967 Women's Tennis Team; co-captain 1966, 1967

Sorority: Alpha Alpha Alpha, Honorary Society of Chemistry Department

SCHOLASTIC RECORD—HIGH SCHOOL

1959–1963 Centerville High School
Centerville, Ky.
Scholastic Average: A minus
Scholastic Recognition:
In 1963, won Kentucky Science Fair prize for an exhibit on the spectroscopic analysis of the stars.
Extracurricular activities:
Tennis Club–1959–1963
Orchestra–1959–1960
Glee Club–1961–1963

PERSONAL

[Follow model of previous résumé]

REFERENCES

School, working, and personal references available

AUTHOR'S NOTE: If the résumé is for a young man, he will probably have to put down his draft status. To leave it out will only make the prospective employer wonder what he's hiding.

WHEN YOU'VE BEEN FIRED

This is sometimes a difficult matter to handle in a résumé. Here are several ways to deal with the problem:

1 If you were discharged because the department was reduced, explain it with a simple sentence: "Reason for leaving: lack of busi-

ness resulted in elimination of all but two senior employees." Or, "Reason for leaving: company reorganization eliminated department."

2 If you were discharged because your work was unsatisfactory, put as good a face on it as you can. One method is to state that this was simply not the proper slot for you. One useful cover-all statement: "Reason for leaving: Position required different skills than I possessed."

This leaves unspoken the fact that you were fired, and is broad enough to encompass everything from incompetence to the fact that your boss didn't like your face.

WHEN YOU'VE BEEN UNEMPLOYED FOR A LONG TIME

Prospective employers like to think that the person they're hiring has been keeping busy. It makes them uncomfortable when they consider hiring somebody who hasn't been keeping his nose to the grindstone.

If you're not exactly the grindstone type: if you've taken a sabbatical for a year or two, if you've looked for work for quite a while and haven't been able to find it, or if personal affairs prevented you from working, then it may be a good idea to conceal this fact—or, at least, not to call attention to it.

How?

Several solutions are possible, depending on your position in life.

1. If you're an upper-echelon executive, or somebody who's had ten or fifteen years of working experience, you might consider using the consultant gambit. It's not unusual for someone who's been working for others for quite a while to try to strike out on his own. And it's not unusual for someone who's tried to strike out on his own to fail. The world, after all, is made up of 99.9 per cent failures, and nobody really holds that against anyone, since we're all pretty much in the same miserable boat.

A "consultant" entry might read like this:

1963–1965: Independent consultant.

or

1963–1965: Independent consultant. Experience showed I was better suited for working within the structure of a company than as an independent entrepreneur.

This second, amplified version subtly tells the prospective employer that you've learned your lesson and are ready to settle down and be the good employee he desperately needs.

Of course, if you actually have tried operating independently, and can describe some of your accomplishments in reasonably glowing terms, by all means do so.

Another gambit that you might use to cover a gap in your career is:

"Supervised personal investments."

This is an impressive-sounding and satisfactorily vague explanation that can mean almost anything you want it to mean. It will work best if you really do have some substantial personal investments in securities or real estate; for then you can explain in the interview that personal affairs kept you too busy to hold down a full-time job.

2. If you're a middle-management person, or if you're a relative newcomer to the job market, your absence from work may not need too elaborate a disguise.

Whatever your explanation, don't apologize. You've done what you've done because you believed it was the right thing to do.

For example, suppose you became fed up with the rat race and decided to become a farmer. You chucked your job, started raising chickens, and lost your shirt. Now, you're back in the market for a job again. How do you describe this in a résumé?

One solution is to be vague about it, if you think that you can tell the story in person more effectively. In this case, you might simply say:

1965–1966 Spent one year in independent enterprise–to be explained in interview.

Another solution is to be quite frank about it, but in terms that reflect credit upon your spirit:

1965–1966 Personal requirements dictated spending a year away from chosen career. At the end of this period, recognized that my greatest abilities did lie in my career field.

You don't, of course, need to explain everything—leave some of the details to the interview. Just be careful to avoid the kind of apologetic statement that gives the impression that you were temporarily insane:

> Quit job in order to make living at farming. Found myself unable to make a go of it, and decided to go back to work.

COVERING LETTERS FOR RÉSUMÉS

A covering letter sent along with a résumé can, if properly written, do a good job of selling your abilities, and of calling attention to your strong points.

In writing a covering letter, a good question to begin with is: "What's the main point I want to get across?" Your answer might be, "My experience," or "My fast rise," or "My general sales ability." Whatever it is, this should be a major point to emphasize in your covering letter. Call attention to it near the beginning, because the prospective employer may be so harried that he won't have time to read anything except the first paragraph or two, before he turns to the résumé.

Again, as with all of your other correspondence, keep the covering letter short.

Here are some samples.

REPLYING TO A WANT AD

When replying to a want ad, remember these points:

1. Read the ad carefully to try to get a feeling for what kind of experience the employer is most interested in. (In the sample letter immediately below, for example, the ad stressed the employer's interest in somebody with a broad background in production, and with some supervisory experience.)

2. It's a good idea to identify the date and newspaper in which

the ad you're answering appeared. The employer may have inserted more than one ad.

3. It's also a good idea to mention the kind of position for which you're applying—for the same reason as in No. 2.

Dear Sir:

Your advertisement for a production manager in the May 12 *Journal* interested me because your requirements closely parallel my working experience.

As the enclosed résumé indicates, I've had more than ten years' experience in all phases of production. For the past eight years, I've supervised a work force of at least a dozen people.

I'll be happy to tell more about my experience in an interview. You can reach me during the day at UN 1-2345, and in the evenings at UN 2-9876.

Sincerely,

Dear Sir:

The sales job which you describe in your advertisement in the *Mirror* of April 19 is one for which I think I can show you some excellent qualifications.

You ask for a "go-getter with proven experience." As you'll see from my résumé, I've turned in an above-average sales record for the past five years, ever since entering the sales field.

While I'm quite happy in my present work, the description of your job sounds even more appealing. I'd enjoy discussing my qualifications with you at your convenience.

Sincerely,

If you're applying for a job for which your qualifications are poor, then your letter might stress your personal qualifications, your zeal, and your willingness to learn:

Dear Sir:

If an ability to take direction well, and to carry out orders faithfully is important to you, then I may be a good man for the job you advertised in the *Chronicle* of August 15.

The job sounds particularly interesting because it is precisely the kind of work I have wanted to do for many years. My working experience thus far has, I think, given me the attitudes and the understanding that would enable me to learn the details of the position you've advertised.

I'd very much appreciate the chance to talk to you, and to get your opinion on whether my background and inclinations would be suitable for the job you offer.

I can be reached by telephone at 398-4123.

Sincerely,

GENERAL COVERING LETTERS

When you're sending résumés to prospective employers, you're at a disadvantage if you don't know exactly what their needs are. In this case, you'll have to take your chances, by trying either an all-purpose letter which calls attention to your availability, or else a more specific letter emphasizing the areas in which you think you're strongest.

I believe the latter choice is preferable. You only live once, and you might as well spend your working hours doing a job for which you feel best qualified. If you emphasize only a couple of points about yourself, you'll lose the interest of some prospective employers who may have a job for you which isn't down your alley, but you'll probably attract the attention of an employer who detects in you a prospective employee who knows what he wants. (And there are certainly few enough of those around.)

One preliminary word before writing your application letter. Presumably, you'll be writing to a company which you think will have a job of the type you want. Try to get the name of the president, and write your letter to him. He may or may not do the interviewing, but even if he doesn't, he'll pass the letter on to the person who does—and a letter coming down from upstairs always carries a bit of extra prestige.

Here are a couple of samples:

Mr. Robert Johnson
President
Johnson Manufacturing Co.
Centerville, Md.

Dear Mr. Johnson:

Having watched your company's growth for several years, I've often felt that I'd like to be able to contribute to that growth by becoming a member of your sales force.

Your company appears to attract men who are capable of growth, and who are willing to shoulder responsibility. As the enclosed résumé will indicate, my working career has been marked by both characteristics.

I think my experience would fit me particularly well for opening new accounts. I'm accustomed to putting in a nine-hour day, plus some homework in the evenings. Hard work doesn't bother me, since I enjoy selling—particularly selling the kinds of products which your company makes.

I'll plan on calling your office on Tuesday, May 14, in the morning, to see whether I might have an interview.

Sincerely,

In the foregoing letter, a couple of points are worth noting. First, if it's a smaller or medium-sized company, it never hurts to praise the top man for the job he's been doing. In a larger-sized company, perhaps, flattery is a bit less effective, but not so much so that you shouldn't consider using a bit of it.

Second, it's a good idea to follow up the letter with a phone call, rather than wait for someone in the company to call you. It shows a certain amount of spirit, and companies like a bit of that.

Here's another example. In this case, the writer has met the addressee, and decides to trade on the acquaintance.

Mr. Howard Hanson
Treasurer
Metallic Cup Co.
New York, N. Y.

Dear Mr. Hanson:

When Bill Jacobs introduced us at the Central Country Club last month, I enjoyed chatting with you about the part you played in the

Democratic primary. I was glad to see that you backed a winning team.

I'd like to ask your advice on a matter pertaining to Metallic Cup. I'm beginning to consider looking for a purchasing agent's position with a new company.

While my present job is satisfactory, my company appears to be in a rather stagnant position, as you may have noticed if you saw the recent Annual Report. The opportunities for growth are quite limited, and since I've always tried to work for a company that seems to promise some possibilities for development, I've been considering looking for a better opportunity elsewhere.

Whether Metallic Cup would have a suitable opening is, of course, something I don't know. But your company is obviously going places. I'd like to explore the possibilities of joining you.

You'll see from my résumé that in each of my jobs, I've been given increased responsibility within a relatively short period of time. Mainly, I think, this is because I've been willing to accept extra assignments on short notice, and because my experience in the field has given me broad contacts that have been useful in emergencies.

I'll plan to call you on Thursday next, to see if we might get together to explore job possibilities further.

Sincerely,

Chapter Five

WRITING TO SCHOOLS AND COLLEGES

The competition for admission to private schools and colleges grows increasingly intense, and from all indications, it will grow more intense in the future. If you're the parent of a child whom you hope to send to a private school or to college, you'll both probably have to write quite a few letters and fill out a seemingly inexhaustible number of application forms. Such letters can be quite important in helping your youngster to gain admission.

In addition to the all-important admission letters, this chapter also discusses a number of the more common types of correspondence to elementary and high schools, such as absence notes, requests for interviews, and consultations.

APPLICATIONS TO PRIVATE SCHOOLS

If you plan on sending your youngster to a private school, you are in one of two situations: either you know which school you want to send him to, or you don't.

If you're not sure of which one would be best suited for his needs, hie yourself to the public library and pick up a copy of either *Private Independent Schools,* published by Bunting & Lyon, Inc., Wallingford, Connecticut, or *The Handbook of Private Schools,* published by Porter Sargent, Boston, Massachusetts. These thick manuals list most of the boarding schools, day schools, and military schools in the country. They also tell a bit of the history, describe the buildings and equipment, the faculty and staff, the size of the student body, admission requirements, costs, and other pertinent information.

Having selected a number of schools you'd like to know more about, your next step will be to write them for catalogs. The catalogs will give you the same information you found in the manuals, but in greater detail. Keep this inquiry letter brief; there's no need to go into detail about your child at this point, since the letter will, in all probability, be thrown out as soon as the catalog is sent. You can send the letter to the school, or to the headmaster if you prefer. In either case, it will undoubtedly wind up on the desk of the secretary in charge of sending out catalogs.

A simple, one-sentence letter like this should do the trick:

Gentlemen:

Please send me the current catalog for your school.

Sincerely,

After you've gone over the catalogs, and have selected those to which you'd like to apply, it's time to send a letter which is a bit more detailed. Here are several points to keep in mind:

Timing: Write for your application as much as a year in advance. Many schools will start interviewing applicants around January or February of the year before they enter. Therefore, if you write for an application form in August or September, and return it by October or November, you'll be adequately protected.

Child's Age: Include the age of the child if he's quite young. Most private schools with a first grade have an arbitrary minimal age at which they'll accept a beginning youngster.

Scholarships: If you're planning on asking for scholarship help, mention it in the letter so that the school can send you a scholarship application form. Failure to do this may delay matters later.

Here are several letters that you might adapt in requesting an application:

Dear Sirs:

My daughter will graduate from the eighth grade at Centreville Public High School this spring, and is interested in attending a private, coeducational high school in the city.

We would appreciate it if you would send us an application form. My daughter would like to enter in the fall of 1967.

We should also like to visit the school and see its facilities. Will you tell us the procedure for making an appointment?

Sincerely,

Dear Sir:

We should like to apply, on behalf of our son, Richard, for the seventh grade for September 1966. Presently, Richard is in the sixth grade at Centreville school.

Please send us the proper application forms, and any other relevant information for parents of prospective candidates for admission.

Truly yours,

Dear Sir:

We are applying to your school because of its outstanding reputation. We are a family of very limited means. However, we feel that we have an unusual child who would be an asset to any school. We, therefore, would also like to request scholarship information, with a view to major assistance.

Yours truly,

Incidentally, the headmaster who provided the last letter commented that "it makes a favorable impression because it's simple and straightforward."

If your youngster is old enough, you might encourage him to write for the application forms himself. This is not an unusual procedure, and it's a good way to get him involved in his own future. Fundamentally, the child need do no more than ask for the application form. But, he may want to add a few flourishes. Don't discourage him; they won't hurt his chances. Here are letters that youngsters have sent to private schools:

Gentlemen:

I should like to obtain application forms for your school.

I am presently in the eighth grade at the Centerville School.

Will you please send me your entrance requirements and examination dates.

Very truly yours,

Dear Sir:

I am now attending Centerville School in Centerville. My academic average at the end of the first marking period was 94.3%. I stand 12th in a class of 190 students.

I would appreciate your sending information about admission to your school in the 1966–1967 semester. I hope to enter in my third year of high school.

Respectfully,

Dear Sirs:

I am interested in attending the Centerville Private School next year.

I am a ninth-grade student in the Gifted Student Program at Midville School, Midville, Kansas.

Last year, I was elected to the school's honor society. This year, I'm editor of the school yearbook.

I would like to go to Centerville because it emphasizes learning and minimizes competition. I also feel that Centerville will provide me with greater opportunities to participate in extracurricular activities such as dramatics and writing.

Please send me an application, and information about your scholarship program, since I would need financial aid.

I would also appreciate an appointment for an interview. I can visit your office any Saturday.

Respectfully yours,

Finally, you may be interested in sending your child to a foreign school. The rules to follow would be essentially the same. Here's the letter that one parent sent not long ago:

Dear Sir:

Please send me an application form and information about entrance requirements for your school.

I am writing on behalf of my son, Julian, who is thirteen years old.

He is now in the tenth grade at Centerville School, Centerville, Utah. This would correspond to Form 3 in your country.

Julian has an excellent scholastic record, and speaks French fluently.

His uncle and aunt, who live in Paris, will provide a home for him there.

Sincerely,

The application form which the school sends you may cover only one sheet of paper, or it may go on for three or four. Different schools, of course, will ask different questions, and their decision about accepting your child will depend on factors peculiar to that school. The most sensible course to follow in filling out the forms is to be honest. One headmaster told me, "Some parents lie about their child having had psychiatric help. There's not much point in trying to conceal it because sooner or later we find out about it, and it doesn't make the parents look very good."

APPLICATIONS TO COLLEGES

Basically, correspondence with colleges is not too dissimilar from that involved with private schools. But a few suggestions are in order about avoiding unnecessary words. Here are some thoughts proffered by college admissions executives:

1 When requesting an application, keep the letter short. One official put it this way: "Too many parents write long letters telling us about their kids, and at the end, they ask for the application. It doesn't do any good to tell us how good your child is—we assume you're biased and we don't read it; we simply don't have the time or the interest."

2 Limit yourself to asking one or two major questions, if you have any. "Many people," said one admissions executive, "ask us a tremendous number of detailed questions about the school. Usually, this is information which they can get from our catalog, and so we frequently don't even bother to answer the questions. We simply send them the catalog."

3 Make sure that you're writing to the right school. Arnold Goren, director of admissions of New York University, gave this example: "We'll sometimes get applications intended for the State University of New York, and they'll sometimes get letters which were meant for New York University. This, of course, just wastes everyone's time."

4 Remember that a college is an educational institution, not a vocational guidance center. Youngsters will sometimes write to a college saying, "I think I may want to be a doctor. Tell me what a doctor's life is like." Schools are rarely equipped to handle this type of inquiry. If you want information about a career, discuss it with the high school's guidance counselor, or check with your library for books on the vocation.

5 In requesting an application, don't try to impress the school with your importance or your important contacts. Generally, it carries little weight. Said one admissions officer: "We have to be like Caesar's wife–above suspicion. We just can't afford to show favoritism to one student because his family may know somebody. Anyway, our general experience has been that Senator Jones has never even heard of Johnny Smith. He may write a letter of recommendation for him, but more often than not, he's simply doing it as a favor for a friend of the Smith's."

THE APPLICATION

Colleges prefer that the student himself, rather than the parent, fill out the application. An admissions officer told me, "The youngster is going to be on his own in school, and we want to get as good an idea as possible of what he's going to be like. Until he arrives on campus, his application form will represent him, and so he ought to make as good an impression with his application as he would if he were coming for an interview."

Judging from the criticisms of many admissions officers, prospective students aren't too careful about this. Admittedly, when a youngster's grades are high, it's not going to count very strongly against him when his application form looks as if it were used to wipe a windshield. On the other hand, as I mentioned earlier, if he's an average student, it may have an effect on the admission department's overall evaluation of him; the prudent student will try to have everything possible working for him, not against him.

Keeping these points in mind, you should now pay very close attention to the following paragraphs. They are adapted from instructions prepared by New York City's excellent private institution, Columbia Grammar School. The suggestions were drawn up under the direction of Headmaster James W. Stern for the guidance of Columbia's students. Because they constitute an extremely knowledgeable and sensible approach to the process of college application, and because much of it is broadly applicable to students in both public and private schools, I'm reprinting much of it verbatim.

Notes for College Applicants and Their Parents

Set aside a drawer at home specifically for college information, applications, etc. Keep all materials in folders. Set up a system so that you can easily find what you are looking for. Instruct well-meaning parents, maids, brothers, sisters, etc., not to "clean out" the drawer or throw away any mail from the colleges.

Applications and Catalogs

1 You may write to any college at any time for its catalog. Once the list of colleges to which you will apply has been determined, you should write immediately to each for its catalog (if you don't already have it) and for its "Application for Admission." You may type or write the letter.

Use your own phrasing, but include the following information:

High School
When you plan to enter college
Request for Application for Admission
Catalog
Your name and home address

Address the letter to Director of Admissions or Admissions Office. Keep the letter short and direct. (See page 126 for a typical letter.)

2 As soon as you receive catalogs and applications for admission:

a. Read each catalog carefully, paying particular attention to requirements for admission and admission tests required.

b. Before you write one single word on the application for admission, read it over carefully to familiarize yourself with what is requested. Check carefully for:

(1) Deposit required, if any, or application fee required.

(2) Can you type the application or are you requested to use your own handwriting? If not specifically stated, you may do as you wish.

(3) Is a photograph required? How many? Always write your name on the back of the picture in case it is detached.

(4) If essay-type questions are asked (autobiographies, compositions, why you have selected that particular college, etc.), write your answers first on scratch paper. Make all corrections before you transfer the final draft to the application. Save your original draft; you may want to read it over before you go for a college interview and you may be able to use all or part of it for another application.

(5) Since all College Board test scores will be reported to the colleges in your senior year–no matter when you took the tests–don't hesitate to discuss them at any interview.

(6) Your nationality or citizenship is: United States, assuming you are a citizen.

(7) When asked to list secondary schools you have attended, this refers only to high school years, unless specifically otherwise stated.

3 Don't hesitate to consult with your school's college guidance counselor if you're not clear about an application question.

4 After completing each application, jot down on a separate

sheet of paper the important information you have supplied. File this or photocopy the application; you may be able to use it on another application, or want to go over it before an interview.

5 It is your own responsibility to handle the applications for admission. No one at school will keep after you to finish them or get them mailed. If you are mature enough to go to college, then you are mature enough to handle this responsibility.

THE SCHOOL RECORD FORM

Each college will require the school to complete certain forms concerning your application for admission. These forms, usually called "The Secondary School Transcript" or "Record" are sent to the school in one of several ways.

1 The college may send it to you when it sends you the application form. It will be separate from the application. As soon as you receive it, look it over to see whether you, personally, have to answer any questions on it. Then turn it over immediately to your school. Don't hold it until you've completed the application form.

2 The college may send it to you attached to the application form, and instruct you not to detach it. This means you must complete your part first, and then turn the *entire* application over to the school. In this case, the application will not be returned to you. Your school will mail it to the college.

3 The college will send the school record form directly to the school when the college has received your application. In this case, you do not have to turn in anything to the school.

RECOMMENDATION FORMS

Certain colleges will send you forms to be filled in by teachers who have taught you or know you well. It is your responsibility to select the teacher or teachers who you want to recommend you.

1 Before giving the teacher the recommendation form, ask him if he will be willing to recommend you. If he is, hand him the form and a properly addressed envelope with a stamp on it.

2 If you are asked to list teachers who will recommend you (on the application), be sure to ask their permission first to use their names.

COLLEGE BOARD EXAMINATIONS AND AMERICAN COLLEGE TESTING PROGRAM

It is your responsibility to take the proper college admission tests at the proper time for each college to which you are applying. What the tests are, and when they are required, can be found in each college's catalog, or in an "Information to Candidates for Admission" guide which some colleges send along with the application, or in both.

All information on the College Board Examinations appears in three publications of the Board: the "Bulletin of Information," "A Description of the College Board Scholastic Aptitude Test," and "A Description of the College Board Achievement Tests." The principal of your school, or the school's college advisor, should be able to supply you with these.

It is also your responsibility to complete the registration form required for each College Board Examination testing program. You can probably obtain these from your principal or college advisor.

The registration form must reach the College Board by a certain date. The deadline for each testing date is listed in the "Bulletin of Information."

It is wise to make up a "college calendar" on which you note all college application deadlines, including such dates as registration deadlines, dates of CEEB exams, application deadlines, interview deadlines, etc.

Certain colleges require the American College Testing Program (ACT) examination. Check the college catalog to find out if you must take this examination. If it is required, see your principal or college advisor for a registration form and information concerning the tests.

COLLEGE SCHOLARSHIP

If you must receive financial assistance from a college in order to attend, it's a good idea to discuss this with your principal or college advisor. He will probably be able to offer good, specific suggestions.

Most colleges are members of the College Scholarship Service (CSS). This is a central clearinghouse for scholarship information and does away with having to file a separate financial statement for most colleges to which you are applying.

The CSS form must be filled out by the parents, not the applicant. The school probably has a supply of these forms, or you can obtain them by writing directly to: College Scholarship Service, Post Office Box 176, Princeton, N. J. 08540. Since the forms change each year, be sure to ask for the form valid for the academic year in which the student is entering his first year of college.

Parents should retain a work copy for their own files in case information supplied to the CSS is needed for other forms during the applicant's senior year.

COLLEGE INTERVIEWS

Consult each college catalog to determine if a personal interview at the college is required, suggested, or not required.

A good procedure to follow is: Visit and arrange for an interview at as many of the colleges to which you apply as you possibly can.

A college visit and interview serves a twofold purpose. It gives you an opportunity to see a school at which you may spend the next four years and to ask any questions you may have concerning that college. It gives a member of the admissions staff a chance to size you up and help determine whether this is a good college for you and, perhaps, what your chances for admission are, based on what you tell him.

Furthermore, if one or both parents go with you to a college, the family enjoys a common experience which can be discussed at home after the visit. Therefore, when it comes time to decide which college you will attend, it can be discussed from firsthand impressions.

Parents are urged to visit colleges with their children; sometimes a parent notices and points out things to an applicant which otherwise may be overlooked.

NOTE TO PARENTS: If you're present during an interview, remember that it is your child's interview, not yours. As much as you would like to have your child say more, or express himself better, or sit straighter, etc., restrain your desire to make corrections or additions. Don't give the impression that your child depends on you to do his thinking and talking for him. College interviewers realize and take into account the fact that they are talking to nervous teenagers who usually cannot handle themselves in an interview as well as adults can. By all means, participate in the interview if questions are directed to you.

1 Colleges do not like an applicant to appear for an interview without a previously arranged appointment.

2 You may arrange for an appointment by letter (addressed to the Director of Admissions) or by telephone. However, some colleges specifically request that all appointments be made by letter; check the catalog or "Information to Candidates" bulletin.

3 If you write for an appointment, give several dates on which you can appear. This may save correspondence if you cannot be seen on the date you select. (See pages 126–27 for samples of appointment-request letters.)

4 Before visiting each college, reread the pertinent sections of its catalog and prepare several questions concerning points which are not covered in the catalog, or points which you would like expanded or clarified.

5 Be yourself during the interview. Don't be afraid to say, "I don't know," if you can't answer a question.

6 Subjects covered in an interview can range from A to Z. The entire discussion may center around you, your interests, activities, likes and dislikes, schoolwork, etc. Then again, it may include current events, your opinions on world problems, a discussion of a recently read book, etc.

7 Don't be disappointed if you travel several hundred miles for a ten- or fifteen-minute interview. The length of the interview does not determine your acceptability.

8 If you know a student who is in attendance at the college, it might be a good idea to write him that you will be visiting on a cer-

tain date, and ask him to show you around. You might see more and meet more students with him as a guide. (See page 127 for sample letter.)

9 After you return home from the interview, write a thank-you note to the person who interviewed you. If you did not get the interviewer's name when called into his office, ask a secretary or an office worker for it after the interview. (See page 127–28 for sample letter.)

10 If you visit a college with another applicant, do *not* arrange for an interview at the same time as his. This is *your* interview and should not be shared with another applicant. (See page 128 for an example of the type of letter that would cover this situation.)

11 Dress simply and neatly. Girls should not overdress or wear excessive makeup.

12 Your application for admission need not be in the hands of the college for you to have your interview. You may have the interview any time, unless a college catalog stipulates otherwise.

13 All applications and interviews should be finished before the Christmas vacation. This is because you will start studying for mid-term exams shortly after Christmas and most colleges start their admission selection work after February 1. Many colleges specifically state that they will not interview candidates after February 1 or March 1.

FIRST-CHOICE COLLEGE

As soon as you and your parents are absolutely 100 per cent certain which college is your first choice, tell your principal or college advisor. This information will be noted on your school transcript and sent to your first-choice college.

You should also write to your first-choice college informing them of your desire to attend, if you're accepted. (See page 128 for such a letter.)

Never tell a college—on the application or in an interview—that it is your first choice if it is not. *Remember: it is not necessary to select a college as your first choice.* Most applicants do *not* indicate a first choice, and it does not in any way affect their chance for admission. They do not make up their minds which college to attend until they hear from all to which they have applied. On the other hand, once you have told the college and your school about your first-choice, if you're accepted, you must attend that college.

Approximately 165 colleges agree to "The Candidates Reply Agreement Date" which is about May 1st each year. Applicants who receive notice of acceptance by these institutions need not reply to them until the agreement date with their decision to attend or to accept financial aid. This enables candidates to consider all available opportunities. Check each catalog to see if that college is a member of the agreement date group.

COLLEGE ACCEPTANCES

1. Let us assume you are applying to four colleges–A, B, C, and D–and you prefer A and B to C and D.

If you are accepted to B before you hear from any of the others, then write to C and D and thank them for their consideration of your application; inform them that you are withdrawing your application because you have made other plans for your education.

Do not wait to do this just to collect college acceptances: you may be keeping another applicant from being accepted. (See page 128 for an example of a withdrawal letter.) If you still prefer A over B, then hold B's acceptance until you hear from A. If A accepts you, then write to B saying that you are flattered to have been accepted, but have made other plans.

If you hear favorably from D first, then hold the acceptance until you hear from another institution on your preference list. In other words, do not collect acceptances. Write a withdrawal letter as soon as you hear from a more preferred college.

2. Remember, *all acceptances are conditional,* based on your completing the senior year with grades comparable to those submitted for three or three and one-half years of high school work. Many seniors feel that the second semester is the time to let down their efforts. This is not true; students have had acceptances turned into rejections because their final grades for the senior year took a noticeable drop.

Criteria for College Admission

Most colleges use the following criteria, in approximately the following order of importance, to select their candidates:

1 Secondary school record
2 School's recommendations
3 College Board scores
4 Character and personality strongly emphasized
5 Extracurricular participation important.

SAMPLE LETTERS

REQUEST FOR A CATALOG AND APPLICATION FORM

Dear Sir:

Please send me a catalog and an application for admission.

I am now a junior at Centerville High School, and plan on entering college in the 1968–69 academic year.

Sincerely,
William C. Smith
2424 Merit Road
Centerville, Calif.

REQUEST FOR AN APPOINTMENT FOR AN INTERVIEW

Dear Sir:

I should like to make an appointment with your office for an interview concerning admission to Centerville College.

I am a junior at Centerville High School, and plan to enter college in the fall of 1969.

Any time on Saturday, November 12, or Friday, November 18, would be convenient for me to visit you.

Sincerely,

The foregoing letter is perfectly adequate, and will do the job nicely. You may, however, want someone to guide you around the school. In this case, you may write:

Dear Sir:

On December 14 through 17, I shall be visiting Centerville, and would like to become better acquainted with your college.

I would be grateful if you could arrange for me to have an interview concerning my admission. Any time during the 14th to the 17th will be satisfactory. I should also appreciate it if you can have someone guide my parents and me on a tour of the college. Again, any time during that period will be satisfactory.

Sincerely,

LETTER TO A STUDENT AT A COLLEGE, REQUESTING HIS HELP ON A TOUR

The letter should include:

1 When you'd like to have him guide you.

2 Whether you'd like to visit any particular part of the campus.

3 A reference as to how long it might take, so that neither of you will feel obligated to spend more time than he desires on the tour.

Dear Joe:

I'm planning to visit Centerville on Saturday, October 14, and hope to spend some time touring the college. As you know, I'm graduating from Midville High this coming June, and Centerville is one of the colleges I'm applying to.

Can you spare an hour or two during the day to act as my guide? I'd be especially interested in seeing the laboratories, because I hope eventually to work in biology.

If you can act as my shepherd, please let me know what time I should meet you, and about how long you think we should spend together.

Sincerely,

THANK-YOU LETTER FOLLOWING AN INTERVIEW

Dear Mr. Smith:

Thank you for spending time with me last Friday when I visited Centerville University.

I enjoyed our discussion, and found it most useful for getting a clearer idea of what Centerville expects from its students and of the many advantages it has to offer them.

I hope that we will have a chance to meet each other again.

Sincerely,

APPOINTMENT REQUEST FOR YOURSELF AND A FRIEND

Dear Mr. Johnson:

On January 13, a classmate of mine, Jane Smith, and I will be visiting Centerville University. We would appreciate it if you could arrange to have a college interviewer see us during the day.

We would prefer to have separate interviews.

Both of us are in our third year at Midville High School.

Will you be good enough to let me know what time I may have an appointment? Also, will you send Miss Smith a letter telling her the time of her appointment? Her address is: 23 Mason Terrace, Midville.

Sincerely,

ACCEPTANCE LETTER FOR COLLEGE

Dear Mr. Johnson:

Thank you for your letter of May 16, telling me that Centerville College has accepted me as an entering student in the 1967 academic year.

It goes without saying that I'm delighted, and that I do expect to attend.

Within the next few days, I shall be sending you the information you requested about my scholarship and about my dormitory needs.

Sincerely,

WITHDRAWAL LETTER FOR A COLLEGE

Dear Mr. Johnson:

Thank you for your letter of May 16, telling me that Centerville College has accepted me as an entering student in the 1967 academic year.

Although I am grateful for your acceptance, I shall be unable to attend Centerville because I have made other plans for my education.

Sincerely,

ADDITIONAL SCHOOL-RELATED LETTERS

Absence–Explanatory Notes

When your child is absent from school because of illness, a short explanatory note to the teacher is normally required.

March 12

Dear Miss Smith:

Tommy's absence during the past four days was caused by a cold and fever.

He seems to be all right now.

Sincerely,

If you expect your child to be absent, explain when and why:

Dear Miss Smith:

We should like to take Tommy on a trip to visit his grandfather next week.

Although we dislike making him miss school, we have been unable to arrange a different schedule.

If you can give him his assignments in advance, we shall try to make sure that he does them while he's away.

Please call me at CE 1-2345 if you foresee any problems.

Sincerely,

Consultations

Requests for interviews with teachers and administrators should:

1 Briefly explain the reason for requesting the interview;
2 Suggest a method for arranging the appointment.

Dear Mr. Johnson:

As the parents of Jim Fletcher, now in his sophomore year, we have been disturbed by his poor academic record during the past four months.

We should like to make an appointment to discuss your ideas about how we might help Jim.

Will you call me at CE 6-7890 any weekday morning to arrange a time when my husband and I might visit you?

Sincerely,

Dear Mr. Harrison:

Earlier this week, you had an advisory session with my son, John Jacobson.

John came home rather discouraged because he felt that the colleges you suggested were not of a high caliber.

I'm certain that you gave him your best advice. However, I'd appreciate it if you'd be willing to spend some additional time in talking to me about the reasons for your suggestions.

If you'll call me at 234-5678, any weekday between 9:00 A.M. and 5:00 P.M., I'll be happy to set up a date with you.

READMISSION REQUESTS

An increasing number of adults are resuming formal studies that were interrupted in their earlier years. This is particularly true of women who have married, have raised a family, and who want to complete their work for a college degree.

In writing for readmission, address your letter to the Dean of Admissions, unless you know of another person to whom you should write. Your letter should:

1 State your purpose;
2 Briefly review your educational status;
3 Describe what you think the next step should be.

Dear Sir:

I should like to apply for admission to Centerville College.

In 1964, having finished my junior year at Maryland State University, I had to leave college in order to support my parents.

Now I shall be able to devote a considerable amount of time to studying.

I'd be grateful if you could write me telling me what steps to take in order to be considered for admission to your school.

Sincerely,

Dear Mr. Jackson,

My advisor, Gerald Davis, suggested that I write you requesting readmission to the Doctoral Program at Teachers College.

In 1960, I stopped working toward my degree, in order to care for my first child.

Next autumn, my second and youngest child will start attending school, and I shall then be able to devote an adequate amount of time to studying for my degree.

I am most eager to return to school, and expect to spend whatever time is necessary in order to do a thorough and expeditious job.

I hope that you and the faculty committee will look favorably on my request.

Sincerely,

Incidentally, the above letter is an adaptation of one which my wife, Susan, sent when she decided to resume her academic career. It pains me to confess that because of my carelessness, she had to undergo a bit of needless anxiety.

In drafting the first letter, I failed to make clear that she would be unable to *start* studying until six months hence, when our youngest child would enter school.

The admissions officer sent back a letter telling her to be prepared to take a readmission examination in four months—an exam that would require at least four months of full-time studying.

Unfortunately, until our child entered school, Susan would be unable to spend *any* time preparing for the exam. And so we had to draft a second letter, spelling out quite clearly when she would be free to start studying, and when she would like to take the exam.

The admissions officer was quite good about it, and granted her request. But in the meantime, Susan underwent a couple of excessively trying weeks, wondering if he would decide that, since she was incompetent to tell them what she wanted, she was obviously not suitable academic material.

The moral: be as specific as possible in describing what you want to do, and when you want to do it.

Chapter Six

TENANT-LANDLORD LETTERS

"Most tenants are more reasonable and more patient than I'd be. They frequently say, 'I don't like to complain, but. . . . ' We reply, 'We want you to complain if things aren't right–otherwise, how can we know what's going on?' We can't possibly know everything that's going on in all our buildings."

This is a direct quote by a senior executive of a major metropolitan real-estate management firm. And it indicates the value of telling your landlord your housing problems. Not all landlords will listen, but it's worth making the effort.

In this chapter, we'll discuss some of the more common problems that occur between landlords and tenants, and suggest ways to achieve more effective action by letters.

To begin with, a bit of common sense is in order. If you live in a house where you're personally acquainted with the landlord; where, perhaps, the landlord actually lives in the building, or where you know him fairly well by sight, then correspondence is probably the last way you'll want to make your problems known to him. The natural thing is to talk things over in a face-to-face conversation.

When you don't know the landlord personally, or when the landlord is a corporation, then the conditions become ripe for letter-writing. Even then, in all likelihood, you'll be making your first contact not with the landlord but with the resident manager, if there is one, or over the telephone with the landlord's office. When face-to-face dialogues fail to achieve what you want, then it's time to sit down and rip off a letter.

TO WHOM SHOULD YOU WRITE?

If you know the name of the landlord, or have already made contact with someone in his office, this is usually the first person to write to.

If you don't know the landlord's name, call the office where you pay your rent and try to obtain the name of a specific person to whom you can write. It's invariably better if you have the name of a person at the head of your letter.

If your building is managed by a real-estate management firm, try to obtain the name of the head of the firm. If his office won't give it to you (some real-estate firms are understandably shy about giving out the names of their chief executives), you may be able to get it by calling your city's real-estate board. If you still can't find it, take your chances and simply write to the office, to the attention of "The President."

If you live in a public housing project, you have a couple of choices, assuming that your relations with the building or project manager have gone beyond the stage where talking will be of any use. One possibility is to write to the municipal housing bureau in charge of your project. The other is to write to a politician who may be able to exert some pressure on the housing officials.

A New York City Housing Authority official vouches for the following story, in which he was involved. A young soldier, newly married, was about to be sent overseas—without his bride. Appeals to the Authority to find an apartment for his wife proved futile. Desperate, or angry, or perhaps just astute, he wrote to President Lyndon Johnson, describing his problem. Within a couple of weeks, a Federal Housing official in New York called the Authority, expressed an interest in the soldier's problem, and managed to secure an apartment for him.

The President probably never saw the letter. One of his secretaries undoubtedly passed it on to the Federal Housing official with a notation that he might look into the matter to see if anything could be done. One can imagine Washington's New York man quite casually calling the city housing agency, and mentioning that the White House had forwarded a letter from the soldier—and did the agency think that anything could be done for the young man? And one can also imagine how the municipal authorities reacted when they heard that the President himself was interested in the case.

You cannot, of course, assume that a letter to the President will solve your housing problems. On the other hand, the incident does indicate that a letter in the right pigeonhole can be useful.

Before providing some sample letters covering a multitude of housing problems, it might be useful to present two groups of suggestions about the principles of good tenant-landlord letters. The first list deals with letters to landlords of private housing; the second, with letters to the management of public housing. If you should find yourself engaged in letter writing with either of these categories of landlord, I'd recommend that you read both lists, since they are by no means mutually exclusive, and you may find that suggestions in one list will be useful if you're writing to a landlord from the other group.

SUGGESTIONS FOR WRITING TO PRIVATE LANDLORDS

If you're already a tenant, and you're not certain that the landlord knows you, include your full name—or the name of the person who is registered as the tenant. Also include your apartment number and your building address. When a landlord of several buildings receives a letter signed with a name and, as the only indication of address, "the tenant in Apartment 3F," it makes it relatively difficult for him to place you. Completely identifying yourself can save your own time and the landlord's.

Include a telephone number where you can normally be reached. If you're usually at home, your home number is sufficient. If you're frequently at another number during the day—say at your regular job, or working for an organization part-time–include that number as well.

Put the date of writing on your letter. Not all letters go directly to the right person. In some cases, they may go through two or three people before reaching their proper destination. As inevitably happens in any office, they may get stalled on someone's desk. If you put on the date, it will get faster attention when it reaches the desk of the person who's supposed to act on it. He'll be able to see, for example, that the letter was written a week or two ago, and will be more likely to hop right on it.

In the body of your letter, be specific about dates. Instead of saying, "About two weeks ago," give the actual date if you can remember it. This frequently helps the landlord's office staff find the appropriate records more quickly.

Finally, even if you're upset about something, try to keep the letter from being supercilious or vindictive. Remember, the person in the office who reads your letter is not the one who failed to fix your leaking faucet, and is probably not the one who neglected to send you the forms you distinctly requested. He is simply an employee of the company who's been hired to do a job, and tries to do it with a minimum of trouble.

If you feel there's been a slip-up somewhere along the line, by all means let the landlord know about it, but try to keep the tone civilized. The staff does probably work hard, and they are probably underpaid; they'll respond to a reasonable plea in the same way that you would if you held their rather harassing jobs.

SUGGESTIONS FOR WRITING TO PUBLIC HOUSING OFFICIALS

Before writing your letter, try to get the name of the person and the department who's responsible for handling your problem. This will help ensure that the letter goes directly to the correct person, instead of drifting around through various offices for several days.

If you can't discover the name of the right person, write to the director of the housing bureau. You can certainly get *his* name.

He may not see the letter; in fact, he probably won't. But his office will route it to the right department. It may take a little longer than sending it directly to the right department, but it will probably get there faster than if you send it simply to the Housing Authority, with no departmental indication.

Try to keep your tone reasonable, and avoid extreme statements. If you write a letter just to get something off your chest, the recipient will simply try to absolve himself of the blame. But, if you approach the recipient as if you were dealing with a difficult problem, he'll tend to approach it in the same way. In other words, don't blame–explain.

Stick to one or two major complaints. You may have a number of grievances that have bothered you over a period of time, but don't drag them all in. To do so classifies you as a crank–and this immediately weakens your position.

If you get a written answer to your letter, and you're not satisfied with it, don't waste your time writing back to the same man. He's made up his mind and you probably won't get him to change it. Write to his boss, who make take a different point of view.

If you're handwriting the letter, keep it short–less than a page. It's not a bad idea to do the same thing if you're typing, but if you really have to make it longer, a typed letter will more likely be read all the way through than a handwritten one.

In filling out forms of any kind, make sure you've filled in all the required spaces. If the instructions aren't clear, attach a letter explaining why you're confused, and if possible, give the alternative pieces of information you think they might want–then let them insert the right one.

Take advantage of anyone you may know, or any special circumstances that will help your case, or that will make you stand out from the thousands of other letter writers. If you know an important –or even an unimportant–politician and you can get them to write on your behalf, by all means do so. If you're infirm in any way, and you think that mentioning your infirmity may help you to get what you want, by all means mention it. In other words, use whatever emotional weapons you can to get what you want.

One final point, applicable to both private and public housing letters. As a general rule, refrain from writing the kind of letter which you feel you have to send anonymously. Unsigned letters are usually treated contemptuously by landlords, and contempt is not the attitude you want any landlord to have toward your correspondence.

SAMPLE LETTERS

COMPLAINTS ABOUT POOR SERVICE

By "service," I mean any of those which a landlord is supposed to provide, such as heat, garbage collection, cleaning of the public areas, painting, etc.

While the following samples deal, necessarily, with specific complaints, you can probably adapt them easily to your own needs if they do not describe your problem precisely.

Plumbing

Dear Sir:

On January 3, last Thursday, your maintenance man came to my apartment to fix a leaking faucet.

Two days later, it began leaking again.

I have tried to reach the maintenance man, but without success.

The constant dripping is running up your water bill. Further, I am afraid that the sink may overflow and cause extensive damage to your floor.

May I urge you to have the maintenance man come again as soon as possible.

I am usually at home between 8:00 A.M. and 11:00 A.M.

Note that the writer emphasizes the expense and possible damage that may result. For a landlord, this is a good reason to take quick action.

Dirty or Cluttered Hallway

Dear Mr. Jones:

For the past two weeks, the halls of this building have not been cleaned.

Not only are they unsightly, but they are a health and fire hazard.

There are now at least half a dozen boxes of garbage and waste in the halls.

Unless you take steps to see that the mess is cleaned up within the next three days, I shall have to notify the Board of Health and the Fire Department.

Sincerely,

Dear Mr. Jones:

An old refrigerator has been standing in the hallways of this house for the past week.

(I believe it was left behind by the tenant in Apartment 6F.)

I think it constitutes a fire hazard, for it blocks off most of the hall.

I am sure that you will want to correct this situation immediately, before it becomes necessary to call it to the attention of the Fire Department.

Will you have it removed within the next week?

Sincerely,

Painting

Although the following three letters deal with the painting of an apartment, they might be adapted for almost any other type of complaint where the landlord has not taken action. The letters begin gently, and become increasingly urgent.

Dear Mr. Smith:

According to the terms of my lease, this apartment was due for a painting about six months ago.

Since I have not heard from you, it occurred to me that you had simply overlooked the matter.

Will you please get in touch with me, or have your painter do so, within the next week?

Sincerely,

Dear Mr. Smith:

Last month, I asked you to get in touch with me about the painting of my apartment. The painting was six months overdue.

I assume that I haven't heard from you because of an oversight.

I call this to your attention again because cracks are beginning to appear in the walls, which, if not attended to soon, may force you to undertake costly repairs.

In the interest of saving your property and your money, I urge you to get in touch with me immediately.

Sincerely,

Dear Mr. Smith:

This is the third letter I have written you about the long-overdue painting of our apartment.

Because the condition of the walls is seriously deteriorating, I shall have to notify the city housing bureau unless you take steps within the next five days to remedy this situation.

Sincerely,

Notice that we have associated the painting of the apartment with the deteriorating condition of the walls. A lax landlord is likely to act more quickly to maintain his property values than to satisfy a tenant's desire for—or right to—a freshly painted apartment.

COMPLAINT ABOUT DAMAGE

Dear Sir:

On Thursday, January 3, a pipe broke on the fifteenth floor of my building and flooded my apartment.

Your maintenance man picked up my watersoaked carpet yesterday for cleaning. However, a friend of mine who is an expert in rug cleaning told me that although the rug might be cleaned, it had been so damaged that it could not be restored to its former condition.

I have had the rug only about six months, and can show you a receipt to that effect. Since it is practically new, I see no reason why I should suffer a loss for which I am not responsible.

Therefore, I will not accept the carpet back. I feel you ought to reimburse me for its replacement cost.

The writer of the above letter may or may not have convinced the landlord to pay for a new rug. In all likelihood, there will be a bit of a hassle before this thing is settled, but at least the tenant has calmly made his point, and has stated clearly and precisely what he expects the landlord to do.

The next letter might have been written by the upstairs neighbor of the man who wrote the first letter. It does an excellent job of describing the writer's unhappy position, and plays beautifully on any sentiment that the landlord may have in his heart.

APOLOGY TO LANDLORD

Dear Sir:

An out-of-town business trip has prevented my visiting your office to apologize for the inconvenience I caused through the flooding of my apartment on March 14.

I feel an explanation is due you.

Bad luck apparently was dogging my steps that day. I had read the notice you posted in the hallways that the water was to be shut off for three hours to make repairs.

In the middle of that afternoon, my wife was brought in by a policeman. She had fainted on the street. I was terribly upset, and went to turn on the faucet to get some water to revive her. There was, of course, no water, and in my confusion, I forgot to turn it off.

I took her immediately to the doctor (Dr. John Jones, 43 Center Street) for an examination. He found a concussion of the brain. I am enclosing his medical report.

Upon returning, I found the maintenance man mopping up the apartment. The water had overflowed, as you know, and had soaked the floor.

Fortunately, there is no damage to the floor or any of the cabinet-work in the apartment. I have since had the floors polished, and they look like new. I have also checked with my neighbors, none of whom suffered any damage from the overflow. I hope you will have a chance to visit the apartment and see for yourself.

As you probably know, my wife and I are on pension, and have a very hard time making ends meet. We are very sorry about this accident, and can assure you that it will never happen again.

COMPLAINT ABOUT AN ACCIDENT

The following letter is a simple, straightforward one which might have been quite angry—and if it had been, would probably not have got the quick action it did get:

Dear Sir:

Since I haven't been able to reach you by phone, I am writing this letter.

On June 3, I visited your office to report an accident that happened to me June 1. The elevator did not stop even with my floor, and as I was leaving it, I fell and fractured a bone in my finger.

Dr. Cecil Smith, 45 Main Street, will confirm this. His telephone number is 617-5454.

Although I have been able to work, I have been suffering a great deal of pain.

I have filled out the accident report your office sent, and now I am waiting to be reimbursed for the doctor's fees. Please let me hear from you within the next week.

CLEARING UP A RENT PROBLEM

The writer of the next letter lives in semipublic housing where his rent is tied to the size of his income. He wrote the letter when he found himself involved in what was apparently an administrative mix-up:

Dear Mr. Smith:

I received a note that you are going to increase my rent because my income has increased.

I believe you have made an error.

On January 3, 1961—three years ago—I became ill and have been convalescent since then, and unable to work. In fact, I retired from my union two years after my illness, and have not worked at all since then.

Please check your records again.

NOISY NEIGHBORS

When you're registering a complaint about noisemaking, it's a good idea to be as specific as possible—as the writer of the following letter was.

Dear Sir:

You asked me to let you know when our upstairs neighbors made any more objectionable noise.

Last night, Sunday, August 2, it hit a new peak between 8:00 P.M. and midnight. It was so bad my wife and I had to leave the house.

I trust you will talk to these people soon.

APPLICATIONS FOR APARTMENTS

If you're looking for an apartment, you're in one of two sets of circumstances: either you're living in a building and you want to change to another apartment in that building or another one owned by the landlord; or, you're an outsider, and you want to get space in a building.

In the first situation, your problem is probably not too difficult, for the landlord probably knows you, and if you've paid your rent regularly and haven't been a troublemaker, he'll probably make some extra effort to retain you as a tenant.

In the second situation, your job may be a bit more difficult, as is the task of any stranger asking for help. The best way to help yourself is to make your needs known as clearly and as completely as possible.

So, if you're looking for an apartment, here's the information you ought to include if you're writing a letter:

- The number of bedrooms you want
- The number of bathrooms you want
- The maximum rent you're willing to pay
- The number of adults in the family
- The number of children, and their ages
- You might also include your employer and your job title, if you think it will impress the landlord.

Here's a letter to a real-estate management firm which incorporates these suggestions:

Gentlemen:

I would appreciate your help in securing an apartment. I have recently been appointed regional sales manager of ABC Corp., and expect to move to Central City next month.

Our family consists of five people: my wife and myself, and three children, aged 6, 9, and 11.

We would like to rent a three-bedroom apartment, preferably with two full bathrooms, or with one bathroom and a lavatory.

We would be willing to pay a monthly rental of up to $160.

I expect to be in Central City in about two weeks, on January 14, and would be available that afternoon to look at prospective apartments. Will you let me know by return mail whether you will have suitable housing for me to look at?

Sincerely,

And finally, it may be useful to review some correspondence of my own involving an elderly relative. As the letters will make clear, she had to seek a new home and applied to the city of New York for an apartment. She received a form letter from the Tenant Selection office which said that she'd first have to obtain an eviction notice from her present landlord. This would have been awkward, and I volunteered to try to get the Housing Authority to revise its decision.

My initial step was to call the Housing Authority's Public Relations office and ask for the name of the man who headed the Tenant Selection Division. I wrote him the following letter. (In the interests of preserving everyone's privacy, I've changed everyone's name.)

Mr. Jack Johnson
Chief, Tenant Selection
New York City Housing Authority
5 Park Place, New York, N. Y.

Reference: Mrs. Anna Smith
Tenant Selection
Committee No. 4321

Dear Mr. Johnson:

The purpose of this letter is to explain some rather unusual circumstances surrounding the housing application of my cousin, Mrs. Anna Smith. This might normally have been written by one of her two children. Since they are dead, I shall try to speak on her behalf.

On September 21st, Mrs. Smith received a letter from the Tenant

Selection Division saying that her housing application could not be processed until the Division had received a final court order for eviction, plus relevant legal papers. This requirement puts Mrs. Smith—and her landlord—in an extremely awkward and distasteful position. The following paragraphs explain why.

For the past ten years, Mrs. Smith has rented two rooms in the private home of Mr. Howard Sales. Mr. Sales is selling the house; his two children are about to be married, and he and his wife wish to move to smaller quarters. The house is on the market, and prospective buyers are now considering it.

Mr. Sales has not served Mrs. Smith with an eviction notice because of their long and close relationship. He was a boyhood friend of her deceased sons. When she became his tenant, she acted as a sort of grandmother in residence, and was the Sales' baby-sitter; in fact, she paid a part of her small rent by her baby-sitting services.

Mr. Sales, a teacher at the Science High School, is a gentle and warm-hearted man. He has done what any gentleman must do: he has told Mrs. Smith he is going to sell the house, and has asked her to find other quarters. (You may check these facts directly with Mr. Sales. His address is 890 Center Street. His telephone number is AB 1-2345.) He knows that Mrs. Smith is in her eighties, and understandably finds quite painful the thought of obtaining a court order against this woman with whom he has had the friendliest relations.

One further point: Mrs. Smith, as the accompanying doctor's statement indicates, suffers from a heart impairment. This makes her situation doubly difficult. First, it sharply restricts her ability to look for an apartment by herself—not an easy task for any woman in her eighties.

Second, her illness makes it impossible for her to climb stairs, and makes it advisable, as Dr. Harris' note says, that she "live in an elevator apartment."

I can understand and agree with the Authority's general requirement for an eviction notice in cases of this sort. At the same time, I'm sure that you consider every applicant individually. I hope that this letter will be of some help in explaining Mrs. Smith's situation, and that you will recommend that her application be processed even though she does not have an eviction notice.

Sincerely,
Lassor A. Blumenthal

Because this letter illustrates several of the points I've discussed earlier in this chapter, it may be well to examine it in more detail for the light it may shed on your own housing correspondence. Here are some of the principles it invoked:

Don't get angry or vindictive: When I first read the authority's requirement for an eviction notice, I felt shock and anger at the inhuman machinery of urban government which in effect dictated that the landlord would have to almost throw Mrs. Smith out bodily before the Housing Authority would take any action. It was a stupid and cruel law, and my first instinct was to write and tell them so.

On reflection, I realized that such a letter would be useless. The Tenant Selection Committee did not make the law; it was merely administering it. If I disapproved of the law, that didn't concern the Authority. If I were to accuse them of being heartless, they would react quite humanly with: "Sorry; we just administer the law, and Mrs. Smith will have to abide by it."

So, instead of being angry, I tried to turn it into a problem with which they could deal as human beings.

Use every advantage you can: The letter is intentionally shot through with emotional appeals. The first paragraph mentions her deceased children. I did not use the word "deceased" because "dead" is a stronger word. Mr. Sales is described as fully as possible, as is Mrs. Smith's long-standing relationship with him. The objective here was to picture two kindly people being caught in a web through no fault of their own. The aim was to help the housing officials *feel* that this was a special situation deserving more attention than routine cases. The medical report was a valid one, and was simply one more weapon in the arsenal.

Keep the tone reasonable: The last paragraph was an attempt to do just this. Its aim was to make clear that I felt the Authority was doing a good job of administering the law, but that this was a case which called upon them to do more than merely administer; they were being asked to behave as the reasonable human beings I knew they were.

I trust that this explanation does not make me out to be overly calculating. Admittedly, it was a carefully written letter, designed to obtain for my relative every possible advantage. But in the great machine in which most of us live today, our strongest refuge often lies in appealing directly to the sympathetic emotions of those who work the levers. They will usually respond favorably because they are more aware than most of the injustices that the machine can cause when it is allowed to run automatically. In effect, what this letter was doing was asking them to switch from "automatic" to "manual" control.

And they did. A few days later, I received a nice reply, not from Mr. Jackson, but from the lady supervisor of another office in his division. The letter said that my relative would probably be unable to obtain City Housing in downtown Manhattan, as she had requested, because the waiting list was so long, but that she would be eligible for housing in another part of the city. If she was interested, she should notify them.

I quickly wrote two letters, one to the lady who answered me, and one to Mr. Jackson:

Dear Miss Anderson:

It was kind of you to let me know, in your letter of October 21, that your office would consider my cousin, Mrs. Anna Smith, when an apartment became available in some part of the city other than Manhattan.

I've spoken to Mrs. Smith, and you should be hearing from her within the next few days, telling you of her willingness to accept.

You're probably besieged daily with scores, if not hundreds, of similar requests. I suspect that your job is a most difficult one, and therefore, I'm very grateful for the encouragement you've been able to offer.

Thank you again for the attention you've given Mrs. Smith.

To Mr. Jackson, I wrote:

Thank you so much for acting on my letter concerning the housing application of my cousin, Mrs. Anna Smith.

I received a pleasant letter from Miss Anderson, supervisor of the Applications Office, yesterday, suggesting that Mrs. Smith may be eligible for apartments in other parts of the city than Manhattan.

Knowing that my cousin will be grateful for reasonable accommodations in almost any part of the city, I've asked her to write to Miss Anderson to that effect.

You've been most kind, and I simply wanted to let you know that I'm quite appreciative of both your understanding and your follow-through.

Since both of them had responded so generously to my request, I thought it only polite to let them know of my gratitude.

At the same time, I made up the following letter for my cousin to sign and send to Miss Anderson:

Dear Miss Anderson:

My cousin, Lassor A. Blumenthal,_____ [Author's note: the letter also included my address], told me that he has received a letter from you suggesting that I might be eligible for City Housing.

I would be very happy if you would consider me for an apartment in any development, regardless of location.

It was kind of you to give me such consideration, and I am very grateful.

Sincerely,
Mrs. Anna Smith

And the result of all this correspondence? Within three weeks, my cousin had moved into her new apartment. But I must admit that it was not in City Housing. The doctor who provided her medical report happened to be friendly with the manager of a large apartment house, and when the latter heard of my cousin's plight, he immediately made one of his apartments available to her.

I'm not sure of the moral of this story. But it had a happy ending —in fact, it had two happy endings. And good letter writing was responsible for one of them.

Chapter Seven

WRITING TO MAGAZINES, NEWSPAPERS, RADIO, AND TV

Every day of the week, you are bombarded by thousands of words and images from the gigantic communications media. Newspapers and magazines try to influence you to believe one thing or another; television and radio programs are largely designed to induce you to buy the product of the company sponsoring the program. In short, you, the reader, the viewer, the listener, are a target.

Must you be a target? Does it do any good to try shooting at the hunters? It does. The mass media welcome letters from the public for a variety of reasons. Sometimes, it's even possible to turn the tables and exert a bit of influence on them.

For example, executives of one national television network received a letter from a rabbi calling attention to the fact that a comedy program had used phrases from Hebrew prayers as pseudo-African mumbo-jumbo. The comedian was warned that his material would have to be screened in the future, and he was further penalized by having a booking taken away from him.

Admittedly, instances of effective reverse pressure are relatively rare. Nevertheless, they do exist. It's worthwhile keeping up the good fight if only to let the mass media know that there are living, breathing individuals with independent minds.

WRITING TO MAGAZINES

Magazines value letters from readers because letters are one of the few ways in which the editors can tell whether they are doing a good job. Just how important some magazines regard reader mail can be judged from *Time* magazine's issuance of a small book for its own employees who answer reader mail. A few lines from the Introduction to the *Time* manual will explain how they handle correspondence:

"Of the hundreds of letters received by the editors every week, *Time* publishes only twenty-five to thirty in the Letters column. These few are chosen for a variety of reasons, but primarily for their interest and readableness. Letters on significant issues, especially those written by qualified authorities, get first consideration. Letters that question . . . *Time*'s handling of the news get particular attention because the editors sometimes like to publish them with a note to explain what *Time* sources were, to clarify misinterpretations, to answer questions, to correct errors. Bright, amusing letters are always welcome, of course, to give the column balance, and to indicate the kind of bright, intelligent readership which *Time* has."

HOW TO GET YOUR LETTER PUBLISHED

You'll increase the chance of getting your letter published if you observe a few rules of good correspondence.

1 *Keep it brief.* Magazines have only a limited number of pages to give to letters. The editors of the letters columns look for mail that expresses in a few sentences the meat of the argument. One editor says, "One of our favorite correspondents is the author, Upton Sinclair. He writes us regularly, sending just two or three handwritten sentences, letting us know exactly what he thinks in no uncertain terms. And because he's always brief and clear, we publish his letters frequently."

2 *Keep it relevant.* This is related to the rule of brevity. If you disagree with an article, say so at the beginning, and tell exactly why in as few words as possible. A letter which wanders all over the lot will stand less chance of being published than one which sticks to the subject. As one editor said, "Some correspondents seem to think they can bully us into publishing their letters by writing at great length. It just isn't so. We don't get bullied, we just get bored."

3 *Be reasonable.* A letter which says, "You're all wet," will not receive nearly as much attention as one which says, "You're all wet.

Here's why," and then gives the reasons. As one editor said, "You should say what you think in the first sentence, and why in the second sentence."

4 *If possible, use a light touch. Time*'s statement that "bright, amusing letters are always welcome" is echoed by the editors of other magazines. Editors like to make their letters columns as readable as the rest of the magazine, but they're often hard put to do it because most letters are serious, even heavy-handed. If you can insert an amusing phrase, the editor will jump at it like a fish at bait.

5 Several other points mentioned by editors as being helpful in letters from correspondents are:

a Don't write a vague letter of praise in the hope of getting it published. While magazines, like anyone else, enjoy praise, they don't like to publish letters which say, "I wanted to tell you how much I enjoy your magazine. I've read it for years." As one editor said, "When we do put in one of these letters, we're always uncomfortable about it. It sounds too much like a puff–as if one of our own editors wrote it."

b Get your letter off early. Often, good letters have to be rejected for publication because they've arrived too late for inclusion. On a monthly magazine, try to send your letter out within the first week or two after you get your copy. On a weekly, if you live any great distance from the editorial offices, send your letter airmail.

c Don't worry too much about the form or the spelling. Editors read everything legible, whether it's typewritten, or handwritten in pencil or pen. One editor of a national publication even recalls receiving one letter written on a paper bag.

d Address your letter properly. Check the letters-to-the-editor column to see if it lists a name and address to whom you should direct your correspondence. Otherwise, address your letter directly to the editor, at the magazine's editorial office. Use the editor's name if it's listed–usually you'll find all staff members listed near the front of the publication, or on the editorial page, if the publication has one. If no editor is listed, send your letter to "The Editor."

Examples

Here is a long letter received by a national magazine:

When I read ________'s article, "Why I Love America" in the January issue, my eyes brimmed with emotions of pride and shame.

Pride for my native land, which I too, love dearly.

But shame, that so many of us "natives" should have to be reminded by an adopted friend of the glories to be enjoyed, of the rights we have, to live, speak and dream in freedom. He has made me want to shout, "Look Americans! Look about you at the opportunities we so casually acknowledge. Look in wonder, look in love, look in peace."

To your author, I extend a hand warm with friendship and love, and say, "thank you" to him for helping me to take a new view of my own land–My America!

Here is how the editors shortened it for publication:

I read ________'s article with pride and shame–pride for my native land that I, too, dearly love. But shame–that so many of us "natives" should have to be reminded by an adopted friend of the rights and glories that we have.

The article made me want to shout, "Look Americans! Look about you in wonder, in love, in peace!"

To your author, I extend a hand in friendship and in gratitude.

Keep it brief and relevant. A physician sent in a letter correcting an error in a magazine's medical column. Here is the succinct version that was published:

You report "old-fashioned measles" to be rubella. Actually, it is called rubeola or morbilli.

Rubella is called German measles or three-day measles. Since many patients are faithful readers of your medical column (they frequently quote it to me) it would be well to have at least one practicing physician check the accuracy of your material.

Add the light touch. The editors smiled when they read this one:

> In your issue of January, on page 15, an Iowa dentist is shown putting steel tooth caps on cows. I've lived in that hard grass country, and will admit that it really would be helpful to cap the cow's teeth with something that will stand the wear.
>
> But I was a farmer and stockman for "nigh on to 50 years" and I never saw a cow with front teeth on her upper jaw. Where did your artist find her? I want to go and see her. I know this new age is faster than I was accustomed to, but I'll still bet you don't have upper teeth in front on anybody's cow. How about it?

The editors shortened this letter for publication, giving just the high point of the humor:

> I was a farmer and stockman for nigh on 50 years, and I never saw a cow with front teeth in her upper jaw. Where did your artist find her? I want to go and see that cow for myself!

WRITING TO NEWSPAPERS

In general, everything that holds true for letters to magazine editors, holds equally true for letters to newspapers. Usually, brevity is important. As the editor of one metropolitan daily said, "We receive *and read* about three thousand cards and letters a month, and we only have room to print about three hundred."

Most newspapers restrict the length of their letters to three or four sentences. A few of the larger papers will give readers more leeway. The *New York Times*, for example, has a maximum rule of eight hundred words, which is more than a full-sized column. Letters of this length, however, are usually printed only if they're by someone who's a known authority in the field about which he's writing.

Most newspapers have certain taboos–subjects which they will not touch in the letters columns. As outlined by one editor, they are:

1 No personal messages, such as "Will that nice boy I met on the beach call me."

2 No poetry.

3 No lost-and-found.

4 No advertising, no matter how subtly disguised.

5 No personal attacks. (This point has to be loosely defined. Public figures such as the President, and members of Congress are usually considered fair game for adverse criticism on public issues. But, unless it's a major topic of discussion, such as a presidential candidate divorcing his wife, the paper won't print it.)

It is hardly necessary to add that papers differ in their taboos. The foregoing list, however, is a fairly common one among reputable papers.

Some newspapers try to make their letters columns exceptionally lively. Says the letters editor of one successful daily: "We like mail if it's violently opposed to an editorial stand that we've taken. A letter that begins, 'How stupid can your editors be?' is more exciting, more likely to be published, than one which says, 'May I take the liberty of disagreeing with your position.' "

Strength in Numbers

There are times when newspapers can serve as a powerful weapon for alerting the public to injustice. Let's take an example of an urban renewal plan which threatens to wipe out a section of a community. The newspaper may have covered the stories in its news columns. It may even have sent out feature writers to tell in depth how the people affected feel about it. But how much more powerful will the voice of the people be if it makes itself heard through the letters column!

Here's what one editor said about the strength-in-numbers policy: "If we receive a few scattered letters on a subject, we'll be less likely to publish them than if we receive four or five or a dozen or more. If we were to receive a lot of letters from the residents of an area that was about to be demolished, we'd be likely to print a lot of them, because we'd feel that this is something of widespread interest. On the other hand, if we receive only a couple of letters from the people affected, we may or may not publish them. It's a case of the squeaking wheel getting the grease."

Therefore, if you feel strongly about an issue, particularly a local issue which will affect you and your neighbors, urge your friends to write their own mail on the subject.

Don't send it all in on the same day, for it will seem too much like a rehearsed campaign, and it will lose some of its effectiveness. But a dozen or two dozen letters spread out over a week or two can be amazingly effective.

SOME GENERAL PRINCIPLES

John Illo is a young, earnest, college instructor, an independent thinker. His name first caught my eye when I was looking for samples of good letters to the editor. Over a period of several months, I found that his name was signed to a number of letters in the *New York Times*. It occurred to me that anyone with such a high batting average might have some useful suggestions about how to get letters published.

He did, indeed. When we met, he told me that letter writing to publications was one of his avocations. And he offered a number of suggestions which I print here, because they are valid whether you're planning to correspond with magazines or with newspapers.

1 Choose a periodical whose views are not radically different from yours. Disagreement is published in letters columns, but disagreement within limits.

2 If the letter is topical, write promptly. A stale letter is like stale news, and editors have little interest in either. Letters to a daily paper should be sent within a day of the news story or column that provoked it.

3 The beginning of your letter should refer succinctly to the story or topic that occasioned it: "Mr. Able believes that fluoridation of public water supplies is a violation of free, individual choice (Newark *Courier-Telegraph,* May 15, 1963)."

4 All letters should be sober and rational for their best effect. The letter of commendation should not gush, the letter of protest should not rage, the letter of complaint should not whine.

5 If you can bring some specialized knowledge to your letter,

it will be more authoritative, and hence, more likely to be published. One way to acquire this knowledge is to set up a file of subjects in which you're interested, and to put in it items that will help you in composing your letters.

6 After writing your letter, let it cool overnight. And then ask yourself: will I want to see this over my name in print next week?

SAMPLE LETTERS

Complaint about Municipal Facility

> The condition of the subway system in summer is a disgrace to this city.
>
> On July 15, at 5:00 P.M., the weather on the street was pleasant, even cool. But when I entered the subway, a thermometer I had with me registered 99 degrees.
>
> I think that in this age of progress, it ought to be possible to find a way to ventilate this subway at a cost that would be within the city's budget.

Note that this first letter has a lively beginning; it registers a complaint, gives a very factual documentation, then calls for action.

Complaint about Government Policy

The writer of the next letter was obviously indignant, even outraged. And he bases his outrage not on a purely personal emotion, but on a statement issued by a civic organization. This lends his letter greater weight and impact:

> Your newspaper reports that the St. Louis Citizens Committee for Nuclear Information says that three thousand children in Utah and Nevada have received excessive radiation doses and that about a dozen will have thyroid cancer.
>
> The federal government explodes the bombs. The federal government establishes radiation controls. But the people of the United States, who have paid taxes supporting the bombs and controls, do not protest.
>
> It is a matter of common sense: you can't explode nuclear bombs without people feeling some effects at least a few hundred miles away. And what about we who live in other parts of the country. Do we

protest? No. What's the use? Parental common sense has little weight in the face of scientists, and the Atomic Energy Commission has reassured us that all is well.

Now, nuclear tests in the air are banned, but for many children, it is too late. The tragedy is that people are helpless before their governments, and when they are not helpless, they are defrauded.

WRITING TO TELEVISION AND RADIO

The television industry spends millions upon millions of dollars to entertain you, to inform you—and to sell you. It is a giant, a rich giant, and perhaps because of its riches, it is sometimes a sensitive giant. It is a giant that is loath to offend, eager to please.

For this reason, you, the viewer, can talk crossly to the giant, and there is a good chance that he will listen. He may not hear the actual words you speak, but he will get the tone of your voice, and he may be moved.

Your letters to the networks *are* read, and they *are* heeded. Your letters have saved a few programs from going off the air; your lack of letters have sent others into oblivion.

In order to understand how to get the most mileage from your letters, you should understand a bit about how networks handle their mail.

All mail comes into the mail room, where it's sorted according to addressee. If it's addressed to an individual, it goes directly to him. (This can be an important point to remember for certain types of letters, which will be discussed further on.) If it's addressed to the network, or to a specific program, it will, in most cases, go to an office generally known as Audience Information.

Audience Information usually consists of a tactful, experienced lady who's been with the network for several years, and knows her way around well enough to answer most letters intelligently, and to route the others to the departments which can handle them effectively.

Unless you're a very important person, it is unlikely that letters which you address to a network executive about a program or a commercial, will ever reach him. His secretary in all probability will send it off to Audience Information to be answered.

However, while the television executive may never see your letter, this doesn't mean that he may not be influenced by it. The networks have set up machinery for getting viewers' opinion through to the top brass. The machinery consists of periodic reports from Audience Information on the nature and number of letters commenting on different aspects of programming.

For example, whenever ABC receives five or more letters on a given subject in a month, that information goes into a report sent to top executives, with excerpts from most of the letters. NBC executives receive a statistical report. It makes no mention of letters about specific programs. Instead, it breaks letters down into the subjects about which they're written.

Thus, under Commercials, the report lists the following categories: Beer and Wine; Excessive Length and Frequency; Offensive–Bad Taste; Sound Levels; Tobacco. It is interesting to note that in one summer month, out of a total of twenty-seven comments on radio and television commercials, eighteen—two out of three—fell in the "Excessive Length and Frequency" and "Offensive–Bad Taste" categories.

Under Programs, the categories range from "Children's Viewing Hours" and "Color" to "Taste" and "Technical." One month not long ago, seventy per cent of the mail was devoted to just four subjects: "Scheduling and Discontinuance of Certain Series," "Practices," "Taste," and "Personalities." By far the largest grouping was "Scheduling and Discontinuance."

Now, since these statistical breakdowns make no mention of which programs the viewer is commenting on, a television executive would have to be a seer in order to know how the viewers are reacting to specific programs. Nevertheless, when there is a great volume of mail on a given subject, the Audience Information department will sometimes make a special call or send out a memo to alert the executives to it. For this reason, it does pay to write.

Mail to the networks generally falls into one of five broad categories. Here is a list of them, along with suggestions on how you, the viewer, can make your letters in these groups most effective.

Programs

This is the largest class, consisting of complaints and compliments about specific programs. Unless a complaint letter is quite specific, it will receive a routine answer.

When writing a complaint letter, be as specific as possible, listing the name of the program, when you saw it, on what station it appeared, and the nature of your complaint.

Tickets for Programs

If you'd like tickets for a specific network show, write to the Audience Information Bureau at network headquarters as far in advance as possible. If you don't particularly care which show you see, but you do want to see some programs on certain days, tell them so. If you do have program preferences, list them in order of preference. Also, don't forget to say how many tickets you want.

Photo Requests

With few exceptions, the networks will not send out photographs of performers. When a letter is addressed to the *network*, the network will usually send back a form letter suggesting that you write to the program itself. However, there is a simple solution to this problem.

Always send your photo requests to the person whose picture you want, in care of the program on which he appears. Send the letter to your local station or the national network. These letters will be passed on to the people responsible for getting out the pictures.

Music

Requests for the names of theme songs or other musical material can be sent directly to the network's Audience Information Bureau. They'll dig up the information and send it to you.

Education

The networks receive many requests from teachers and students for various kinds of information about television and radio. Some networks used to practically write students' term papers for them. But they've grown more sophisticated now, and will generally send out simply a few brochures or a reference bibliography. NBC, incidentally, is generally reputed to have the best selection of brochures on the television industry and television as a career.

Miscellaneous

The American public seems to feel that the networks are a reliable source of general information, and the networks have responded by doing their best to oblige. They are constantly receiving–and answering–such queries as: "Where can my daughter learn reweaving?" and "How do you get the effect of fog on a theater stage?"

Here, incidentally, is a moneysaving tip. There's no need to enclose stamps or a self-addressed envelope when you expect an answer. The networks will pay the postage on their own mail, even when they're doing you a favor. Indeed, one network spokesman said, "We never use the envelopes or stamps that readers send in because our own stationery looks so good; we think it helps impress on recipients what an excellent network we are."

HOW TO PRESSURE THE NETWORKS

While network executives are admittedly sheltered from viewer mail, they do, as we have noted, feel the effect of a volume of mail on any given subject. The following suggestions will help increase the weight of your complaints or compliments on specific programs or commercials:

1 State your credentials. If you hold any executive title in your company, or in your town or city government, or even in a reasonably well-known organization, get it into the letter. If you are a member of an organization, church, synagogue, club, etc., mention this in your letter. A routine letter of complaint signed by a member of a

Kiwanis chapter or church group will probably receive more attention than a good letter signed by a "nobody."

2 When a show is sponsored by only one or two companies, send a copy of your letter to the sponsor. Individual sponsors have little control over what goes into a program supported by several companies; but if they are the sole or the sharing sponsor, they are much more sensitive to viewers' comments. A few letters can go a long way, here.

3 When writing a letter of complaint or comment to a network show, send a carbon to the local station. They usually like to know what the local viewers are thinking, and if they get enough comment on one side of a question, they'll add their pressure to yours.

4 Make sure that you know what you're talking about. It is not unusual for the networks to receive letters complaining about shows that have appeared on other networks.

Also, it's a good idea to make sure that you've seen the show before you complain about it. Here's a specific example of what the networks don't pay attention to, as related by one executive:

"Every time we televise a rodeo, we get a spurt of letters protesting our treatment of the animals–even though we always have a humane society administrator on hand at every show. While we do read the mail that comes in on the subject, we give little credence to the following kinds of mail:

"First, if it comes in before the show has been televised. We can't pay much attention to somebody who criticizes something he hasn't seen.

"Second, if it comes in three or four or more weeks after the show. This indicates to us that the viewer hasn't seen the show himself, but that he's been urged to write by somebody else–a friend, or perhaps a magazine.

"Third, if he says in his letter something like, 'I wouldn't be caught dead watching that show.' If he's not going to watch it, we're not going to pay much attention to his criticism."

These three rules can be considered valid for all types of programs.

One final point is worth mentioning. Networks and stations, for all their faults, are not utterly spineless. They do have some sense of responsibility to the public, and when they are bold enough to step into an area of controversy, they will usually not be intimidated by threats of boycotts, nor will they be influenced by vituperative letters. If you see a television show which you think is in bad taste, or unfair, or poor for whatever reason, by all means let the people responsible know about it. But remember that your letter will have greater weight if it is rational and thoughtful.

SAMPLE LETTERS

Note: Be certain to include your return address when you expect a reply.

Educational Requests

Gentlemen:

We are conducting a Reading Workshop for selected high school teachers from the state of Alabama, and are collecting materials for distribution to the group. The number of participants is thirty.

Will you kindly send us sample copies of available materials on reading or related literature where possible.

Yours truly,

Gentlemen:

I would be greatly interested in reading the script to a program televised yesterday evening (over your station in San Francisco) which reported on a convention in Chicago of pilots who had participated in the raids on Hiroshima and Nagasaki in August, 1945.

I missed seeing this program myself, but I feel it would be most useful to me, as I am engaged in research that bears on problems of the psychology of nuclear armament.

I would be glad to reimburse you for the expenses that this request might entail.

Sincerely,

Note: The request for scripts of programs is a fairly common one. In some cases the networks can supply them; in some cases, they cannot. The author of the letter above, not knowing the name of the program, wisely wrote the network. If, however, you know the name of the program, write to it directly, in care of the network.

Music Request

Gentlemen:

I would appreciate some information concerning your television program "The Match Game."

I would like to know the name of the theme song, and where I may obtain the music in sheet form or on record.

Sincerely yours,

Congratulatory Letter

Dear Sirs:

I congratulate you on the excellent presentation by Frank McGee on the Supreme Court decision last Monday night.

Not only was the narration well written, but the presentation was completely objective, allowing the viewer to make his own decision for or against the Supreme Court's decision.

I felt that the closing quote by the United States senator summed up the situation ideally.

Congratulations again on this type of public service programming by your Public Affairs department.

Sincerely,

Letters like this help to keep such shows on the air.

Critical Letters

This was written to the producer of a well-known children's show by an irate mother:

Dear Mr. _______:

Your program is the sole television program permitted in this house for our three-and-one-half-year-old daughter. As you must know, your word is almost law. Just your having said something, makes it so.

On occasion, I sit with Elizabeth and we enjoy the hour together. I have always objected to several of the commercials on the show. Candy of any sort, and chewing gum of all kinds should, I think, be mentioned at the discretion of parents or physicians or both, not dangled enticingly from the TV screen.

I know you have to have a sponsor, but it seems to me that you ought not to need to stoop to unhealthy foods, and certainly unnecessary ones. (I am not a food nut, incidentally, but I feel that sweets should not be emphasized unduly.)

Sincerely,

The producer of the show sent an answer explaining that he does not have control over commercials as long as they are in good taste and not truly harmful.

Here's a letter protesting poor programming practices, sent to the owner of a local television station:

Dear Sir:

May I protest the avalanche of family-comedy programs you have been showing in the evenings during the past two months.

I counted twenty-three last week alone.

Your station has a responsibility to serve all members of the community, and certainly there are not many who can digest this tiring repetition night after night.

As the comptroller of the ABC Co., I am in frequent contact with leading Centerville businessmen. In private conversations, many of them have expressed feelings similar to mine.

We look to you for more diverse programming. If it is not forthcoming, some of us will simply turn to other stations. Others will protest to the Federal Communications Commission when your license is due for renewal.

Will you please give us fare that is worthy of our intelligence?

Sincerely,

And here's one protesting a program that the writer felt showed poor taste. It was sent to a network president.

Sir:

On February 25, your local affiliate, in Centerville, Mass., broadcast the network program "Burlesque Again."

As a responsible parent and as the chairman of the Centerville Youth Group, I protest the shoddiness of this show.

The leers, the double entendres, the overstuffed and underdressed girls, and the questionable comedians, all left a very bad taste in my mouth.

I suspect it is not a show of which you, personally, are proud. And while I cannot expect you to censor every program, I can hope that you will encourage your staff to be a little more intelligent, a little less sleazy.

We look to you for entertainment and information; you gave us cheapness.

Please do whatever you can to see that this sort of program is not repeated in the future.

Sincerely,

And finally, here's a plea to save a program:

Dear Sir:

My family and a multitude of my friends have enjoyed Lily Smith's program, "It's Your World," for many years.

And so, it came as a great shock when we read that her show will end in two more weeks.

Mrs. Smith is one of the most intelligent and perceptive interviewers that has ever appeared on television in this area. Her frequent involvement in controversy had made her that much more interesting.

Television offers my friends and myself little enough that is worth watching. Mrs. Smith is always an exception.

I write not only for myself, but also for many of my acquaintances. Please keep her with you–and with us.

Chapter Eight

WRITING TO YOUR CONGRESSMAN

A couple of years ago, Henry S. Reuss, a Democratic congressman from Wisconsin, introduced a bill that would establish in Congress an Administrative Counsel to expedite complaints from the public. The congressman's bill was born of desperation, for, as he explained in an article in the *New York Times Magazine*: "A member of Congress today is a harried man. The days are hardly long enough for him to think and act soundly on all the great issues of war and peace, national prosperity and civil rights. Yet these are only part of his burden. The Congressman and his staff must also cope with an astounding amount of constituent business—the requests and demands from voters that require him to serve as their mediator with the Federal Government . . . he cannot give it less than his best—even though it can take up as much as 90 per cent of his time."

Representative Reuss admitted that his bill was moving very slowly through the mazes of Capitol Hill, and since it looks as if a long time will pass before a citizen can be sure of getting a quick reply to a letter, the problem with which we will deal in this chapter is: How can you, as an independent citizen, get answers to your questions, or action on your complaints, or an ear for your opinion, from elected public officials?

To obtain the answers, I asked several representatives and senators a number of questions about how best to get their attention. Not only were their replies helpful, but they also provided me with letters which they felt were above average. This chapter will present their answers and a number of effective letters they received.

HOW TO CORRESPOND WITH ELECTED OFFICIALS

Five representatives and senators have provided detailed answers to my questions on how best to correspond with them. They were Representative John V. Lindsay, 17th District, New York (Mr. Lindsay has since been elected mayor of New York); Representative Leslie C. Arends, 17th District, Illinois; Representative Robert W. Kastenmeier, 2nd District, Wisconsin; Senator Carl T. Curtis, Nebraska; and Senator Thomas H. Kuchel, California.

My first question was: Do you read all the mail sent to you by voters, or does your staff screen it and route only the most important letters to you?

Most replied that an administrative assistant either screens their mail, and briefs them on its contents, or else goes over it with them. Typical was Congressman Lindsay's response: "I read most of the mail sent to me by voters. I receive a minimum of fifteen hundred letters a week and I try to skim all of it. All carefully written letters, important gripes, Dear John letters, and letters that 'say something' are, of course, put at the top of the pile and, of course, I read those with care."

Note the four categories of letters which Congressman Lindsay pays the most attention to. Later, we'll explore these in some detail.

Are elected officials influenced by the volume of mail on a subject? To find out, I asked two questions:

1 Does the quantity of the mail you receive on an issue ever influence your thinking or your efforts in regard to that issue?

2 Are you influenced to any extent by write-in campaigns on an issue? I'm referring specifically to large numbers of letters, all of which express the same opinion in identical, or nearly identical words.

The answers boiled down to "Yes" and "No," respectively.

Senator Kuchel said letters are very useful. He wrote: "Let me point out that California has dire need for federal aid in many fields, such as operation of schools, construction of public works projects, planning of transit systems, and the like. My attention has been directed to possible shortcomings in pending legislation relative to such matters because informed officials and private citizens have taken the time and trouble to write me setting forth basic facts meriting consideration."

Senator Curtis, in answer to question 1, said: "It is the quality of the letters. By that I mean the person *who gives the reasons* [italics mine] for his position is definitely more helpful. . . ."

Said Congressman Lindsay: "Quantity of mail is important, but quality is of far greater importance. Much quantity mail can be inspired mail. *The least effective kind is a form that has obviously been received from someone else by the sender or which is clipped from a newspaper* [italics mine]. Nevertheless, quantity is important on a given issue as it indicates that large numbers of people may be affected one way or another by governmental position or by a vote."

Congressmen Kastenmeier and Arends indicated that the volume of mail will cause them to explore an issue more closely. Said the former: "I think the quantity of mail influences my political thinking about an issue only slightly. It ordinarily, however, will not alter my judgment or decision or about how I shall vote on a particular issue. It might well keep me from pursuing a given matter more aggressively or it might tend to temper my opposition to a piece of legislation."

Said Congressman Arends: "Quantity of mail causes me to give the matter a 'second look,' but doesn't necessarily change my position. *The source is more influential than quantity.*" (Italics mine.)

Next, I asked them what they considered to be the characteristics of a good letter. Here are the individual qualities mentioned:

1 Individuality and creativeness

2 Questions should be framed so as to evoke an individual response rather than a form response

3 The writer should show some knowledge of the issue

4 He should show personal viewpoint as distinguished from an inspired form letter

5 The letter should be legible

6 The letter should be short

Finally, I asked what were the most common flaws in mail from constituents. Here are the answers:

"1 The writer states his position on legislation, but doesn't explain the problem in his community, or how the law would affect his business or give other reasons for the position he takes.

"2 The most common flaws are oversimplicity and triteness, especially in dealing with very complex issues.

"3 Hostility in the writer's attitude, thereby constituting a bar or a defect in communication.

[Author's note: I believe that the congressman was saying, in a polite way, that if you get sore with him, he's likely to feel, "You can go to the devil."]

"4 Representative's name misspelled and incorrectly addressed.

"5 Confusion between a bill in Congress and one pending in the State Legislature.

"6 Lack of reply address.

"7 Typed rather than signed signature."

Finally, I asked legislators whether they preferred that mail be sent to their offices or their homes. Without exception, they preferred their offices. Frankly, there is some question in my mind whether you, as a constituent, might not get faster action by writing to the representative's home, simply because most constituent mail *will* go to his office. Letters to the home, on the other hand, might tend to get more personal attention.

However, John Lindsay presented a very strong argument for not sending it to the home:

"Letters from the public should always be addressed to the office. Many people go to some lengths to find out the home address to send it there on the thought that it will receive faster and more personal attention.

"In my own case, this is not true. Sending letters to the home, either the New York home or the Washington home, merely delays. I find myself traveling back and forth from New York so much that a home letter can be delayed as much as a week more than if it were sent to the office.

"Nevertheless, many people persist in sending the stuff to the home. Very often letters sent to my New York home will be batched up and forwarded to Washington, which means another few days in the mails.

"Unfortunately, too many people think that a Member from New York spends all his time in New York instead of in Washington. Then, too, with four kids around and a busy household with no help, I have found that mail sometimes gets lost that goes to the home."

At this point, it will be a good idea to summarize the congressmen's answers in order to understand how best to get a quick, informative answer from them, or in order to ensure that they pay attention to your letter.

1 If you're making an inquiry you should:

a. State your request in the first paragraph.

b. Explain the reason for your request. This will help guide the representative in giving you a more precise answer.

2 If you're expressing an opinion on an issue or a bill, you should do the following things in order to give it more weight:

a. State your position in the first paragraph; be quite specific about the measure to which you're referring. If it's about a bill up for consideration, give the number of the bill if you know it.

b. Explain the reasoning behind your position in the next paragraph or two.

c. Avoid copying a form letter that may have been provided by a club or association. You might use it as the basis for a letter of your own, but put your letter in your own words.

3 Regardless of the reason for your letter, you should

a. Keep it short. Congressmen are reluctant to wade through more than a single page.

b. Make it legible—a typed letter is easiest to read. If you don't have access to a typewriter, be sure your handwriting is decipherable.

c. Include your return address. It goes without saying that your signature should be easily readable.

d. If you have an official position in connection with some organization interested in a measure or an issue, mention it, either listing your title below your signature or incorporating it into the body of the letter.

SAMPLE LETTERS TO ELECTED REPRESENTATIVES

LETTERS ABOUT SPECIFIC BILLS

The writer of the letter below gives a good, personal reason for his position. He might have bolstered his argument, however, by describing his income in greater detail. A little drama never hurts.

Dear Mr. Congressman:

I strongly urge you to assist in having Bill H.R. 1811 passed.

It would be of considerable help to those, such as I, who are handicapped, to have a $600 tax exemption. My income has been reduced considerably, even though I have tried to keep as busy as is physically possible.

Respectfully,

It may be useful to remind the representative of the effects of legislation on his constituents.

Dear Congressman Smith:

Passage of the Wheat-Cotton Bill (H.R. 6196) would in effect be equivalent to a tax on bakery products, since it would mean an increase in wheat and flour prices.

I feel that such increases would result in further hardship for the needy, and would render a disservice to all your constituents as well. I respectfully urge you to vote against it.

Yours very truly,

A little humor can make a letter stand out from the run of correspondence. Avoid, however (as this letter does), sarcasm. Cutting humor makes representatives bleed, and a bleeding congressman is an angry congressman.

Dear Sir:

I am opposed to the recent action of the House Health and Safety Committee in approving H.R. 4731.

This bill will repeal a section of the 1906 Food, Drug and Cosmetic Act which keeps candy makers from using "non-nutritive ingredients" in their products.

I do not wish to eat talc when I eat candy. Maybe talc has some nutritive value, but being a conservative, I don't like getting used to it.

While normally I vote Republican, I voted for you in the last election because I felt you had a slight edge over the Republican incumbent.

I trust that you will continue to follow through with the admirable work you have done. And I am confident that you will do what you can to keep candy adulteration from becoming legal.

Sincerely yours,

LETTERS ABOUT GENERAL ISSUES

The letter following is a beautiful example of simplicity and clarity. The writer is restrained, informal, and direct. If you were a congressman, wouldn't you be proud to have constituents who could write like this? You'd be very inclined to listen to them.

Dear Congressman Smith:

I have been very interested in the Peace Corps and have followed its progress with pleasure. Noting the success of this program in other countries, I would like to suggest a "Domestic" Peace Corps. Our young people could help the American Indians, the itinerant workers, and the people who live in depressed areas.

I'm sure the problem has already been called to your attention, but I should like to add my concern.

Sincerely,

The personal touch in the following letter certainly helps its effectiveness. The congressman's own wife probably has the same complaint.

Dear Congressman Smith:

I feel that Air Pollution Control is one of the most important issues facing us today.

It is more dangerous than such diseases as lung cancer and heart disease because it affects not just a few thousands, but millions of people.

My venetian blinds, window sills, floors, etc., have to be swept and washed with soap and water daily. Inhaling this soot *must* be detrimental to our health.

Won't you please see what can be done to eliminate this serious condition? It is vitally important.

Sincerely yours,

The next letter enclosed a newspaper clipping about the writer's topic. This is an effective way of dramatizing a letter. If the clipping is a small one, paste it to a separate sheet of paper so that it doesn't get lost, and put it behind–not in front of–your letter, so that the representative doesn't get distracted by the clipping before he reads your letter.

Dear Mr. Jones:

I should like to call your attention to the enclosed article, which appeared in the Centerville *Journal,* of July 3.

I cannot understand why former Attorney-General Biddle insists on pushing the slab design of the Franklin D. Roosevelt Memorial down the throat of the Washington Fine Arts Commission.

Both the Commission and the House seem to feel, as I do, that the slab design was unsatisfactory.

I object to these gigantic "idiot cards" and I object to Mr. Biddle's bullying. I hope that you will support the Fine Arts Commission at the proper time.

Sincerely yours,

ADAPTING A FORM LETTER

As we noted earlier, elected representatives will pay less attention to a form letter than to an original composition. If an organization to which you belong suggests that you send a letter to your congressman, and provides a model, adapt it so that it comes out in your own words. Here, for example, is a letter that was published by the National Restaurant Association as a model for its members. Wisely, NRA offered the letter merely as an aid, so that its members could send their own versions:

> Dear Congressman ________:
>
> I am writing because a bill presently before your committee contains a provision which would seriously harm my business if enacted. I know you don't want to do anything to hurt the restaurant business but, believe me, this Tax on Tips bill would do just that.
>
> I run a small place (twenty-five employees) and we all get along fine. My waitresses don't want to tell anybody their tips and they will resent having to do so. If I have to give them tax receipts instead of paychecks, they are going to quit. I won't be able to convince them that I have to do it that way.
>
> I run my own place and keep my own books but I've got all I can handle. If I have to do all the government's bookkeeping, I'll have to hire a bookkeeper at least three days a week. My profits are too low to permit this. I'd do it now if I could. My payroll taxes last year were more than my profit. Please don't raise them now.
>
> Please eliminate the Tax on Tips.

Before giving some alternative samples that I've made up, I'll quote the suggestions that the National Restaurant Association offered its members. They're an excellent guide in adapting all kinds of form letters:

1 Tell your congressman why you are opposed to the measure. Use your own words.

2 Give him examples based on your personal experience.

3 Tell him what you would do if the legislation were to become law.

4 Don't just oppose. Give your reasons and give another solution if possible. For example, NRA's alternative solution to the problem of giving employees credit for tips toward Social Security benefits is to treat tips as self-employment income.

Alternative Letters

Dear Congressman Smith:

The Tax on Tips clause in H.R. 1 will do severe damage to my business, and I hope you will oppose it.

As the owner of a small chain of restaurants in this city, I operate on a profit margin of 3 per cent. According to my own calculations—and this has been confirmed by my accountant—the profit margin will drop to 1.5 per cent if the Tax on Tips bill becomes law. In short, my already narrow margin of profit will be cut in half.

As you know, this is a profit level at which it is almost impossible to conduct a business. For this reason, I suggest that you eliminate the Tax on Tips clause from the bill, and let stand the present method of treating tips as self-employment income.

Sincerely,

That letter emphasizes the profit-margin problems, but it expresses the same idea as the model letter. The next sample emphasizes the effect the bill would have on employees:

Dear Congressman Jones:

On behalf of my waiters, I should like to express my opposition to Section 205 of H.R. 1, the Tax on Tips clause.

Smith's Restaurant, of which I'm the owner, has seven people waiting on customers. I have explained to them how the clause will affect their tips. Six of the seven said they were opposed to the measure because they feel it's none of my business how much money they make in tips. And, as one of them said, "I think that the tax is one more government grab for power. Why do they have to pick on the little guy?"

As far as I'm concerned, the tax would be a burden; as far as my employees are concerned, they would resent it. I hope that as our representative, you'll take our feelings into account when you vote on this measure.

The final alternative letter emphasizes why the writer thinks a different method of handling the measure would be superior.

Dear Congressman Smith:

Section 205 of H.R. 1, the Tax on Tips bill, is a poor way of achieving a worthy end.

I speak as one who owns a restaurant with seventy-five employees, fifty of whom serve the public.

The weakness of Section 205 is that it will seriously damage the relationships between employers and employees. While I sympathize with the government's need for money, I feel that it shouldn't be done at the expense of good human relations. This is an unsound way to run either a government or a business.

A superior way of collecting this money would be to lay the burden of payment on the employees rather than on the employers. This is the way it is now done in a number of other areas, for example, with court reporters who sell transcripts of trials. They, and not the courts, must report this extra money.

Don't you agree that it's unfair to single us out for special treatment? I hope that you will vote against this measure because it is discriminatory to our type of business.

Sincerely,

SHORTENING THE LONG LETTER

When we're very excited about an issue, we tend to talk about it. When we write letters about an issue that concerns us very much, we tend to do the same thing, and will often write two or three pages to get our point across. In writing to congressmen, this is cutting our own throats. They simply don't have time (and, some would argue, the powers of concentration) to wade through a long letter. Therefore, if you want to get something off your chest, by all means put it in writing—and then trim the letter down to its essentials. You'll get a much better hearing.

This point applies to all letter writers in general, but I suspect it's particularly applicable to political conservatives. Judging from the samples the congressman sent me, conservatives tend to write dreadfully long messages. This may be one reason why they are not as successful in lobbying as they might be. They get carried away by their dedication, and their representatives simply don't have the patience to read all about it.

By way of illustration, I reprint below a couple of typical letters which should *never* be sent to congressmen. The first one is a general letting-off of steam, and while it may serve as therapy for the writer, it is little better than a crank letter as far as the representative is concerned. Remember: if you're going to send a man a letter, let it be about *something,* not about everything, as the following example is:

Dear Sir:

I am nauseated and sad as all God-fearing Americans must be. Today we are told that Russians, with malice and in cold blood, murdered three more unarmed Americans. Our people must now or never take a positive stand, not with mere diplomacy, but with a majority of our senators and congressmen passing a resolution to protect ourself in any part of the world. The Russians and all other Commies must realize that payment is long overdue, and that we will extract payment for our dead.

We concentrate upon illegal acts of certain people for political reasons with the end results that minor penalties are imposed. We hear the courts ruling against God, against big business, and against the police, as we read about rulings favoring Communist subversive activities. Minority groups press to hide criminal truths as they also press to conceal the real perpetrators of President Kennedy's untimely and gruesome murder as well as the events that followed.

Our leaders allow Communism to spread to all parts of the world, collecting ransom as it destroys not only the Monroe Doctrine, but also our Constitution. They get military treaties favoring themselves, and they exploit taxes earned by honest toil to buy wheat or any other product they can lay their dirty blood-covered hands on.

In the name of Almighty God, I earnestly request that we stand up forthrightly. Let the Congress halt the activities of misguided men who have brought out the Cuban, Panamanian, South Vietnam, Congo, Laos, and many other shameful situations . . ."

Et cetera, et cetera, et cetera.

The letter tries to cover everything that irritates the writer, and as a result, it loses its meaning. Far preferable would have been a series of short letters sent over a period of weeks, each one touching on a different subject. This, at least, would have made the senator aware that he had one constituent who was following the news and who had some strong opinions about it.

The next letter is one that would have benefited from severe cutting. Just how it might have been cut, I'll indicate after you've looked at the original version.

Dear Sir:

After much deliberation and many discussions, I have come to the conclusion that the Civil Rights bill is a dangerous one affecting all the people of our democracy.

The bill grants no freedom—instead it deprives many freedoms. I'm against no one because of his color—that's not his fault. And I'm against no one because of his religion—that's his privilege, even if he wants to be an atheist. I'm just an advocate of free choice, and I hope you are too.

If the pushers of the Civil Rights bill think that by passing it they will abolish discrimination, they are sadly mistaken. Today in business many young people are being turned down on jobs because they don't have a college education. Is this not discrimination? Would you pass a bill against that? When I go to the store to buy soap and I purchase a cake of Ivory, I'm discriminating against Lava, Dial, Zest, Palmolive, and Lux. Is this not discrimination? And it is the same principle as the one in the Civil Rights bill.

I believe in a democracy and I wish more of the senators did, too. The Civil Rights bill would make us an extremely socialistic nation ruled almost completely by a small group of power-happy government officials. This is all wrong and I don't want to live in a country like that.

If at all possible, I would like to know who is going to say whether or not a person committed a discriminatory act. I would like to know where in the bill it defines discrimination, race, or religion. How can the Senate possibly pass this bill and have it enforced when these important words are not even defined?

If this bill is passed, including such things as making a barber cut a specific person's hair, or making a woman give a massage to a specific person, the Senate will violate the Thirteenth Amendment which states, "Neither slavery nor involuntary servitude, except as a punishment for crime whereof the party shall have been duly convicted, shall exist within the United States, or any place subject to their jursidiction." I hope we are not going to be punished. Besides, I'm antislavery.

If I'm correct, Lyndon Johnson, when a senator, said he hoped a bill like this would never pass. I hope this is not a football game with President Johnson as the quarterback of the political football team.

Please vote NO on this bill and keep freedom for all under a democracy.

Sincerely,

The main flaw in this letter is that it tries to say too much. It should have been a first draft. And then, if you were the writer, you could have asked yourself: "What's the most important point I'm trying to get across?" That point could have served as the heart of the letter, and the rest could have been condensed or eliminated.

My own feeling is that the strongest argument raised is the constitutional one, and therefore, this should have come first. I would then have sketched in some of the other reasons briefly, and mailed it off. Here's how it might have then read:

Dear Sir:

I believe the Civil Rights bill is unconstitutional.

The Thirteenth Amendment states that "neither slavery nor involuntary servitude, except as a punishment for crime whereof the party shall have been duly convicted, shall exist within the United States. . . ."

The Civil Rights bill will make a barber cut a specific person's hair, force a woman to give a massage to a specific person. This, I believe, is certainly a form of involuntary servitude, and hence, it would be unconstitutional.

There are many other reasons for opposing the bill: it doesn't define many important terms, such as "discrimination" or "race," and it would subject us to more federal power.

Because of these reasons, I hope you will vote against this bill.

Sincerely,

Chapter Nine

WRITING TO GOVERNMENT AGENCIES

The first thing to be said about government agencies is that the people who staff them are nervous, harassed, overworked, and underpaid, and they are frequently confused, inadequate, and tardy in their correspondence. In short, they are exactly like the rest of us.

Most government agencies receive an enormous volume of mail. To cite a few examples: the Postmaster General receives between 175,000 and 200,000 letters a year; the Secretary of Labor between 50,000 and 60,000; the Food and Drug Administration of the Department of Health, Education, and Welfare answers about 30,000 from consumers a year; and the Secretary of H.E.W., all by himself, gets over 18,000 letters a year.

In the face of this welter of correspondence, the basic rule in writing to any government agency is: make it easy for them to reply. Above all, this means adhering to the rules we laid down in the first chapter: be accurate, brief, and clear.

Because each agency deals with a different kind of problem, this chapter will deal with several major departments individually. I've selected those cabinet offices and independent agencies that get the bulk of correspondence from the public. In each section, we'll consider what sort of problems they handle, and how you can best get your request or opinion across to them.

Not all problems, of course, have to do with the federal government. You may, of course, want to write to your local government for information or to express an opinion. In the second part of this chapter, we'll describe how one group of people has done this most effectively.

THE UNITED STATES GOVERNMENT ORGANIZATION MANUAL

Before we discuss the different federal government offices, it's appropriate to say a few words about the *United States Government Organization Manual.* This book is published annually, and gives a complete guide to the functions of virtually every department in the legislative, judicial, and executive branches of the government. It lists the names of the chief officers in the departments, and contains a series of organization charts which show quite clearly the relationships of the agencies to one another. For the dedicated letter writer, or for anyone who is merely interested in how the extensive Washington bureaucracy is organized, I recommend it highly. It costs $2.00 and can be obtained from the Superintendent of Documents, Government Printing Office, Washington, D.C. 20402.

In the following section, most of my descriptions of the offices' functions have been adapted from the *Manual.*

Cabinet Offices

DEPARTMENT OF AGRICULTURE
WASHINGTON, D. C. 20250

The Department acquires and diffuses useful information on agricultural subjects. It does research not only in agriculture, but in nutrition, home economics, conservation, and other areas. In addition, it administers national forests, aids in soil and water conservation, disposes of surplus agricultural commodities, gives grants-in-aid for the national school lunch program, and makes loans to farmers and farm groups.

In 1963, Agriculture Secretary Orville Freeman held a series of meetings with farmers to get their thinking about what kind of farm programs they wanted. Because he could not answer all questions at the meetings, he urged farmers to write to him. He received around twenty-five hundred letters, and many of these comments helped shape the national wheat program, which was enacted in 1964 by Congress.

Thus, the Department does pay attention to correspondence from the public. In fact, the Secretary regularly receives a cross-section of the mail on major subjects of interest, plus a daily listing of the mail showing the number of letters on different subjects.

WHAT'S WRONG WITH YOUR LETTERS?

The Department says that the most common faults in letters from the public are illegibility, and letters that are rambling and therefore hard to understand. This underscores the point we've made before: keep your correspondence brief. A good letter, says a Department spokesman, "will state the writer's views simply and briefly in the writer's own words and cite any pertinent data; if it makes several different points, each is easy to identify."

WHO CAN HANDLE YOUR PROBLEM?

There are a dozen agencies in the Agriculture Department, each dealing with a different set of problems. A very good way to find out which agency can best handle your problem is to write to the Department and ask for publication No. PA-542, "You and the USDA." Address your request to Office of Information, U. S. Department of Agriculture, Washington, D. C. 20250. A postcard will bring faster action than a letter; be sure to enclose your return address.

Incidentally, the Department also will send free up to ten different publications in response to any one request. Many of these brochures are helpful to nonfarm residents, as well as to farmers. For example, the Department will send you guides explaining how to buy a variety of agricultural products, such as cheeses, eggs, and meats, how to prepare foods, how to build cabinets, how to control pests, etc. If you ordered these from the U. S. Government Printing Office, you'd have to pay for them, but you can get them for nothing from the Agriculture Department. A good way to find out what *is* available is to write the Department at the address given above and ask for "Miscellaneous Publications No. 959–A Consumer's Guide to USDA Services." Now for some sample letters:

ON PUBLIC POLICY

If you plan to write to the Secretary of Agriculture about a matter of public policy, such as pending legislation, or a departmental policy, you might follow this formula:

1 Give your opinion.
2 Give the reasons for your opinion.
3 Urge a specific course of action.

Here's a model you can adapt to your own needs:

Dear Mr. ________:

I believe the Agriculture Department is (acting wisely or unwisely) in (supporting or opposing specific legislation; following a specific practice or policy).

The (legislation, practice, or policy) will (help or hurt) people like myself who are (explain why you're interested in the matter under discussion).

My reasons for believing the Department is (acting wisely or unwisely) are:

First–

Second–

Third–

For these reasons, I believe you should (describe the course of action).

Sincerely,

A letter following these principles might read as follows:

Dear Mr. ________:

I believe the Agriculture Department is making an error in planning to testify in favor of the bill to increase import quotas for Argentine beef.

The bill will cause severe damage to domestic ranchers like myself, who are barely able to obtain prices high enough to cover our costs.

Statistics published by the Department's local Extension Office support this contention.

Last year, these figures show, the average rancher in this area made less than 2 per cent profit on beef sales. (I am enclosing a copy of this report, with the relevant statistics underlined.)

My second reason for thinking the Department should oppose the liberalized quotas is that . . .

My third reason is that . . .

For these three reasons, I believe you should support present quotas on Argentine beef, and oppose any increase.

Sincerely,

REQUEST FOR INFORMATION

Requests for information should be brief and specific. They should include any information you think might help the Department to fill your request.

Office of Information
U. S. Department of Agriculture
Washington, D. C. 20250

Gentlemen:

Please send me a list of Agriculture Department publications on the stocking and maintenance of ponds.

I am planning on creating a pond on my property. It will measure about 200 by 300 feet.

Sincerely,

DEPARTMENT OF COMMERCE WASHINGTON, D. C. 20230

The Department fosters, promotes, and develops foreign and domestic commerce, the manufacturing and shipping industries, and the transportation facilities of the United States. Among its subordinate agencies are the Bureau of the Census (Washington, D. C. 20233), the Patent Office (Washington, D. C. 20231), and the Weather Bureau (Rockville, Md. 20852).

The Commerce Department, quite naturally, deals primarily with businessmen and with business problems. Thus, according to one executive in the Department, the attitude of American businessmen, as expressed in their letters to the Department, was a factor in the approval of wheat sales to Russia. Many letters are passed on to the

Secretary, mainly those which (a) reflect *reasoned* criticisms of the Department's policies and programs, or (b) offer constructive suggestions for a change.

In writing to the Commerce Department about matters of public policy or when requesting information, follow the principles discussed on pages 182–83, concerning letters to the Department of Agriculture.

DEPARTMENT OF DEFENSE
THE PENTAGON
WASHINGTON, D. C. 20350

The Defense Department consists of the Departments of the Army, the Navy, and the Air Force. Presumably, correspondence from the public can occasionally light a fire under the Secretary of Defense. In fact, the Department admits that his trips to Vietnam and his widely publicized visits to installations scheduled for shutdown a couple of years ago were the result of public concern that was expressed through the mails.

Unless you're a fairly important person, the chances are that the Secretary won't see a letter you address to him. However, *somebody* will probably answer in fairly short order.

REQUESTING A FAVOR

Bureaucrats are humans, and they will respond to a letter which gives them a reason for acting like human beings. A request for special treatment is a good place to set forth the human factors which prompt the letter. Here's one sent to the Department of Defense not long ago:

Dear Mr. McNamara:

If you could postpone my father's retirement from the Navy for one year, I should be enormously grateful.

I am seventeen years old, and for the last sixteen years, we have moved every two and a half years to a new Navy station.

I did not mind when I was younger, but since entering high school, I have been terribly distressed by our having to move. I've been fortunate in having been able to spend the last two years at Centreville

High School. It is an excellent school, and I have finally established myself here, and have made a very good record.

Next year will be my senior year. However, my father is being retired (after twenty-one years in the Navy), and because he must go where he can obtain a job, we will be forced to move again. This will mean, of course, that I shall have to start in a new school all over again.

I have tried, without success, to make other arrangements to stay here for my last year. Consequently, I turn to you as my last resort.

Would there be any possibility of having my father's tour of duty extended for one year? He is due to be retired within the next few weeks, and we are planning to leave in July.

I will appreciate any solution to my problem which you may be able to suggest.

Respectfully,

P.S. My father is Lt. Cdr. John Smith, Serial No. 456789, attached to COMFAIR WHIDBEY, Whidbey Island Naval Air Station, Whidbey Island, Washington.

Note that this letter begins with the specific request in the very first paragraph, then goes on to give the reasons for the request, and winds up by repeating the request again. The "P.S." at the end, by identifying the writer's father, makes it easier for the bureaucrats to check the father's records.

OFFERING AN OPINION

Dear Mr. McNamara:

I am opposed to our continued military presence in Southeast Asia.

There is a serious possibility that military operations there will spark World War III. I am sure this is true if we continue our present course, and particularly if we expand the war as advocated by all of the Republican presidential contenders.

I am in accord with those who believe that De Gaulle's proposal of neutralization should be given careful consideration.

Alternatively, I suggest that the United Nations peace-keeping forces be introduced to the area. The fact that they have not leaves serious doubts about the rightness of our intervention.

Yours truly,

This letter is a good one because it gives the reason for the writer's opinion, and suggests a solution that he believes would be superior to the one now being followed.

DEPARTMENT OF HEALTH, EDUCATION, AND WELFARE WASHINGTON, D. C. 20201

The Department was established to improve the administration of those government agencies whose major responsibilities are to promote the general welfare in the fields of health, education, and social security. Among its subordinate groups are the Office of Education, the Public Health Service, the Social Security Administration, the Welfare Administration, the Administration on Aging, the Vocational Rehabilitation Administration, and the Food and Drug Administration.

A special word is in order about the Food and Drug Administration because this group touches so closely upon the health and even the lives of many Americans. According to FDA officials, most correspondence which they receive deals with inquiries or complaints about food labeling, the safety of certain food ingredients, pesticide control programs, the safety and effectiveness of drug products, and reports of suspected foods, drugs, and cosmetics.

Your best bet, if you're not sure of which FDA branch to write to, is simply to address your letter to Food and Drug Administration, Washington, D. C. 20204. The department's mail-processing system will probably route the letter fairly quickly, and you save yourself the time that you'd lose if you addressed the letter to some individual who wasn't the right one to handle your problem.

WHAT YOUR LETTER SHOULD INCLUDE

If you're writing about an unsatisfactory product, be sure to include the following details, which the FDA needs in order to follow up a complaint.

The kind of product.

The brand name.

The name and address of the manufacturer, packer, or distributor. (This will appear on the label.)

Any code marks or symbols. (These are usually embossed on the ends of cans.)

The name and address of the store where the article was bought.

The approximate date of purchase.

If you refer to published articles or news reports, it will be a help if you refer to the date of the article, and where you read it. Even better, include a copy of the article.

It's also a good idea to have your letter refer to only one subject. As one spokesman said: "The value of any exchange of correspondence is considerably diluted when letters run to several pages and discuss several subjects."

GETTING FAST ACTION

The first thing the Department looks for in its correspondence is whether the letter concerns a matter that might pose a threat to health. So, if this is your concern, say so right at the beginning. If you feel it's an urgent matter, you might do much better to telephone your district office.

LETTERS OF INQUIRY

Dear Sirs:

I am interested in obtaining information concerning the new pill, Smithereens. Have you approved this as a safe and effective nasal decongestant?

Sincerely,

Gentlemen:

Could you tell me if vitamin products sold by discount companies, bearing a name not well known, can be relied upon as containing the vitamins and quantities indicated on the label?

I have a catalog which offers such vitamins, and as my husband and I are approaching retirement and must be scrupulously careful of our expenditures, this would give us quite a saving if the vitamins are as advertised.

My physician has prescribed a B-complex capsule which he wishes me to take regularly; it bears a name which I can call for over the counter. However, the discount company's price is much lower, and the saving would help us.

Sincerely,

Gentlemen:

Would you please tell me if the ABC hair dye is harmful in any way. ABC is manufactured by ABC Co., Centerville, Iowa.

Gentlemen:

I would appreciate very much your opinion as to whether the labeling of our salve complies with the Federal Food, Drug, and Cosmetic Act. As suggested, I am sending you the complete quantitive formula of this salve showing the kind and proportion of each ingredient, and two copies each of the tube and carton labels and the leaflet which will be enclosed in the carton with the tube.

Yours truly,

COMPLAINTS

Dear Sirs:

I would like to report that a can of peas my wife opened last night contained the enclosed stone. I am also enclosing the label from the can, and the end of the can bearing raised letters and numbers. This food was purchased last Saturday at the Centerville Chain Store, Centerville, located at the corner of Smith and Main Streets.

Sincerely,

GENERAL

Dear Sirs:

I am concerned about the radiation of food products. Enclosed is a clipping from *Parade,* March 22, 1964. The rays are called "clean" but have we done enough research on radiation to know the answer yet?

I hope that labels on irradiated products will clearly state that fact.

Sincerely,

Dear Sirs:

Please send literature about the food and drug laws and their enforcement by the Food and Drug Administration.

I am planning to use the material in a report I'm writing for a college course in government administration.

Sincerely,

DEPARTMENT OF THE INTERIOR
WASHINGTON, D. C. 20240

The Department of the Interior deals with the public mainly in connection with three subjects: recreation, the national parks, and the American Indian. Since the Secretary receives about twenty-one thousand letters a year, he obviously can't read them all. However, he will be given a good cross section of mail, and the best way to increase the chances of having him read your letter is to relate it to something that he's expressed a public interest in.

For example, Stewart L. Udall, Secretary of the Interior when this chapter was written, is an outspoken defendant of conservation, and letters referring to important conservation problems are likely to attract his attention. Here are three letters that the Department sent me, which they felt were well written.

LETTER REQUESTING A SPECIFIC WRITTEN RESPONSE

Dear Mr. Udall:

Your reference last Monday at the Rensselaerville Institute to William Faulkner's comments regarding the destruction of the historic courthouse in his home town leads me to send you the enclosed data on the Centreville Courthouse. [The enclosures consisted of a short brochure describing the courthouse's 160-year-old history, plus a newspaper article about its impending destruction to make way for an office building.]

I am sure you will agree that a tragedy of the first order is imminent. This fine Courthouse was built right on the edge of the great Adirondack wilderness in 1878, in one of the most historic areas in the United States.

Would you be willing to address a letter to me, pointing up the moral you so vividly expressed last week in the Faulkner anecdote?

The State Historical Society, the State Bar Association, and all the civic leaders of the Centreville area are actively supporting this effort.

We will be very grateful for your consideration.

Very sincerely yours,

Note that this letter doesn't bother to repeat the details of the brochure enclosed. It assumes that the Secretary is interested enough to read the brochure; the writer isn't pounding him on the head.

If the brochure had been a long one, it might have been useful to have put in a postscript calling his attention to the pages that would be most relevant.

ASKING FOR PERSONAL HELP

Flattery never hurts. The writer of the following letter praised the Secretary's book in his opening paragraph. No author can ignore a letter that begins this way.

Dear Mr. Udall:

I have read your book, *The Quiet Crisis,* with intense interest. The forthright manner in which you present the case for America's outdoor recreation causes me to ask for your help in connection with a recreation area which, although small, may be worth salvaging.

I own an outdoor recreation area in Stateville which has existed for more than one hundred years. Its principal asset is a lake of some 175 million gallons of fresh water. My property taxes amount to about 1 per cent of the township taxes.

Experts in the Stateville Division of Fish and Game say that the lake is one of the best fishing lakes in the state. It is also a potential source of potable water.

Without asking my permission, the local township not long ago ran storm water drains into the lake, causing considerable silting. Recently, they ran a sanitary sewer into it. I took the matter to court, and obtained an injunction against them—I'm told that this is the first time the state courts have ever granted such an injunction.

I'm enclosing a copy of a news release which appeared in the local paper at the time, and if you're interested, I can furnish a copy of the judgment.

Despite the injunction against the town, the county government has started using the lake for storm water draining. I now have a suit against them, which will come up for trial in about six months.

The county has enlisted the aid of the State Highway Department. Most of the county highway engineers are incensed that anyone should question their God-given rights as "highwaymen." For example, in my suit against the township, one state engineer testified that in his thirty years of service, no thought had ever been given to the rights of private property owners or the "other uses" of property. He said, in effect, that the "highest use" of property was for highways.

As a former member of the State's Planning and Development Council (1957–1962), I'm familiar with the state Outdoor Recreation Programs. In fact, I've made several dozen speeches advocating a green-belt program around our urban areas.

The state has asked me to contribute the lake as a part of this program, but until I can make sure that the highwaymen won't steal this little bit of American heritage by ruining its recreation value, I intend to retain title to it.

I therefore intend to resist these "modern land raiders," as you call them. But I can't do it alone. I am not asking for monetary help, but I do need qualified witnesses who are dedicated to the preservation of America's heritage of outdoor recreation areas. Can your Department make available to me one or two consultants who would be willing to testify about the value of preserving our outdoor recreation areas, and of the importance of not using them as sewage dumping grounds? My attorney tells me that the trial will probably go to court in about sixteen months.

I hope that you will be able to help me.

Admittedly, this letter is longer than most letters should be. But the writer had a good story to tell, and he told it completely, using the minimum number of words.

See, also, how he quietly placed himself on Udall's side by mentioning his membership in the State Planning and Development Council. This paragraph serves two purposes: it shows the Secretary that the writer is a man of repute, and that he is interested in the same goals as the Secretary.

BRINGING A SPECIFIC PROBLEM TO THE BUREAUCRAT'S ATTENTION

Dear Sir:

Recently, I read with horror the enclosed article in the *New York Times* about spraying sagebrush. Apparently, both the Department of the Interior and the Department of Agriculture are involved in this, so I am also writing to Secretary Freeman.

Also, I enclose a relevant excerpt from Justice Douglas' book *My Wilderness,* which condemns the spraying program as a crime against the general public, which really owns the lands.

From a conservation standpoint, large-scale destruction of sagebrush is shameful enough. From an economic standpoint, it is sheer stupidity and a contradiction to other federal policies.

The purpose of the spraying is to enable our ranchers to range more animals. Yet, Congress is considering imposition of beef import quotas because of domestic overproduction.

Surely it is madness for the federal government to listen to the appeals of the stockmen for higher beef prices and also to their appeals for killing publicly owned sagebrush in order to grow more beef. Surely, a man of your wisdom and influence can do something about this insanity.

Please tell me: what can I, as an individual, do besides writing my senators and congressmen? Do you think a taxpayers' suit against the federal government would do any good? Have you any other suggestions?

Sincerely,

DEPARTMENT OF JUSTICE
WASHINGTON, D. C. 20530

The chief purposes of the Justice Department are to help enforce federal laws, to furnish legal counsel in federal cases, and to interpret the laws under which other departments act. It conducts all suits in the Supreme Court in which the United States is concerned, supervises the federal prison system and, through the FBI (Washington, D. C. 20535), investigates violations against federal laws. It also represents the government in legal matters generally, rendering legal advice and opinions, upon request, to the President and to the heads of the executive departments.

Apparently, however, many people think that this isn't enough, for they write to the Department on an enormous variety of subjects. Said a letter which the Department wrote me recently: "Some write about individual problems involving civil rights, veterans seek assistance in securing employment, and various other problems. Prisoners complain of police brutality, unjust sentences, and unfair trials, others seek pardon or parole. (Many of these are state prisoners who misdirect their mail to this department.) Others seek financial assistance and legal assistance. Some seek help with their marital problems. Others complain of land, insurance and postal frauds. Some seek assistance in locating missing relatives. Reports of corrupt officials—state, local and municipal and in unions—and of breakdowns of law and order, are detailed by many writers."

The Department's ability, or willingness, to cope with these matters is, of course, defined fairly sharply by law. In general, where a federal law has been violated, the Department will have an interest. But where the matter is of local concern, it's probably beyond the Justice Department's power to do anything about it.

My suggestion is, then, that if you have a complaint about a violation of federal law that you think the Department might be able to answer, by all means write them about it. They'll let you know whether they can help. (It may take some time to get an answer. They receive between 130,000 and 200,000 letters a year; it took them three months to reply to a not very urgent letter of mine.) And unless you're quite sure of where to send the letter, direct it simply to the Department of Justice, Washington, D. C. 20530. The Department handles all the mail for the bureaus it contains, and will direct your correspondence to the right place.

DEPARTMENT OF LABOR
WASHINGTON, D. C. 20210

The Department is concerned, of course, largely with management-labor matters, such as working conditions, the length of the work week, or overtime pay. Of course, it also helps frame labor legislation, and your letters on this area may help the Secretary by making him aware of your feelings.

When writing to the Labor Department about matters of public policy, or when requesting information, follow the principles discussed on pages 182–83, concerning letters to the Department of Agriculture.

POST OFFICE DEPARTMENT
WASHINGTON, D. C. 20260

Not long ago, the Postmaster General instituted an economy drive reducing some Saturday window services and parcel post service. The Post Office Department was promptly deluged with mailed protests, and shortly after, a directive went out to the regional directors telling them to use a little discretion. As a result, your post office is probably now offering far more service than it would have had the public taken the order submissively.

HOW TO GET THE TOP MAN'S ATTENTION

When John Gronouski was Postmaster General a couple of years ago, he issued instructions to his staff on the type of letters that were to be passed on to him. They serve as a useful guide in getting the attention not only of the Postmaster General, but, probably, many other top officials as well. Here are the letters that Mr. Gronouski wanted to see:

1 *Those coming from people or places familiar to him as part of his past service or experience.* If you can dig up any personal connection between yourself and the addressee, mention it in the letter.

2 *Intelligent, thoughtful letters from students,* particularly when the letters deal with issues relating to the Post Office Department and to education and economy, areas of his special interest.

3 *Letters of complaint or commendation that indicate a special trend either by sheer number or by the vehemence of attack.* This doesn't mean that if you're vituperative, he'll be interested. It does

mean, however, that if you're angry about something, and a number of other people are angry, at least some of your letters will get through.

4 *Intelligent and timely comments on his speeches or public utterances.* If you can tie in your letter with something he's recently said that's come to your attention, he'll be more interested. This, of course, is known as the principle of feedback. Bureaucrats tend to feel somewhat isolated in Washington and they relish the knowledge that someone outside is aware of them. One may take it as a general rule that if the thing we all love the most is to hear ourselves talk, the thing we love next is to see others listen to us. By relating your letters to an official's comments, you get him at his weakest spot.

DEPARTMENT OF STATE
WASHINGTON, D. C. 20520

The State Department's main job is to act as chief advisor to the President in the field of foreign policy.

The Secretary of the State Department will not, in all probability, read your letter. As one of his subordinates explained: "Perhaps no other Cabinet officer has such a great demand on his time. In addition, the Secretary is frequently out of town or out of the country." In other words, unless you're his mother or his child, you probably won't get an answer from him.

In fact, you may consider yourself fortunate if you get any answer at all. A State Department newsletter indicated that at the beginning of 1962, there was a backlog of 18,000 pieces of unanswered mail. Three months later, it had climbed to 39,000. By now, they probably have a special warehouse to store it in.

Even if you do receive an answer, it may not have been touched by human hand. The department uses a number of automatic typewriters which are activated by paper tape with holes punched into it. If your letter can be answered in a routine fashion, a secretary will simply press a button next to her typewriter after she types in your name and an introductory acknowledging paragraph, and the paper tape will activate the keys, punching out a standard message.

Don't be resentful. Most large companies and government offices use these labor-saving devices. And anyway, there probably isn't too much that you could say to the Secretary of State that will change his mind. This is true even if you write in as part of a mailing campaign. The State Department is particularly apt to receive this kind of literature, and it treats it with little more than, at the most, a minimal acknowledgment.

THE TREASURY DEPARTMENT
WASHINGTON, D. C. 20220

Besides managing the financial affairs of the nation, the department controls the coinage and printing of money. The Coast Guard, the Bureau of Narcotics, and the Secret Service are under its jurisdiction, also. The Internal Revenue Service is also part of the Department. The IRS's address is 12th Street and Constitution Avenue, N.W., Washington, D. C. 20224.

Letters for the Treasury Department generally fall into two categories: those asking for assistance or information, and those commenting on Treasury policies. If you're writing about a personal tax matter, be as specific as possible. If it's in reference to a disagreement between you and the tax people, give the dates of past correspondence, and the names and addresses of the officials with whom you've corresponded. It may also help if you include photocopies of past correspondence, in order to save the Treasury officials from spending time in going through the files.

If you're commenting on Treasury policies, don't expect the officials to pay too much attention to you unless you're an expert in finance. As they say, in their own defense, "high level policy issues today are complicated and generally very sophisticated. One has to be well trained and experienced in areas such as federal income taxation and international finance before he can add constructively to many of the pending policy issues with which the Secretary of the Treasury would be concerned."

When writing to the Treasury Department about matters of public policy, or when requesting information, follow the principles discussed on pages 182–83, concerning letters to the Department of Agriculture.

Independent Agencies

FEDERAL AVIATION AGENCY
WASHINGTON, D. C. 20553

The FAA's main jobs are establishing safety regulations for planes and pilots, testing safety equipment, establishing air navigation facilities, and administering air traffic rules.

When you want to complain about low-flying airplanes zooming over your house, or about a pilot who took you straight through a lightning storm on your last flight, shoot a letter off to the Federal Aviation Agency. They'll route it through channels, and eventually, somebody's wrist may—or may not—be slapped, and you may get some satisfaction. In any event, write directly to Washington rather than the local office. Here are some typical letters that the Agency has received recently:

REQUESTING INFORMATION

It will help the agency to give you what you want if you tell them briefly what you're going to use the information for, as does the writer of the following letter in his first and second paragraphs:

> I am requesting information from your Agency to be used in a report I'm writing for our local Army base. The report will deal with obtaining FAA aviation ratings.
>
> In our group there are many pilots, aircraft mechanics, radio repairmen, air traffic controllers and others who, with a little guidance, could obtain and utilize such ratings for their personal benefit. Many of my fellow aviators, for example, don't understand the requirements and procedures for obtaining a private pilot's license, although many of them are fully qualified. My article would assist by outlining the many ratings available and the procedures involved.
>
> I would appreciate information outlining the examinations, waivers,

and other procedures that an individual would meet in pursuing these ratings.

I know that this is a large request. However, my purpose is to help my associates to do a better job. I feel that this will promote the field of aviation.

Sincerely,

When you want several kinds of information, you can make the officials' job easier—and get a faster reply—by listing each item separately, as in the following letter:

Gentlemen:

I'm doing research on air transport, and would appreciate your sending me any free literature on the following areas:

1 Routine duties and responsibilities of pilots;
2 Routine duties of other crew members, including stewardesses;
3 Safety procedures in handling air cargo.

Also, can you send me a list of all publications, whether free or not, available from your Agency.

Sincerely,

COMPLAINT ABOUT THE AGENCY

Dear Mr. Halaby:

As one who travels often by air, I am concerned about the accidents which have been occurring to jet airliners.

I would like to ask several questions: Do we know what is causing such incidents as the Texas DC-8 dive and the Lake Pontchartrain accident?

If we do know, what steps are being taken to prevent repetitions?

If we do not know, what recommendations are being made to the public?

I believe that your Agency should provide the public with information about these crashes. I don't like to feel that I'm traveling in a device which may very well kill me while your experts are finding out *why* it does the killing.

If there is uncertainty about the causes of the accidents, then I think the machines should be kept on the ground until the problems are solved. Or, alternatively, your agency should warn the public that it must travel at its own risk while the investigations are proceeding.

Sincerely,

FEDERAL COMMUNICATIONS COMMISSION
WASHINGTON, D. C. 20554

Like a mother hen, the FCC hovers nervously over our radio, wire, and cable communications networks. Charged with regulating these forms of interstate and foreign communication its major duties include the licensing and regulating of radio stations and operators, the allocation of radio-frequency bands to radio services and stations, and regulating the interstate and overseas operations and rates of United States telegraph and telephone companies.

FCC critics regularly accuse the Agency of being unresponsive to the needs of listening and viewing public. But I suspect that the Agency is no more derelict in its responsibilities than most other government organizations which deal mainly with a few large and powerful pressure groups. When the public complains loudly and vehemently enough, they may act; otherwise, there is a strong tendency to let things stand as they are.

WHOM TO WRITE

Address your letters to the Secretary of the FCC; of course, he probably won't see it, but it will be routed to the right department. You can expect an answer to a routine letter a couple of days after it's been received. If you've a complaint about a specific program or station, you'll still get an immediate acknowledgment and probably, after the Commission has investigated the complaint, a more detailed reply.

When writing to the FCC about matters of public policy, or when requesting information, follow the principles discussed on pages 182–83, concerning letters to the Department of Agriculture.

FEDERAL TRADE COMMISSION
WASHINGTON, D. C. 20580

The encouragement of competition is the FTC's function. While a considerable amount of time is spent in dealing with complex business affairs involving monopolies and restraint of trade, a considerable amount is also spent in coping with con men who prey on the general public, namely, you.

The FTC can't imprison, fine, or assess or award damages, but it can issue a "cease and desist" order which will temporarily, at least, stop the illegal practices. If the order is violated, then the FTC can take action in the courts, through the Justice Department.

If you feel you've been victimized by a crooked businessman, it may pay to notify the FTC. While they won't interfere in private disputes, they are empowered to take action if the offense appears to be against the public interest–in other words, if it's happened to a reasonably large number of people. Some of the more common complaints in which the FTC becomes involved are:

The Fake Bargain When a store advertises falsely that prices are "cut in half" or are "greatly reduced," or that an item "formerly sold for" so much.

The Vanity Appeal If a salesman approaches you with the story that you are one of a few specially selected people in your community to receive a product at a reduced price, and induces you to sign a contract for the item which you could buy at that price anywhere–just as long as you had sufficient funds to make a down payment.

The Last Chance When a salesman tells you that this is a one-time offer and that if you don't take advantage of it now, you may never be able to buy it at this price again–and it remains at that price the next month and the next and the next.

The Instant Fortune Here, the company falsely offers that you can earn up to so many dollars per week. Frequently, these claims are grossly exaggerated, and you have to invest a considerable amount of time and money before you discover that you've been bilked.

Even if you're a prudent consumer you may be fooled by these operators, and while you may not be able to get your money back, your complaint may put the man out of business.

The Inheritance Gimmick In their attempts to find a debtor's employer so that they can attach his wages, debt-collection agencies have used this technique for years. Despite its hoariness, it has continued to work for them. Here's how they operate: You receive a letter in an official-looking envelope. It may come from Washington, D. C., and carry the name of what sounds like an imposing government department. The letter will say (a) that you have some money due you, and that in order to collect it, you must fill out an enclosed form giving your name, address, and place of employment, or (b) that the federal government is making a legitimate demand for this information.

The purpose of the inquiry, of course, is to put some sort of attachment on your salary. But, because the agency is lying, it is engaging in a deceptive practice, and the FTC is empowered to investigate. (Incidentally, as the FTC says, "the promised 'fortune' that finds its way to the hapless 'heir' is never more than a dime.")

WHOM TO WRITE AND WHAT TO SAY

If you've been victimized by a crooked operator, you can write simply to the Federal Trade Commission, Washington, D. C. 20580. Your letter should include the following information:

1 Describe the nature of the practice. Include specimens of advertising or labeling. If there's nothing in writing, summarize the oral representations made.

2 Give the name and address of the person you're complaining against.

3 State why you think the practice is misleading or unfair.

4 Indicate why you think the practice is used to sell goods across state lines. (The FTC can act only in interstate commerce affairs.)

You'll probably get an answer within a week or ten days, which will tell you whether the Commission is going to investigate.

The following letter will serve as a model you can adapt to your needs:

Gentlemen:

I should like to register a complaint about (the nature of the complaint).

The company involved is (name of company).

I think the company has engaged in misleading and/or unfair trade practices for the following reasons:

(Describe briefly the events that took place.)

I believe the company operates across state lines because (give reasons why you think so).

I believe the Commission should investigate this matter, and (describe what course of action you think suitable).

Will you tell me what action the Commission will take?

Sincerely,

A letter which followed this model might read like this:

Gentlemen:

I should like to register a complaint about fraudulent pricing and breach of contract.

On January 3 of this year, a salesman from the ABC Sales Corp., 123 Main Street, Centerville, Md., called at my home and offered to reshingle my roof at what he said was a "special introductory price" of $500.

In return, I agreed to give him the names of five people who would agree to listen to his sales pitch.

I went to considerable trouble to obtain these five names.

I also paid a $125 deposit.

I have since discovered that most firms in this area charge about $300 to do the same job.

Further, although five months have passed, the roof has still not been shingled, despite several telephone calls that I've made to the company.

I am enclosing a copy of the contract I signed with the representative.

Since ABC Sales Corp.'s address is in an adjoining state, I believe this company is acting in interstate commerce, and therefore comes under your jurisdiction.

Will you be able to act in this matter, and either compel the company to honor its obligation or return my deposit? Also, will you be able to make them cease from offering a "special price" which is substantially higher than that of other firms in the area?

Sincerely,

DECEPTIVE ADVERTISING

The trouble with many complaint letters the FTC receives is that they are long on indignation and short on facts. A good letter need not be long, and it should cover the points listed above. Here are a couple of samples:

Gentlemen:

Enclosed is an advertisement from the Centreville Department Store offering Japanese transistor radios at "less than half the usual price." This advertisement appeared in the Centreville *News* of June 23, 1965, on page 12.

I purchased one of these radios last week. A few days later, I found the radio on sale in another store at exactly the same price. On checking with the manager of the Centreville Department Store, I was told that the store thought the radios were sold at twice the advertised price in other cities.

I believe the FTC should investigate the matter because these radios, having been made overseas, obviously must be involved in interstate commerce. Further, the store has run similar advertisements in the past, which I suspect are equally fraudulent.

Please let me know what action you intend to take.

Sincerely,

A letter describing an oral fraud might follow the following format:

Gentlemen:

This evening I was visited by a door-to-door salesman who said he represented the ABC Encyclopedia Co.

He told me that because of my high reputation in the community, I had been selected to receive a special low price on the 1965 edition of the encyclopedia. The price he quoted was $485. I happen to have checked prices recently, and know that this is about $40 more than the encyclopedia sells for in the stores.

The salesman's name was Homer Smith, and he said he worked out of the Encyclopedia's Middle Western office.

Because these encyclopedias are sold all over the country, I suspect they would come under the jurisdiction of the FTC. I would appreciate your investigating this company, in the hope that their fraudulent practices can be stopped.

Sincerely,

VETERANS ADMINISTRATION
WASHINGTON, D. C. 20420

Most VA correspondence is of a highly personal nature, dealing as it does with benefits such as compensation, pension, education, GI loans and insurance.

If you have to write to the VA about a benefit, your best bet is to contact the regional office in your own state, since most VA records are kept there, rather than in Washington.

The one exception is GI life insurance policies. These are administered at VA centers in St. Paul, Minn., Denver, Colo., and Philadelphia, Pa. Where your records are located depends on where you live. In all likelihood, if you have a policy, or are going to write on behalf of someone who has a policy, there will be a slip of paper along with the policy indicating which office has the records.

The list below gives the regional offices of the VA:

Alabama
  Montgomery
Alaska
  Juneau
Arizona
  Phoenix
Arkansas
  Little Rock
California
  Los Angeles
  San Francisco
Colorado
  Denver
Connecticut
  Hartford
Delaware
  Wilmington
District of Columbia
  Washington
Florida
  St. Petersburg
Georgia
  Atlanta
Hawaii
  Honolulu
Idaho
  Boise
Illinois
  Chicago
Indiana
  Indianapolis
Iowa
  Des Moines
Kansas
  Wichita
Kentucky
  Louisville
Louisiana
  New Orleans
  Shreveport
Maine
  Togus
Maryland
  Baltimore
Massachusetts
  Boston
Michigan
  Detroit
Minnesota
  St. Paul
Mississippi
  Jackson
Missouri
  Kansas City
  St. Louis
Montana
  Fort Harrison
Nebraska
  Lincoln
Nevada
  Reno
New Hampshire
  Manchester

New Jersey
Newark
New Mexico
Albuquerque
New York
Albany
Brooklyn
Buffalo
New York City
Syracuse
North Carolina
Winston-Salem
North Dakota
Fargo
Ohio
Cincinnati
Cleveland
Oklahoma
Muskogee
Oregon
Portland
Pennsylvania
Philadelphia
Pittsburgh
Wilkes-Barre
Philippines
Manila
Puerto Rico (and Virgin Islands)
San Juan
Rhode Island
Providence
South Carolina
Columbia
South Dakota
Sioux Falls
Tennessee
Nashville
Texas
Houston
Lubbock
San Antonio
Waco
Utah
Salt Lake City
Vermont
White River Junction
Virginia
Roanoke
Washington
Seattle
West Virginia
Huntington
Wisconsin
Milwaukee
Wyoming
Cheyenne

Address your correspondence to the Manager of the VA regional office.

The most important item in all VA correspondence is positive identification of the veteran. Just the name alone isn't enough, since there are about twenty-two million living veterans, and thousands of them have exactly the same name. The information you should include is:

1 The veteran's claim number. This should appear on the policy, or on other correspondence from the VA about the policy.

2 If the veteran has no claim number, or if it's unknown, give his birth date, the branch of the armed forces in which he served, and the dates of his entry into and discharge from the service.

COMPENSATION OR PENSION LETTERS

Manager
Veterans Administration Regional Office
Boston, Mass. 02203

Dear Sir:

I have moved and would like my compensation checks sent to my new address. To identify my account easier, my old address was 8 Swallow Street, Boston, Mass. The new address is 2026 Market Street, Lynn, Mass.

Charles P. Knudson
(C-2-305-etc.)

INSURANCE

Manager
Veterans Administration Regional Office
Seattle, Wash. 98121

Dear Sir:

Please tell me when my next insurance premium is due. If you have already notified me, I have lost the letter.

My insurance policy number is V-3325.

EDUCATIONAL BENEFITS

Manager
Veterans Administration Regional Office
Chicago, Ill. 60612

Dear Sir:

I have heard that you offer educational opportunities to the children of veterans who died because of a disability received in the line of duty while on active military service.

I have a daughter, 18, and two sons, 12 and 16, whose father died last year from a chest ailment which had been ruled service-connected. His name was Peter Paul Manley and he served in the Navy from October 29, 1942, to January 31, 1946. His birthday was March 2, 1919. He was born in Albany, N. Y., and he went into the service from Biloxi, Miss.

I would appreciate information as to what I must do to obtain any educational benefits for which the children may be eligible.

Marion B. Manley

PENSION

Manager
Veterans Administration Regional Office
Pittsburgh, Pa. 15222

Dear Sir:

I am sixty-seven years old. My health is poor and I can't work any more. Am I eligible for a veteran's pension?

I served in World War I from October 2, 1918, to December 3, 1919. I was in the Army, and my serial number was 234 81 82. I also served in the Navy from June 12, 1944, to February 12, 1946, in World War II. My Navy serial number was N23333.

GI BILL

Manager
Veterans Administration Regional Office
Muskogee, Okla. 74401

Dear Sir:

I should like to know if I am entitled to benefits under the GI Bill.

I served in the Army from May 1, 1960, to May 15, 1963. My service number was B-3-405-678.

If I am entitled to any benefits, will you please tell me:

a. What they consist of, and,

b. How I should apply for them.

Sincerely,

HOSPITAL ADMISSION

Manager
Veterans Administration Regional Office
Phoenix, Ariz. 85025

Dear Sir:

My father, a World War I veteran, is quite ill and needs hospitalization.

I do not know his VA file number or his service number. But the following information may be helpful:

His name is John Hazard Smith. He was born April 3, 1890, in

Kansas City, Mo., and he enlisted in the Navy in 1916, when the U. S. entered the war.

Can you tell me if he is entitled to treatment at a Veterans Administration hospital?

And if he is entitled to treatment, what steps do I take to have him admitted?

Sincerely,

PERSUADING LOCAL POLITICIANS

Are your streets dirty?

Are your police invisible?

Are factory smokestacks polluting the air in your neighborhood?

If you live in a community where the local government officials aren't doing their jobs properly, or where a situation exists that needs improving, you may be able to effect improvements if you write the right kind of letter to the right people.

The politicans in your local government will probably be at least as responsive to certain correspondence as will those in the federal government. But you'll have to apply essentially the same principles if you expect to get action.

One success story that came to my attention has so many instructive points that I think it would be helpful to give the complete background. I first heard about it through an article in the *New York Times,* written by reporter Bernard Stengren.

The article said:

> Trees probably will continue to cast their shadows on east 48th, 49th and 50th Streets because residents have demanded vigorous enforcement of the parking rules.
>
> The relationship between tree preservation and parking enforcement was described yesterday by Peter Detmold, Vice President of the East 49th Street Association.
>
> "Back in 1958, there was a lot of talk about widening streets because traffic was piling up," he said.
>
> "We knew that traffic conditions were bad in our neighborhood, but knew also that if streets were widened, we'd lose our trees."

Members of the association, which is made up primarily of homeowners and tenants east of Lexington Avenue on the three streets, decided that if parking rules were enforced, there would be no need for widening the streets.

The result was a campaign that has caused officials of the Traffic, Police and Highway Departments to marvel at community determination and to wish at times for a little complacency.

The residents demanded that parking rules be enforced continually and impartially, even on persons who lived, worked or did business in the neighborhood.

The basic regulation in the neighborhood is no parking from 8:00 A.M. to 6:00 P.M., Monday through Friday. Telephone calls and letters to the police pointed out violations and demanded the ticketing of vehicles breaking the rules. . . .

Mr. Detmold said yesterday that residents had become so used to empty curb lanes that they called the association as soon as illegal parkers began to appear. The association investigates and calls the Police Department, if the situation warrants.

"The police are very cooperative," he said, "because they know we'll go right up to the commissioner, if necessary."

After reading this article, I had a lengthy interview with Mr. Detmold. He told me that letters played an important role in his group's successes, and he offered the following suggestions:

First, always approach the man at the top. "If you write to the low man on the totem pole," he said, "he'll ask his superior about it, or perhaps his assistant, and before anything is done, the matter is likely to get lost. Therefore, we almost invariably write to the Commissioner of the Department concerned."

Second, write to the press. Said Mr. Detmold: "Letters printed in the newspaper are efficient because politicians read them, and they pay attention to them. They know that bad publicity in the press can hurt them."

Third, know whom you're writing to. Said Mr. Detmold: "It may be a good idea to call first and talk the problem over with the official, then write a follow-up letter confirming the conversation.

"Always make sure to get the full identification of the person you're talking to. For example, if it's a matter for the police, we'll get the name of the officer we're speaking to, his badge number and his rank. When we write the follow-up letter, we refer specifically to the conversation and the man."

Fourth, send multiple copies when necessary. "Sometimes," said Mr. Detmold, "officials play musical chairs, telling us to talk to another department. In this case, we blanket them all, writing copies of the same letter to all of them."

Fifth, don't make the letters too short. Said Mr. Detmold: "We find that short letters are read quickly and usually ignored. A long letter will be more annoying–and this is probably a basic principle: irritate the politician until he does something. You may run the risk of a backfire, of course, but it's also a most effective way to get them to act."

Mr. Detmold also made this point: "You can't always rely on letters alone. Sometimes you may have to go down to the Commissioner's office and talk to him. We occasionally go down as a group."

Sixth, it helps if you can write your letter on organizational stationery. Politicians tend to pay attention to organizations because they know that organizations are made up of people, and people mean votes.

Here are some of the letters which the East 49th Street Association has sent to New York City officials.

REQUESTING INFORMATION

Note the firm, polite, businesslike tone of this letter:

The Hon. John Smith
President, Borough of Manhattan
Municipal Building
New York 7, New York

Dear President Smith:

In connection with our Association's interest in street widening in Manhattan, we would appreciate your providing us with the following information with respect to the recently announced plans to widen portions of 24th, 39th, 44th, 48th and 55th Streets:

1. The reason for selecting these streets for widening; and
2. The title, date, and nature of the reports upon which the widening

decision was based, together with the names of the agencies which prepared the reports.

Thank you for your cooperation.

Very truly yours,
James Amster
President

ASKING FOR HELP

The Hon. Nathan Mills
Commissioner
Department of Parks
64th Street & Fifth Avenue
New York 21, N. Y.

Dear Commissioner Mills:

While August may seem a strange month in which to raise a problem concerning snow removal, this Association lost three trees this year on our street in consequence of last winter's storms. We were informed today by your forestry division that the trees were killed by salt deposits thrown around the trees last winter.

Our sidewalks are shovelled clear. Salt is rarely, and then only sparingly, used. But the streets are heavily and repeatedly salted after each storm, and then plows shovel the mess up on the sidewalks and around the trees. Since we assume that this is a city-wide problem, we wonder if your Department might want to give some thought now as to ways in which further losses of our trees can be prevented.

We would appreciate any suggestions you may have as to how this association can take motion on its own to assist in combatting this problem.

Very truly yours,
Peter Detmold
Vice President

(Copies of this letter were sent to four other city commissioners, having responsibility for sanitation, snow removal, and general administration.)

CORRECTING A DEFECT

The following letter gives all the data needed to correct a missing traffic sign. Further, its second sentence explains succinctly why the sign should be replaced.

Department of Traffic
100 Gold Street
New York 38, New York

Gentlemen:

It has been called to the attention of the Association that one of the parking regulation signs governing the block of East 49th Street between Second and Third Avenues is missing. Since this tends to trap motorists into parking where it is illegal to do so, we would appreciate having this sign replaced as rapidly as possible.

The sign in question stood in front of 254 East 49th Street. Both the sign and the pole to which it was affixed have vanished.

Very truly yours,
Peter Detmold
Vice President
Parking & Traffic Committee

REQUESTING ACTION

John Q. Anderson
Department of Parks
64th Street & Fifth Avenue
New York 21, N. Y.

Dear Mr. Anderson:

The Charlotte Hunnewell Martin Memorial Tree Fund of the East 49th Street Association wishes to plant six trees this spring in front of the following locations. Would you be kind enough to re-survey the requested sites, and arrange for applications if they are acceptable?

Two trees on the southwest corner of 48th Street and Second Avenue (opposite 249 East 48th Street).

Two trees in front of the Midtown Hospital, 309 East 49th Street. The preferred sites are those flanking the entrance to the hospital.

Two trees on the southwest corner of 49th Street and First Avenue. I believe the address of the building occupying the corner site is

346 East 49th Street, but in any event, the desire is to have the trees on 49th Street as close to the corner of the south side as conditions will permit.

The Memorial Tree Fund is a permanent part of our Association now, and we anticipate continued plantings by it until we are fortunate enough to have no room left for trees.

Very truly yours,
Peter Detmold
Vice President

ARRANGING AN INTERVIEW

When a new official comes into office, it's often good practice to meet him face to face, particularly if you think you may have dealings with him later. Here's the letter the Association sent to the new traffic commissioner:

Dear Commissioner Jones:

Would it be possible for the Executive Committee of East 49th Street Association to have a short conference with you at your office some time in the near future?

Our association has been involved in matters of direct concern to the Department of Traffic over the past several years, and we would welcome the opportunity of presenting our problems and our views to you in person.

If this is possible, would you be kind enough to have one of your staff let our office know what time would be satisfactory to you?

And may we welcome you to your most difficult post, and express the admiration which all of us have felt for the way in which you have gone to work on problems which for so many years seemed without solution.

Very truly yours,
The Rev. Warren W. Ost
President

This is a beautiful letter. It's polite, and it's direct. The very first sentence states the request. The second explains the reason for it. The third explains how the request can be fulfilled. And the fourth closes the letter on a friendly tone. It is not surprising that within a few days, an appointment was made by telephone. And here is the confirming letter:

CONFIRMING AN APPOINTMENT

Dear Commissioner Jones:

This letter will serve to confirm the appointment made today by telephone for the Executive Committee of this Association to meet you on Wednesday, March 28, at 2:00 P.M. at your office.

At your request, I append below the names of the members of the Executive Committee who will attend the meeting, according to our present understanding of each individual's ability:

[A list of five officers and their titles appeared here.]

Our Vice President (Lowell K. Hanson) has a conflicting appointment and will probably be unable to attend, and our Treasurer, Jack Mognaz, is currently in Europe on business.

Very truly yours,
Peter Detmold
Vice President

OFFERING TO HELP OFFICIALS

When the local police officials started to enforce parking regulations, some residents of the area protested. The Association hopped right on top of the situation with this letter to a top official:

Dear Mr. Hagan:

We have learned today from Sergeant Hanley of Safety Unit B that the police have had some complaints from residents of East 49th Street about having received parking tickets. Since the East 49th Street Association wishes to have the parking regulation enforced on our street —even at its own expense and at the inconvenience of the membership —I wonder if you would be interested in having our Parking & Traffic Committee help answer these complaints.

If so, the Association, through this Committee, would be pleased to learn of the nature of the complaints, and would try to see that the responsible persons are advised of the need to have illegal parking tagged on East 49th Street.

We would be happy to cooperate in any way with both Safety Unit

B and the 17th Precinct in any problems arising out of the enforcement of the parking regulations.

Even though when the shoe fits, it pinches, the Association much appreciates the work your department is doing in eliminating the parking mess.

Very truly yours,
Peter Detmold
Parking & Traffic
Committee

REQUEST FOR INFORMATION

Public officials will occasionally announce new programs with great fanfare. After reaping the benefits of the publicity, they may let the whole matter drop. At other times they may go ahead quietly with a plan, and sometime later announce decisions that seem to take no account of the voters' wishes. Inquiring letters, such as the following one, may help forestall these tactics. Note that the first two sentences review the history of the inquiry, and the final sentence asks for a specific answer.

The Hon. R. A. Mason
Commissioner, Department of Traffic
100 Gold Street
New York 38, New York

Dear Mr. Mason:

Several times over the past three years (in 1959, and again in 1960) this Association has written to you about a promised survey of traffic conditions on East 49th and East 50th Streets. We were told at the time of each inquiry that the survey had not been completed, but was under way, and that we would be advised when it was finished.

May we renew our request at this time that we be informed whether this survey has ever been made, and if so, that we be permitted to study its contents?

Very truly yours,
Peter Detmold
Vice President

DEMAND FOR ACTION

When fast action is required, a telegram can be an effective means of getting your message across. Although there's a tendency to use words sparingly in a telegram, there is a psychological advantage if you send a longer rather than a shorter message. The reader is likely to feel that you are (1) very much concerned about the matter because you've taken the trouble to go into your demand in detail (2) a person of some means, and hence, by inference, of some importance.

The following telegram is an example of an effective message that stopped the politician dead in his tracks; it was sent to the then borough president of Manhattan, a man who, in most other communities, would be the equivalent of the mayor:

> The East 49th Street Association protests the order from your office requiring the widening of the south side of East 48th Street at First Avenue in front of the new United Engineering Center.
>
> The order to the owners of the building constitutes a direct violation of the letter sent by your office to the Local Community Planning Board for District No. 6, dated May 4, 1961, and signed by William Gibney, which stated that "no street widenings are contemplated in the area between 42nd and 49th Streets."
>
> This spot widening effectively prevents civic improvements such as the planting of street trees, and this Association which had a commitment for street trees at this location, now finds that commitment cancelled.
>
> The East 49th Street Association asks you to take the following immediate action:
>
> 1. Provide this Association, and all other interested agencies, with the reasons and circumstances for ordering this spot widening, including a copy of the order, the date the spot widening was first considered by your office, and the names and titles of the officials who participated in the decision.
>
> 2. Take immediate action to rescind this order and issue a new order for the restoration of the area subjected to widening.
>
> Time is of the essence in this problem.
>
> James Amster
> President

Much of the strength of this message comes from its tight organization, an organization which can serve as the model for other similar messages. Note these points carefully:

1 The first sentence identifies the writer, tells how he feels (i.e., "protests") and describes specifically what he's protesting about ("the widening of the south side . . . ," etc.).

2 The second and third sentences explain the reasons for the protest. Sentence two explains that the order is directly contrary to a previous statement made by the executive. Sentence three suggests why the order will be bad for the community.

3 The fourth sentence requests specific action. This is always quite important in a protest, for if it's left out, the official, even if he's willing to cooperate, may not know what you want of him. In this case, there can be no doubt.

The first demand, requesting names, titles, and reasons behind the action, is to provide the group with leads to other officials who can be pressured, in case the recipient of the telegram is reluctant to cooperate.

The second demand carries the protest to its natural conclusion: that the order being protested be rescinded.

It is debatable whether the final sentence, "Time is of the essence . . ." adds anything to the telegram, but I think that even though it is a cliché, it does add a note of urgency, and therefore, I'd not object to it.

Chapter Ten

WRITING FOR CLUB MEMBERS

Sooner or later, to many men and women, comes the moment of truth: they are elected to a post of responsibility in a church, charity, or business club. This might mean being called upon to raise funds, plan entertainment, or publicize the club's activities. This chapter is devoted to helping make some of these organizational duties more bearable. We will discuss three of the most common types of club communications: publicity, fund raising, and program planning.

Your club may be a community organization or the local chapter of a national group. In either case, it becomes your job to tell the truth—or as much of it as will bring credit upon the organization—to the general public. At the least, this means persuading the local newspapers to carry news about the club's activities. And, if you are more than ordinarily ambitious, you may also try to persuade the community's radio and television stations to devote time to the club.

If you find yourself in this position and are worried about doing a competent job, this chapter will provide you with some guidelines. It can't, of course, turn you into a professional public relations counselor, but it will give you enough basic knowledge so that you'll do as well as any of your predecessors, and probably a great deal better.

GETTING ACQUAINTED WITH THE EDITORS

Once you've taken the mantle of publicity chairman on your shoulders, one of the first things you'll want to do is meet the editors of your local newspapers. You'll be relying on them to publicize many of your club's activities, and both you and they will be able to do a better job if you understand each other's problems. Frankly, though, it's more important for you to understand their problems than for them to understand yours.

You can do the job by telephone, but it's better if you meet each local editor for a brief face-to-face chat. Call him first for an appointment, for if you drop in around deadline time, when he's rushing to get out the newspaper, he'll probably give you very short shrift. When you meet him, get the answers to these questions:

- To which editor should you send news about your organization?
- What are the deadlines for daily and Sunday editions?
- To whom should you send suggestions for feature stories or human interest articles?

Make a note of this information; you'll find it invaluable in getting your publicity releases in time to the right editors.

SELECTING NEWS THAT'S FIT TO PRINT

In preparing newspaper publicity, you should first put yourself in the editor's shoes. One of his main jobs is to print as much news as possible that will interest his readers. Therefore, before you sit down to write, ask yourself: "Why is this important or interesting to the readers?"

If you're honest with yourself, you'll probably find that some of the items you're writing about will have general interest, and some will not. The latter category will generally include routine meetings open only to the membership. Don't expect the newspaper to give you any great amount of space for these. If the publication has a regular column covering regular meetings, the best you can hope for, unless you have a remarkably complaisant editor, is a notice in that column.

Now, let's turn to events of more than routine interest. Among these might be included meetings featuring a well-known speaker or a high official; or the kickoff of a special campaign, such as a fund-raising drive; or the election of new officers. Here, two possibilities are open. You can try to get the newspaper to send a reporter to cover the event, or you can write your own press release and hope the paper will publish it.

If you want a reporter on the scene, submit a press release about the event at least forty-eight hours in advance. This will give the editor a chance to decide whether it's worthwhile sending a reporter. But, recognize that the editor will have many similar demands: his staff can cover only a few of them. So, your best bet is to play it safe and plan on writing your own press release.

WHEN TO WRITE THE RELEASE

When you're submitting an after-the-event publicity release, send it in the day the event occurs. If it's a night event, send it in the next day. This is vital if you're submitting the news to a daily paper. It may be a little less important if it's a weekly. But, even in the case of a weekly, the sooner you get the item to the editor, the better. He, too, likes fresh news, and if the event happened the day before he receives it, he'll be more likely to feel that it deserves attention than if it happened three or four days before.

You may be able to save yourself a last-minute rush by submitting the item before the event takes place. For example, you know in advance when your group is going to hold an election or a banquet; and if there are going to be speakers, you may even know what they're going to say. If you have this information, send in your story about two days in advance of the event, with a notation on the top right corner of the first page: FOR RELEASE: TUESDAY, FEBRUARY 13.

Of course, should the event fail to occur, let the editor know immediately, by phone. This will save both of you embarrassment.

For very important affairs, you may be able to get extra publicity by handing in your story considerably in advance of the event. Here's what the Wilmington (Del.) *News-Journal* suggests to publicity chairmen in its area:

> When your organization plans a special event, send the information about three weeks before, so we can plan to run an advance story the

coming week. If you send another story, perhaps adding names of committee chairmen, send this in about a week before, changing the lead [the first paragraph] so that it is different from your first story.

It is often wise to telephone the department head or include a little note with your advance story, so he or she will have an idea about the amount of publicity to be released. Often, such advance knowledge will give the department head time to plan a staff-written feature story or pictorial layout based on your tentative publicity. Many times you can get far better coverage than you thought possible—although at other times it may be less than you hoped for.

If you want someone to cover a special program, please see that tickets are sent to the department head in plenty of time, and arrangements made. Follow this up with a phone call to ask if someone can come. The staffs try to cover important and interesting events, but, of course, this cannot always be done.

HOW TO PREPARE THE RELEASE

There's a fairly standard format which virtually all newspapers prefer for news releases. If you follow the nine suggestions below, you'll satisfy almost any editor.

1 Use 8½″ x 11″ paper.

2 Type the story, if possible. If you haven't a typewriter, write clearly, preferably on lined paper, and always print the names of any people you mention. Spell all names correctly. Most papers prefer that married women be identified by their husbands' name; for example, Mrs. John Smith.

3 Write on one side of the sheet only. When typing, double-space.

4 Leave a margin of about one and one-half inches on both the left and right.

5 Put your name, address, and phone number in the upper left corner, so that the editor can reach you for further information. You may also give the name of anyone else who can provide the same information.

6 Below your name, briefly indicate what the story is about.

7 Start the text of the story about one-third of the way down

the page. (This will give the editor room to insert special notations, headlines, etc.)

8 Try to limit your item to one page. Contrary to a popular impression, newspapers usually have much more news than they can print. A major task of most editors is to condense the items they receive. The less condensing the editor has to do, the more welcome will your story be, and the more easily will it slip through to the printed page.

9 Keep your paragraphs short. Newspapers rarely put more than two sentences in a paragraph. If you have just one sentence to a paragraph, it's perfectly acceptable.

Here's the format of a good press release:

FROM: Centerville Parent-Teacher Association — FOR RELEASE August 23, 1966
Mrs. John Jones, President
617-5389
Mrs. David Smith, Publicity Chairman
SUBJECT: PTA Election

Mrs. John Jones, 22 Main Street, Centerville, was elected president of the Centerville Parent-Teacher Association last night.

She succeeds Mrs. Eleanore Cage.

Other officers elected were Mrs. Joseph Moore, vice-president; Mrs. Tina Larson, secretary; and Mrs. Arthur Pine, treasurer.

The new officers will be installed at the annual meeting next fall.

END

WRITING IN NEWSPAPER STYLE

If you study your local newspaper, you'll find that most of the news stories follow a standard format. The first two or three sentences will present the most important information. Less important information appears at the end.

There are two reasons for this. First, a newspaper tries to get the reader's interest by calling his attention to the exciting things going on in the community. Therefore, the editor puts the most important information at the beginning, where it will be likely to catch the scanner's attention.

Second, the length of a printed story is frequently dictated by the amount of space on the page. If there's not enough room for the entire story, the easiest way for the editor to shorten it is to lop it off at the bottom. When the story is properly written, no important information will be lost. In a long story, the editor should be able to cut off several of the concluding paragraphs without losing any important information.

WHAT IS THE MOST IMPORTANT INFORMATION?

In a good newspaper story, the lead, i.e., the opening paragraphs, will give five pieces of information, called the "Five W's." They are:

WHO (did it)
WHAT (happened)
WHERE (did it happen)
WHEN (did it happen)
WHY or HOW (did it happen)

Here are some suggestions on how to construct a good lead. They appear in a booklet, "Help for the Publicity Chairman," published by the New London (Conn.) *Day.*

"The publicity chairman untrained in news writing usually builds his story chronologically–he begins his account with the earliest fact and ends it with the latest, like the minutes of a meeting. This is exactly opposite to newspaper style.

"Let's take a simple example.

WRONG, OF 'MINUTES' METHOD

> Welfare Fund Campaign workers met last night. President Public presided. Campaign Chairman Jones assigned solicitors to districts and showed a movie of how to ask for donations. The goal for this year was set at $50,000. Mr. Public caused quite a stir by saying he will donate whatever amount the workers collect in the first week of the drive. We should get at least $5,000 the first week.

"This contains several errors. . . . Use full names and identifications. Give enough facts so the reader who is not a member of your organization will understand. Don't use personal pronouns like 'we.' Attribute opinions to someone.

RIGHT, OR 'NEWS STYLE' METHOD

Whatever amount is collected during the first week of the Welfare Fund campaign which opens next Monday, April 1, will be matched by Fund President, Earl Z. Public.

The industrialist made this announcement at a meeting of campaign workers last night at the YMCA, at which the fund goal was announced as $50,000.

Mr. Public declared that judging from previous years' experience, solicitors should collect about $5,000 the first week.

Ernest X. Jones, campaign chairman, assigned solicitors to districts and showed a sound film on proper solicitation methods."

Several additional points that will help you to get the editor's attention are these:

1 Where you're reporting about a speaker, *what* he said is more important than the fact that he spoke. Mrs. Smith of the Golden Age Club may not care that Mr. Eggers spoke to the Kiwanis, but she might be interested in reading *what* he said about Medicare.

2 By all means, when a group of committees has been appointed, list the names of the committee chairmen. Don't, however, include the names of all committee members near the front of the story. As a general rule, where you have a lot of names to include, list them at the end of the story. If the editor feels they're important enough to be included, he'll leave them in; if not, he can cut them out easily.

3 When you become publicity chairman, study your local news-

papers. Notice the kinds of stories they use—which ones go on the front page, which in the society and club columns, and which on general news pages inside. You might find it useful to cut out various types of stories from the paper and follow their pattern when a similar situation arises in your own organization.

4 Don't telephone your publicity, as a general rule. It interrupts the editor's work, and further, you run the risk of getting names copied incorrectly. If there's a last-minute change in a publicity release you've already sent in, then of course it makes sense to use the phone and tell the editor about it.

HOW TO HANDLE NATIONAL PUBLICITY RELEASES

If you're the local publicity chairman of a national organization, you will probably receive press kits from headquarters. Typically, they will be sent out when the organization is conducting a national fund-raising drive, or when it's embarking on a new program.

The surest way to kill your chances of getting publicity is to take the kit to the newspaper.

Your newspaper is always looking for a local angle. Unless the editor finds something about the local chapter in the kit, he probably won't be able to use the release. Your job, then, is to find a local angle for the story.

Some national organizations make this easier for you by preparing a press release which enables you to fill in local information. A typical example would be:

> ________ has been appointed chairman of the ________ (name of town) fund-raising drives of the National Sewing Circle.
>
> The appointment of ________ was announced last night by chapter president, Mrs. ________, at the Circle's monthly meeting at the home of ________.

In this case, all you need do is fill in the blanks. If, however, the release hasn't been prepared this way, then you'll have to find some other local angle. Your best bet is to ask yourself: what people in the community will this affect? For example, if you can put in the names of club members who will be active in the campaign, or the drive, or whatever the activity is, then you'll have a good chance of getting the newspaper to print it.

Sometimes you may find the local angle is built right into the story. If you receive a publicity release from national headquarters which names individuals and tells about their background, check to see if any of them are mentioned as having been born, educated, or employed in your area. If so, you might do as some publicity people do, and simply encircle the name of your community on the release so that the editor will immediately see its local news value.

If this information doesn't appear on the front page, you might fold the pages back over so that the encircled item appears on top; or you might attach a note to the first page calling the editor's attention to the page on which it appears.

In summation, then, use national publicity releases primarily as a guide for your own local release, which should stress facts that will interest the local newspaper and the local community.

GETTING PICTURE COVERAGE

There are two ways to get pictures of your organization's events into the newspapers. One is to have the editor send a photographer to cover the event. The other is to have your own photographer take pictures.

Getting the Newspaper to Send a Photographer

If you can persuade the editor that an event is large enough or of sufficient general interest to warrant sending a photographer, there's a good chance that the paper will use the picture, since the editor will have invested the man's time in the assignment. How, then, can you best persuade him to send a photographer?

The first rule is, give him time—at least a couple of days' notice. You may simply call the editor one or two days before the event and explain that you'd appreciate it if you could get picture coverage. Also, explain why you think it would be worthwhile to have a photographer on the job. Will something unusual be visible that will help make the picture stand out? Will an important official be present?

These are things that will tempt an editor.

A better way to do this is to send out an "informational" news release in advance of the event. The purpose of the release is to give the editor a clear idea of what will take place.

A publicity executive of the YMCA suggests following this procedure: Address the informational release to both the City Editor and the Picture Assignment Editor. The former may want to send out a reporter; the latter may want to send out a photographer. The YMCA will also try to make the release as visual as possible.

Here is a copy of a release which the YMCA sent out to New York City newspapers:

INFORMATIONAL RELEASE

Attached is a program and time schedule for the ground-breaking ceremonies tomorrow (Saturday, October 23) at 2:00 P.M. in connection with the construction of a new YMCA building in Eastern Queens (Hillside Avenue at 239th Street, Queens Village, N. Y.).

The city of New York is erecting a platform for the guests of honor, and the contractor will have a piece of construction equipment—a bulldozer and truck loader—on the scene. This will be the first new YMCA building in New York City in nearly ten years. The building, costing one million dollars, will contain an Olympic-size swimming pool, a gymnasium, meeting rooms, and other facilities to make it a complete Community Center large enough to accommodate more than 1500 families.

The building will be situated on two acres of land formerly belonging to the State of New York as a part of the ground occupied by Creedmoor State Hospital. In order for the YMCA to purchase the property, it was necessary for an Act to be passed by the State Legislature and signed into law by Governor Rockefeller. This Bill was introduced by Queens Assemblyman Fred W. Preller in 1963, and he will be one of the guests of honor to "man" a shovel at the ceremony.

PROGRAM

Ground-Breaking Ceremonies
Eastern Queens Extensions of Central Queens Branch of the
YMCA of Greater New York
Saturday, October 23, 1965
2 P.M.
Hillside Avenue at 239th Street, Queens Village, N. Y.

1:30–2:05 *Selections by The Martin Van Buren High School Band*
Maurice Bleifeld, Principal
H. Allan Orshan, Chairman of Music
Leo Palminteri, Conductor

2:05 *Call to Order*
Chester Schwimmer, Master of Ceremonies
Member of Central Queens YMCA Board of Managers
Co-Chairman of Ground-Breaking Ceremonies

2:06 *Presentation of Colors*
Color Guard, John F. Princ Post, V.G.W. 6478VFW
Frederick H. Spiegel, Commander

2:07 *The National Anthem*
Irene Handler – Soprano
The Martin Van Buren High School Band

2:10 *The Invocation*
Father Daniel J. Halloran, Pastor, St. Gregory's R. C. Church

2:12 *Introduction of Representatives on the Platform*
Chester Schwimmer – Master of Ceremonies

2:35 *The Initial Ground-Breaking*
The Hon. Fred W. Preller, State Assemblyman, 29th District, representing the State of New York
Dr. Harry A. La Burt, Director of Creedmoor State Hospital, representing Creedmoor
The Hon. Mario J. Cariello, President of the Borough of Queens, representing New York City
Chris de Neergaard, Chairman of Eastern Queens Extension YMCA and member of Central Queens

YMCA Board of Managers, Co-Chairman of Ground-Breaking Ceremonies, representing the YMCA

2:36 *Prayer of Dedication*
The Rev. W. John Derr, Pastor, Holy Trinity Lutheran Church

2:40 *Introduction of Speaker*
Chester Schwimmer, Master of Ceremonies

2:42 *Address*
The Honorable Mario J. Cariello
President of the Borough of Queens

2:55 *The Benediction*
Father Daniel J. Halloran, Pastor, St. Gregory's Roman Catholic Church

2:59 *"America" (All Sing)*
Irene Handler
The Martin Van Buren High School Band

A YMCA spokesman says that this program may be too precise for newspaper purposes, but he suggests that some kind of time schedule should be given for the photographer's use. And it's certainly better to be over- than under-cautious.

Arranging for Your Own Photographer

If you can't get a guarantee from the editor that he'll send a photographer, or if you want to make doubly sure that suitable pictures are sent to the paper after the event, you may want to arrange to have photographs taken yourself.

It's a good idea, before you hire a photographer, to ask the editor whether he thinks that the paper might print a picture if one is submitted. If he's doubtful, remember that you may be going to the expense for nothing.

If you or someone in your organization takes the picture, keep in mind these suggestions, culled from a booklet published by the Macon (Ga.) *Telegraph and News:*

> Limit the number of people in the picture. If you try to use too many, the picture will be so crowded that no one can be recognized.

The picture should help tell your story. The group should be doing something, rather than merely looking at the camera.

Props, or an unusual setting, or action at the scene of the event will all help give your picture news value.

If the picture shows preparation for an upcoming event, make arrangements to have it taken well in advance so that the picture can be used before the event.

If you send a picture with your release, it should be a glossy print with the names of those in the picture and your own name, address, telephone number, and organization written on a slip of paper and pasted or taped at one edge to the back of the photo. Most papers prefer a print measuring 5″ × 7″, or 8″ × 10″. There's no need to send the negative.

Don't type or write on the back of the photograph. This damages the print and can result in bad reproduction.

Don't be disappointed if an unsolicited picture isn't used. Some pictures are not suited to newspaper reproduction methods.

OBTAINING FREE RADIO AND TELEVISION PUBLICITY

Broadly speaking, there are three kinds of radio and television publicity that, with good planning, you can probably obtain for your organization. News announcements about your group are the first kind. The second kind consists of free advertising, otherwise known as public service announcements. These are short announcements about your organization or about some of its activities. The third kind consists of more extensive publicity–the best example is an interview with somebody associated with your organization.

HOW TO OBTAIN NEWS-ANNOUNCEMENT PUBLICITY

Make it a habit to send news releases to radio and television stations as regularly as you do to newspapers. It probably won't be worth your while to send out notices of routine meetings, but if your club is undertaking any special activity, it's worth letting the stations know.

Check your local television and radio schedules for programs which specialize in local news. Call the station and find out to whom you should send announcements for this program.

Keep your news releases short, your sentences bouncy. Use the present tense as much as possible in order to create a feeling of immediacy. Write the release in capital letters.

Here's an example of a radio or television news item:

NEWS RELEASE

THREE CENTERVILLE HOUSEWIVES ARE CONSIDERABLY RICHER TODAY BECAUSE THEY WERE KIND TO THEIR NEIGHBORS. THE LADIES HAVE WON A TOTAL OF ONE THOUSAND DOLLARS IN A CONTEST SPONSORED BY THE CENTERVILLE CHAPTER OF THE GOLDEN AGE CLUB. EACH OF THE PRIZE WINNERS WAS SELECTED BY A GOLDEN AGE CLUB COMMITTEE BECAUSE OF A KINDNESS SHE HAD PERFORMED FOR A CLUB MEMBER.

MRS. JOHN ROBINSON HAS WON FIRST PRIZE OF FIVE HUNDRED DOLLARS BECAUSE SHE SAVED THE LIFE OF EIGHTY-TWO-YEAR-OLD MR. THOMAS ALGERNON BY MOUTH-TO-MOUTH BREATHING WHEN HE SUFFERED A HEART SEIZURE OUTSIDE OF HER HOME LAST AUGUST. MRS. MAY ATHERTON TOOK SECOND PRIZE OF THREE HUNDRED DOLLARS. MRS. ATHERTON DROVE NINETY-ONE-YEAR-OLD TESSIE DINGER FIVE HUNDRED MILES LAST SPRING ON A THREE-DAY VISIT TO A DINGER FAMILY REUNION IN SMITHVILLE. AND MRS. JACK LALLY HAS WALKED OFF WITH THE THIRD, TWO-HUNDRED-DOLLAR PRIZE BECAUSE SHE RESCUED WILLIE, THE SEEING-EYE DOG OF BLIND, SEVENTY-THREE-YEAR-OLD HOWARD PEMBERTON, WHEN WILLIE BECAME SEPARATED FROM HIS MASTER DOWNTOWN LAST CHRISTMAS IN THE MIDDLE OF A LARGE SHOPPING CROWD.

SO FAR, NONE OF THE LADIES HAVE DECIDED WHAT THEY'LL DO WITH THE MONEY. BUT THE FEELING OF ALL OF THEM SEEMS TO BE PRETTY WELL SUMMED UP BY MRS. ROBINSON, WHO SAID, WHEN TOLD OF HER AWARD: "MY GOODNESS, I HARDLY EXPECTED A PRIZE FOR DOING WHAT JUST SEEMED TO COME NATURALLY."

PREPARING PUBLIC SERVICE ANNOUNCEMENTS

The public service announcement is essentially a free advertisement. Radio and television stations usually use them at the end of a program, when they have unsold advertising time. In a certain way, they like to have these items because they're profitable. The station's auditors list them as a charitable contribution, and when the station makes its report to the Federal Communications Commission, it will usually mention that it has devoted a certain amount of time to public service activities. This makes the FCC look more kindly upon the station's application for a renewal of its license. There is, of course, also the fact that the station owner may actually have a few drops of altruism in his blood, and may want to help promote worthwhile community activities.

Your job is to put public service announcements about your organization in a form that makes them easy to read, and to get them to the right person. As with the news releases, it's a good idea to call the station and ask to speak to someone who can tell you where to send your spot announcements. You might help the man along by asking him to suggest individual announcers or programs which have a record of using public service announcements.

Typewrite and triple-space your spots, writing on one side of the page only. They should be written so that they will take a specific amount of time to read. The standard lengths are 10, 20, 30, and 60 seconds, and this length should be indicated at the top of the page. It's a good idea to send in several announcements of varying lengths, and it won't hurt to send in a couple of each kind. Never let them exceed one page in length, and if possible, use soft paper which won't rustle when it's handled. Staple them together behind a cover sheet which gives detailed information about the source of the announcements.

Here are some spot announcements prepared by the YMCA in New York. Follow this format in your own club's releases.

YMCA OF GREATER NEW YORK

FOR RELEASE:
SEPTEMBER 24th
through
OCTOBER 11th, 1965

Francois L. Sheats
Director of Public Relations
422 Ninth Avenue
New York, New York 10001
LAckawanna 4-8900
(Night Phone: POrt Washington 7-0566

SPOT ANNOUNCEMENTS
(60, 40, 30, 20, and 10 SECONDS)

FOR

BROOKLYN YMCA TRADE SCHOOL
BEDFORD YMCA
1115–1121 Bedford Avenue
Brooklyn, N. Y. 11216
MAin 2-1100

Leona Rudman
Radio-TV Assistant
YMCA OF GREATER NEW YORK
SPOT ANNOUNCEMENTS
BROOKLYN YMCA TRADE SCHOOL

FOR RELEASE:
SEPTEMBER 24th
through
OCTOBER 11th, 1965

60 SECONDS

WHY DO SO MANY MEN TRAVEL FROM ALL FIVE BOROUGHS OF NEW YORK CITY TO ATTEND THE BROOKLYN YMCA TRADE SCHOOLS? . . . BECAUSE THEY CAN LEARN A TRADE IN ONLY TEN WEEKS . . . AT EITHER A DAY OR AN EVENING SESSION . . . IN WORKSHOPS WELL-EQUIPPED WITH TOOLS AND MACHINES USED IN INDUSTRY. THE "Y" OFFERS YOU SUCH A SHORT TRAINING COURSE BECAUSE YOU LEARN BY DOING . . . AUTO MECHANICS, RADIO AND TELEVISION, MACHINE SHOP, OIL-BURNER SERVICING, REFRIGERATION, GAS AND ELECTRIC WELDING, HELIARC (HEELI-ARC) WELDING, MOTION-PICTURE OPERATING, AND OTHER SKILLS. YOU CAN GET A GOOD JOB AS SOON AS YOU FINISH YOUR TRAINING AT THE YMCA TRADE SCHOOL IN BROOKLYN. REGISTRATION IS GOING ON NOW. PHONE MAIN TWO . . . ONE ONE HUNDRED.

—E N D—

YMCA OF GREATER NEW YORK
SPOT ANNOUNCEMENTS
BROOKLYN YMCA TRADE SCHOOL

FOR RELEASE:
SEPTEMBER 24th
through
OCTOBER 11th, 1965

40 SECONDS

THERE'S A SHORTAGE OF SKILLED WORKERS IN NEW YORK CITY . . . AND THERE'S A GOOD JOB WAITING FOR YOU . . . IF YOU LEARN A SKILL AT THE BROOKLYN YMCA TRADE SCHOOL. YOU CAN TAKE A TEN-WEEK OR THIRTY-WEEK COURSE . . . DAY OR EVENING . . . IN MACHINE SHOP, AUTO MECHANICS, RADIO AND TELEVISION, MOTION-PICTURE OPERATING, AND MANY OTHER INDUSTRIES. THE CLASSES INCLUDE WORKSHOPS, WELL-EQUIPPED WITH TOOLS AND MACHINES, AND YOU LEARN BY DOING. YOU CAN REGISTER NOW AT THE BROOKLYN YMCA TRADE SCHOOL. PHONE MAIN TWO . . . ONE ONE HUNDRED.

—E N D—

YMCA OF GREATER NEW YORK
SPOT ANNOUNCEMENTS
BROOKLYN YMCA TRADE SCHOOL

FOR RELEASE:
SEPTEMBER 24th
through
OCTOBER 11th, 1965

30 SECONDS

NEW YORK CITY NEEDS AUTO MECHANICS, MACHINISTS, RADIO AND TELEVISION REPAIRMEN, MOTION-PICTURE OPERATORS, AND OTHER SKILLED WORKERS. YOU CAN GET A GOOD JOB IF YOU LEARN THESE SKILLS AT THE BROOKLYN YMCA TRADE SCHOOL . . . IN A TEN-WEEK COURSE . . . DAY OR EVENING SESSION. "Y" WORKSHOPS ARE WELL EQUIPPED WITH TOOLS AND MACHINES USED IN INDUSTRY . . . AND YOU LEARN BY DOING. REGISTER NOW. PHONE MAIN TWO . . . ONE ONE HUNDRED.

—E N D—

YMCA OF GREATER NEW YORK
SPOT ANNOUNCEMENTS
BROOKLYN YMCA TRADE SCHOOL

FOR RELEASE:
SEPTEMBER 24th
through
OCTOBER 11th, 1965

20 SECONDS

YOU CAN GET A GOOD JOB IF YOU LEARN A TRADE AT THE BROOKLYN YMCA TRADE SCHOOL IN BROOKLYN. REGISTER NOW FOR A TEN-WEEK COURSE IN AUTO MECHANICS, MACHINE SHOP AND MANY OTHER SKILLS. PHONE THE BROOKLYN "Y" TRADE SCHOOL AT MAIN TWO . . . ONE ONE HUNDRED.

—E N D—

YMCA OF GREATER NEW YORK
SPOT ANNOUNCEMENTS
BROOKLYN YMCA TRADE SCHOOL

FOR RELEASE:
SEPTEMBER 24th
through
OCTOBER 11th, 1965

10 SECONDS

YOU CAN GET A GOOD JOB IF YOU LEARN A TRADE AT THE BROOKLYN YMCA TRADE SCHOOL. REGISTER NOW. PHONE MAIN TWO . . . ONE ONE HUNDRED.

—E N D—

GETTING A RADIO OR TV PROGRAM BUILT AROUND YOUR CLUB

If you're really enthusiastic about your job of publicity chairman, you may try to interest a radio or television station in devoting one or several programs to your club. What's the best way to go about it?

One of the most intelligent set of suggestions I've seen appears in an excellent book published by the League of Women Voters of the United States, and called *Tips on Reaching the Public*. While the book is written for publicity chairmen of the League, its information is invaluable for publicity chairmen of almost any organization, and I recommend it highly if you're looking for a more detailed discussion of public relations. It costs $1.25, and you can order it from the League of Women Voters of the United States, 1026 17th Street, N.W., Washington, D. C. 20206.

The following suggestions are based on the book's recommendations:

If you're starting cold, try writing a letter to the station—either to the owner of the station, or to a particular program.

Indicate that you're familiar with the programs they produce.

Establish that your group is a worthwhile community organization by describing some of your activities.

Make clear what you're asking for: a guest appearance on a certain show, three or four weeks of programs, an announcement, etc.

Point out why you think the program will interest the station's listeners.

Indicate when you'll make a follow-up telephone call, either to ask for a personal interview, or to discuss further plans.

In a personal interview try to find out what the station would like and then try to fill that need.

Here's a letter that you might send, based on the previous suggestions:

Dear Mr. Station Owner:

May I suggest an idea for a program based on activities of the Centerville Volunteer Fire Department. The program would, I believe, fit in well with your current series, "Your Community in Action."

The Volunteer Fire Department services Centerville and three outlying towns. Its members are drawn from all parts of the community, and include a bank president and a school janitor. In the past year, it has prevented at least seven major fires, and five citizens of Centerville are alive today who would have been burned to death if the Volunteers had not saved them.

The program might follow the general format of the "Your Community in Action" series. That is, it might last for one-half hour, and would be moderated by your regular announcer, John Jones.

We think that listeners will find the program interesting because it directly affects their own safety and their own lives. We think listeners may also be interested in finding out about the new and unusual fire-fighting techniques which the department uses, and about some of the more exciting events of two recent major fires in Centerville. The program might also offer suggestions for making the listeners' homes safer from fires.

I plan to call you next Wednesday morning, June 9, in the hope of setting up an appointment to discuss this program with you further.

After you've made the initial contact with the station, you, or some other person–and only one person–should have the responsibility of working with the station. To make your relationship effective:

1 Ask for time only on the merits of the program idea; don't try to use pressure.

2 Be reliable, prompt, and trustworthy.

3 When proposing a single program, furnish a specific outline.

4 When proposing a series of three or four programs, take an outline of the series to the station, a comprehensive outline for at least one program, and a promotion plan for the series. If it's for television, bring ideas on visuals, but be open to the station's suggestions.

5 When planning to broadcast an event for which site and hour cannot be changed, notify the station as soon as details are known.

6 Do as the producer suggests. He has the know-how for what can and cannot be done.

7 If a script is used, provide copies for the director, the sound man, each member of the cast, the writer and the chairman.

8 Use the program as the basis for a news release in advance of the program, in addition to a listing in the newspaper log and television guide. If there's a chance that the program will make news, alert reporters or fill them in after the broadcast is over. Coordinate your own public relations with those of the station's public relations department.

9 Don't hesitate to ask for station plugs of the program in advance. They're important in building up an audience.

10 Give credit to the station as co-sponsor in all publicity.

11 After the program is over, notify the station of any reactions your group has received.

12 The chairman or president of your club should be present at all broadcasts to make guests comfortable, check the script, and congratulate the participants on their splendid performance.

FUND-RAISING LETTERS

In addition to obtaining publicity for your organization in the public media, you may also be called on to do some writing for other purposes. Two of them which we'll discuss in the balance of this chapter are: fund-raising letters and speaker solicitation letters. For advice on what a good fund-raising letter should contain, let's turn to the experts—those responsible for directing large charitable trust funds which regularly contribute to worthwhile causes.

The people who run these funds are a hardheaded lot, and they have established certain criteria which an organization should be able to meet in order to be considered worthy of a contribution. If you can meet *their* requirements, you can meet almost anybody's.

Following is a checklist—arranged alphabetically by type of organization—of the things these people look for in deciding whether to contribute.

In constructing your letter, you probably won't be able to cover all of these points. But you should think about which ones might be most helpful to your cause, and make some reference to them in your letter.

At the end of this section, you'll find sample fund-raising letters for various types of institutions.

HEALTH AND WELFARE ORGANIZATIONS*

1 Is the board an active and responsible governing body, serving without compensation, holding regular meetings, and exercising effective administrative control?

* Based on standards established by the National Information Bureau, Inc.

2 Does the group have a legitimate purpose? Does it avoid duplicating the work of other sound groups?

3 Is there reasonable efficiency in program management, and reasonable adequacy of resources, both material and personnel?

4 Does the organization consult and cooperate with established agencies in the same or related fields?

5 Does it use ethical methods of publicity, promotion, and solicitation of funds, avoiding exaggerated and misleading claims for prestige or fund-raising purposes?

6 Can the group provide an annual audit prepared by an independent, certified public accountant or trust company?

7 Is there a detailed annual budget, translating program plans into financial terms?

HOSPITALS

1 If the letter is soliciting funds for a new facility, does it establish the need? Pointing to an objective survey by an independent, qualified person or team is a good way of doing this.

2 Is the hospital efficiently managed? Are its officers willing to discuss their financial records and their administrative procedures?

3 Is there broad public support for the campaign?

4 Is the board of trustees composed of reputable people?

5 If the campaign's purpose is to carry out a research project, is the medical staff of sufficiently high caliber to do the job well?

6 If the campaign is for a new building, will the building overlap other community projects?

7 Is the new building designed to serve its function well?

LIBRARIES

1 What is the purpose of the donation? A new building? More books on certain subjects? Improved services?

2 How will the contribution benefit the donor? If the request is to a corporation, will it benefit the employees or their families? If it's to individuals, will it benefit them or their families?

3 Is this new building or service really needed? Try to show that it is both reasonable and necessary to collect money for this purpose.

4 Will the gift be used for the general welfare, rather than for just a small, select group?

5 The recipient may be interested in how the library's present income is spent, and how it will spend its gifts in the future. Can you include an annual report or a proposed budget?

MUSEUMS

1 Does the museum exhibit a record of industry, imagination, alertness, and a sense of public responsibility?

2 How far will the museum go in acknowledging contributions to exhibits? What services will it extend to contributors?

3 Is the museum making good use of its resources?

4 What is the purpose of the campaign? How will it benefit the community?

PARKS AND PLAYGROUNDS

1 What is the purpose of the gift? Many people think that public parks and playgrounds are wholly supported by government. Make clear why your request is not being supported by this source.

2 If the request is to a company, make clear whether you expect this to be a one-time donation, or whether it's a long-range program which you hope will be supported for a definite or indefinite number of years.

3 If the money is to be used to establish a new playground or park, is the location a good one in terms of its benefits to the community?

SCHOOLS—COLLEGES AND UNIVERSITIES

1 Has the school demonstrated qualities of leadership?

2 Is the institution efficiently run?

3 Is the institution solvent, or does it have a good chance of becoming solvent without the contribution?

4 Will the contribution benefit the donor directly or indirectly?

5 Is the request for a one-time contribution or for a repetitive one?

6 Has the school been accredited by any professional organization? If not, why not?

SCHOOLS—INDEPENDENT

1 Is it clear that this is a nonprofit school? Donors will give more freely if it is.

2 Are the head of the school and the board of trustees qualified and capable?

3 Is the school doing worthwhile work, and has it shown signs of growth and innovation?

4 Is the gift being requested for only this one time, or is the request for a regular gift?

SCHOOLS—PUBLIC

1 Will the project for which a contribution is being requested benefit the entire community, or all of the school's children?

2 Do the school authorities in general support the project?

SOME ADDITIONAL HINTS

In composing your fund-raising letter, keep these points in mind:

First, the letter should offer some reason for giving that will appeal to the reader's emotions. When you've finished writing the first draft, ask yourself, "Would I be interested in reading beyond the first paragraph of this letter?"

Second, the letter should back up the emotional appeal with a few hard facts which will help the reader to feel that he should back up his emotions with hard currency.

Third, if you can afford it, enclose a stamped, self-addressed envelope. This usually increases the rate of returns.

Fourth, if possible, personalize the letter by putting the addressee's name on the salutation. "Dear Mr. Jones" is more effective than "Dear Friend."

Fifth, consider listing the names of the board of directors or the chief officers on the letter. This may help establish the reputability of your organization, particularly if it's a new one.

SAMPLE FUND-RAISING LETTERS

Dear Fellow Citizen:

What is your child's health worth?

Five dollars? Ten? One hundred?

In the town of Centerville, there is a sick child whose parents cannot pay even $5 to care for her.

Will you help this youngster?

You can–through the Centerville Child Care Group–the only organization in Centerville which underwrites the medical bills of those children whose families are too poor to afford even minimal medical care.

Last year, the Group helped more than 5000 youngsters. This year, we expect to help more than 6000.

Since the staff of the Child Care Group is almost entirely voluntary, virtually every penny you contribute will be used to help the children, not for administrative expenses.

And further, your contribution will immediately double in value, because it will be matched by a special, one-year grant from the Crowder Foundation.

The enclosed brochure will tell you more about the Group.

After reading it, will you send your contribution to help a youngster who needs your support?

Sincerely,

Mrs. James Patterson
Chairman
Centerville Child Care Group

On the back of the next letter was a filled-out application blank for a children's camp. The front of the letter read:

Our 41st Year
Camp Season, 1967

Dear Mr. Johnson:

James, a copy of whose application appears on the reverse of this letter, seeks permission to go to camp.

As a social worker and a worker with boys for over forty years, I am naturally concerned with the future of our youth, especially as applied to the present wave of juvenile delinquency.

I am, however, convinced that sending an underprivileged boy to camp is one of the greatest deterrents to delinquency, and the most effective means of making him aware that "life is real–life is earnest, and 'jail' is not its goal."

No boy is born vicious. Viciousness is thrust upon him by the unfortunate accident of his environment. Give him a chance and he will rise to heights of character that will ennoble him and everyone who extends a hand to help him.

Give this boy, and all our boys, a chance to achieve the heights of honor, of loyalty, and of godliness, and you will serve these boys well.

Will you please return James's application blank with your check if you possibly can? It costs $60 to send him to camp for two weeks, $30 for one week, and $5 for a day. I assure you he will be grateful, and so will I.

Yours very sincerely,

John Connolly, Director

Mark Mason President
William Bush Vice-President
Howard Flower Treasurer

Please make checks payable to Boys Camps, Inc.
(All Contributions are Deductible from your Income Tax)

Dear Mrs. Madison:

In this envelope you will find the Centerville Library's Annual Report.

But don't be fooled. It does not tell the real story.

For the Report talks about statistics, and statistics are not the Library's real story: people are the real story.

People such as the 84-year-old lady who visits the Library every Friday at 3:00 P.M. to pick out two mystery novels because, as she told our librarian, Miss Finch, "These give me all the excitement I need to keep on living."

And people such as the 17-year-old boy from the wrong side of Centerville who recently wrote us from college: "I never would have gotten here if you hadn't encouraged me to use whatever brains I have. If I ever make anything of myself, I'll have you to thank for it."

You've undoubtedly guessed that the purpose of this letter is to ask you for a donation, to help meet our operating budget of $13,000.

With your donation, we will be able to help the people who rely on the Library for knowledge and for excitement.

Will you send us your check so that we can continue to help?

Joseph B. Blackwell
Chairman
Centerville Library Committee

P.S. Our operating budget this year is a modest 10 per cent above last year's budget. If it's possible, will you increase your contribution over last year's amount by at least 10 per cent—to help us help people?

Dear Member:

With your help, the Centerville Museum of Art will shortly be able to embark on a project that will place it in the front rank of comparably-sized museums in this country.

The project, called Art of Our Ancestors, will be a permanent exhibit devoted to the works of painters and craftsmen who lived in this region in the eighteenth and nineteenth centuries.

In this time of transient values, when we all wonder if anything will be worth passing on to our descendants, the project takes on special meaning.

For, it will preserve a segment of our history which helped make us the dynamic community we are today.

Many of the works which we hope to include in this exhibit are still in private hands, within the community. But they are being dispersed throughout the country by piecemeal sales, at auctions, and through the purchases of art dealers who know that their value will increase in the future.

By supporting this project now, you can help to preserve this heritage for your descendants.

We will welcome a contribution of any size. But if you are able to donate at least $25, your name will be inscribed on a bronze plaque which will be mounted near the entrance of the new exhibit.

And a contribution of $100 or more will entitle you to bring an unlimited number of guests to the Museum at no admission charge, for as long as you remain a member.

I'm sure you will agree that this exhibit will help fulfill one of the most important functions which any museum can serve: helping our citizens recognize and appreciate their cultural heritage.

Will you help that realization come true—for yourself, your fellow citizens, and for the generations which will come after us?

Your check, payable to the Centerville Museum of Art, will help make this dream come true.

Sincerely,

John Retina
Chairman
Friends of the Centerville Museum

Dear Fellow Citizen:

We will shortly be breaking ground for the construction of a cancer research building for the Centerville Community Hospital.

We need your help to make the project successful.

Here are some of the reasons why I think you will want to contribute to the Building Fund.

First, there is an urgent need. There is no other facility of a similar type within a five-hundred-mile radius of Centerville.

Second, many of your friends and neighbors have already pledged their help. Among the organizations supporting the drive are the Kiwanis, the Daughters of the American Revolution, the Junior League, and the leaders of the Centerville Catholic, Protestant, and Jewish congregations.

Third, the building will incorporate many of the newest innovations in cancer research, including a new cobalt radiation therapy device which has proven extremely successful in halting the disease.

Fourth, the new unit will be staffed by some of the leading physicians and research people in this part of the country, including many of the teaching staff at the Centerville Medical College.

But perhaps the most important reason is that the new building will stand as a bulwark of defense against a killer that threatens every one of us in Centerville.

We have now reached the halfway mark in our goal of raising five million dollars for the new building.

Will you help us go all the way?

Your contribution, which is tax deductible, will be put to work immediately.

Sincerely,

Mrs. Aline Benton
Chairman
Centerville Fund-Raising Committee

P.S. Please make your check payable to the Centerville Hospital Building Fund.

SPEAKER SOLICITATION LETTERS

If you are writing letters to obtain speakers who will address your organization, include:

1 The date of the meeting
2 The subject you'd like the speaker to talk about
3 The reason for the meeting
4 The approximate length of the talk
5 The total time the speaker's presence will be required
6 The time of the meeting
7 The address of the meeting place
8 Whether you'll pay a fee for the speech
9 Whether you'll pay for the speaker's traveling expenses and his accommodations
10 It may also be helpful to give a brief description of the organization, so that the speaker can slant his remarks appropriately

SAMPLE LETTERS

To an Individual

Dear Dr. Trundell:

Will you be able to address the Centerville Three O'Clock Club on Saturday, April 23?

The Club is composed of Centerville elementary and high school science teachers. The purpose of the organization is to learn about new developments in science that may help our teaching.

Your current astronomical research is of great interest to all of us. The members would be particularly eager to hear about your ideas concerning life on other worlds.

The meeting will be in the auditorium of the Centerville High School, Main Street and Arbuthnot Road. If you can come at 1:00 P.M., we will have about ten minutes of preliminary business, and will introduce you at about 1:10.

You might plan to speak for about thirty minutes, followed by fifteen or twenty minutes of questions from the audience.

Although we are unable to pay a speaker's fee, we shall be happy to reimburse any out-of-pocket expenses you incur in traveling to and from the meeting.

If you are unable to be our guest on April 23, would you consider talking to us at a subsequent meeting on Saturday, May 17, or Saturday, June 20?

I shall look forward to hearing from you, and I know that all the members will be delighted if you can accept.

Sincerely,

Jonathan Bingle
Program Chairman

P.S. If you would like to use any visual aids, please let me know what you'll need in the way of equipment, screens, or other accessories.

To a Company or an Association

Gentlemen:

Can you provide our organization with an after-dinner speaker on January 15?

We are an investment club with twenty-five members who meet monthly to review our portfolio, and to learn from the professionals about good investment practices.

We would expect to introduce the speaker at 9:30 P.M., and would anticipate his talking for about thirty minutes, followed by a fifteen- to thirty-minute period in which he would answer questions.

We would be delighted to have the speaker join us for dinner, which begins at 8:30.

The speech would be of particular interest to our members if it dealt with the subject "Five Stocks that May Split in the Next Year."

An alternative subject would be: "How to Analyze Your Portfolio's Past Performance Intelligently."

The meeting will be in the Burberry Room of the Hogan Hotel.

Will you let me know by letter or telephone if you can fill this request?

Yours,

Earl Fultz
President

To One of Several Speakers

If you expect the speaker to be one of two or more, explain who else will be speaking and what the format will be:

Dear Senator Johnson:

We would be most honored if you would be one of the two featured speakers at the state meeting of the United Veterans Association.

The Association has a national membership of thirty thousand, all former members of the armed forces. Our objective is to promote welfare benefits for wounded veterans.

There will be about three hundred in the audience–the heads of virtually all of the state chapters.

We have been following your fight in the Senate against increased pensions for veterans, and would appreciate the chance to hear your arguments first-hand.

The second featured speaker will be Congressman Virgil Applegate, who, as you know, favors larger veterans' pensions.

Your remarks might revolve around the topic, "Why I Oppose Greater Benefits for Veterans." (Congressman Applegate has agreed to discuss his reasons for favoring increased benefits.)

We've planned the following schedule for the evening:

7:00 to 8:00 Dinner
8:00 to 8:05 Introduction of the first speaker
8:05 to 8:25 First speaker
8:25 to 8:30 Introduction of the second speaker

8:30 to 8:50	Second speaker
8:50 to 9:30	Speakers answer questions from the floor
9:30	Meeting concludes

Also attending the meeting will be Governor James Ambrose, who will act as our master of ceremonies, and the mayors of Centerville and Amityburg.

We will be able to offer you a modest speaker's fee of four hundred dollars, and will reimburse you for first-class plane fare from Washington and back, for your overnight stay at the Major Hotel, and for incidental expenses which you may incur.

Can you let me know by November 15 whether you'll be able to accept? Your presence will add both distinction and honor to our meeting.

Sincerely,

Leslie Buckland
Director

Chapter Eleven

WRITING CLASSIFIED ADS

Paul Schultz, the Classified Advertising Manager of the Indianapolis *Star and News,* and a former president of the Association of Classified Advertising Managers, recently described for me his conception of a good classified ad.

"Letter writing and classified ads," he said, "have very much in common. Each of them is an instance of 'people talking to people.' Both are meant for a specific person, but may be read by many. I have found that to project one's personality in any letter is most desirable.

"To this extent, a classified ad can stand the same test. Boil it all down, and it means, 'Be yourself.' "

This rule holds for most of the classified ads you'll have occasion to write. Whatever the reason for the advertisement, you'll be trying to talk to the reader clearly and succinctly. I know of no better advice on this subject than that offered by C. M. Carroll, Classified Advertising Manager of the *New York Times,* who makes these three suggestions for writing a good classified:

Make it clear–if it can be misunderstood, it will be.

Make it true–use facts, and understate rather than overstate.

Make it complete–leaving information out can mislead and confuse.

Mr. Carroll made these suggestions specifically in reference to real-estate classifieds, but they are applicable to all types of ads–

whether you're selling a house or a boat, or looking for a job or for an apartment.

I would add one other suggestion. If you have an item to sell or rent, mention the price if possible. Readers may suspect the worst if price isn't mentioned, and they're likely to ignore the ad in favor of one which is more specific about price.

Because the *New York Times* probably carries more classified ads than any other paper in the world, I asked them for help in preparing this chapter. They were most generous in their response, and provided me with a great deal of information. Much of the following material is based upon an extensive checklist which *New York Times* classified-ad-takers use in helping advertisers to construct good, strong, complete, informative advertisements. Where it has seemed worthwhile, I have added other material in the form of examples and suggestions from other sources. Your local newspapers may vary somewhat from the models suggested here, and of course, it's a good idea to examine them for significant differences.

DISCRIMINATION IN CLASSIFIED ADS

Many newspapers do not now permit advertisements that discriminate against race, religion, or national origin. Federal and state regulations are becoming increasingly strict in this respect, and advertisers should be aware of it for their own protection. The prohibitions will vary from region to region, and even from newspaper to newspaper within a city. It may be helpful to read the regulations which the *New York Times* applies to different types of classifieds:

Help Wanted

Advertisers may not specify the religion, race, color, or national origin of the applicants they seek, except under (a) Household Help Wanted, where *only* national origin may be indicated; (b) when based upon bona fide occupational qualifications. No advertiser may state his own religion, race, color, or national origin in the Help Wanted columns.

An exception to the rules above is made only in the advertising of charitable or religious nonprofit organizations, which may indicate their own religious affiliations. They are permitted to use such phrases as "Jewish philanthropic organization," "Counselors wanted for camp operated by Congregational Church," etc.

Such wording as "state nationality," "give place of birth," "state religion," etc., is not acceptable.

"Send photograph" or "include snapshot" may not be used. Advertisers may not refer to the complexion of the applicants sought.

Business Opportunities

In Business Opportunities advertisements, advertisers may not specify their own religion, race, color, or national origin, nor that of the persons with whom they seek connection, except in the advertising of charitable or religious nonprofit organizations. Here, religion, race, color, and national origin of the advertiser may be indicated.

Real Estate and Apartments

Such phrases as "state religion," "Christian community," "restricted community," or "near Catholic and Protestant churches" are not accepted.

Rooms and Board

Advertisements offering rooms and board may not specify religion, race, color, or national origin of either the advertiser or the person sought. The word "restricted" may not be used. "Kosher cooking," "dietary laws observed," "French cuisine" are acceptable.

Situations Wanted

In the Commercial Situations Wanted columns an advertiser may state his own religion, race, color, or national origin when such information constitutes bona fide occupational qualifications. Under Household Situations Wanted an advertiser may specify his own race, color, or national origin (not religion).

Tutors and Private Instruction

No reference may be made to the religious affiliation of tutors or prospective employers.

Other Exceptions

The advertiser may state his own religion, color, or national origin in the following classifications: Apartments and Rooms to Share, Apartments Wanted, Board Wanted, Real Estate Wanted, and Rooms Wanted.

A WORD ABOUT TYPE SIZES

If you study the classified advertisements in this book and in your own local newspaper, you'll of course notice that the type is set in different sizes. Selecting the right type for your ad is a matter of balancing aesthetic, economic, and advertising sense. The smaller the type size, the more words you'll be able to get into a given amount of space, and the less expensive the ad will be. On the other hand, you lose the attention-getting value of larger type faces. As a general rule, a larger type face for the headline will get more attention. If you really want to set your ad apart, you'll leave an extra line or two blank between the headlines and the text of the ad. Usually, these blank lines, or "white space" as they're called, are charged for according to the number of lines they occupy.

Here are the sizes of the types most commonly used in classified ads:

This is an example of
24-point type

This is an example of 18-point type

This is an example of 14-point type

This is an an example of 10-point type

This is an example of agate type

Now on to the actual makeup of your want ad.

ANNOUNCEMENTS

There are about ten types of announcements which you may have occasion to make in the classified sections. The following list describes them, suggests the information that should be included, and gives examples of each kind.

ANNIVERSARIES

Information to include:

1 Family name
2 Full name
3 Address
4 Anniversary
5 Date
6 If there is to be a reception, state when and where

Example:

Jones Mr. and Mrs. Herbert W. Jones of 000 West 120th Street announce their 50th wedding anniversary, March 20. At home after 8 P.M.

ANNULMENTS

These announcements refer to the annulment of engagements and are acceptable only with the consent of both persons concerned.

Information to include:

1 Family name of man
2 Family name of woman
3 Name of parents, relative, or guardian making the announcement
4 Address of parents, relative, or guardian making the announcement
5 Given names of woman
6 Full name of man
7 Address of man

Example:

Smith-Jones Mr. and Mrs. Robert Jones of 000 West 76th Street announce the annulment of the engagement of their daughter, Ella May, to John Smith, of 000 West 92nd Street.

CARD OF THANKS

Information to include:

1 Family name
2 Full name
3 Address

Example:

Jones Mrs. Herbert W. Jones and family of 000 St. Nicholas Ave. sincerely thank their friends and relatives for their kind expressions of sympathy in their recent bereavement.

BIRTHS

Information to include:

1 Family name
2 Full name of parents
3 Maiden name of mother
4 Address of parents
5 Sex of child
6 Name of child
7 Place of birth (if in institution)
8 Date of birth

Example:

Jones Mr. and Mrs. Arthur D. Jones (nee Mary Louise Smith) of 000 Parkside Ave., Brooklyn, N. Y., announce the birth of a daughter, Mary Elizabeth, at the Caledonia Hospital, October 21.

It is becoming somewhat common to insert a less formal and more exuberant notice, such as: Mr. & Mrs. Arthur D. Jones of 000 Park-

side Ave., Brooklyn, announce the birth of Myra, a sister to Jack, George, and Harriet, etc."; or, "Jack, George, and Harriet Smith are overjoyed by the arrival of their baby sister, Myra, etc."

The practice is questionable. It elevates the children while it diminishes the importance of parents. My suggestion is that you suppress any inclination to turn childbirth into a family picnic. This is a place for dignity and maturity, and the traditional, formal notice is one way of asserting it.

ENGAGEMENTS

Information to include:

1 Family names of man and woman
2 Name of parents, relative, or guardian making the announcement
3 Address of parents, relative, or guardian making the announcement
4 Given names of woman
5 Full name, address of man

Example:

Brown-Read Mr. and Mrs. Henry J. Read of 000 West End Avenue announce the engagement of their daughter, Mary Jane, to Mr. Harold M. Brown, of 000 Columbia Heights, Brooklyn.

Example (announcement by someone other than parents)

Mr. and Mrs. John Smith of 000 West End Avenue announce the engagement of their niece, Mary Jane, to Mr. Harold M. Brown, of 000 Columbia Heights, Brooklyn.

Example (announcement when parents are divorced)

Mr. and Mrs. John Jones of 000 West End Avenue, announce the engagement of Mrs. Jones' daughter, Mary Jane Smith, to Mr. Harold M. Brown, of 000 Columbia Heights, Brooklyn.

Example (*announcement when one parent has died*)

Mrs. Henry J. Read of 000 West End Avenue, announces the engagement of her daughter, Mary Jane, to Mr. Harold M. Brown, of 000 Columbia Heights, Brooklyn.

UNVEILINGS

Information to include:

1 Last name of deceased
2 Full name of deceased
3 Time and place of unveiling

Example:

Blackmer A monument to the memory of the late Henry Robert Blackmer will be unveiled at Woodlawn Cemetery, August 18, at 2 P.M. In case of rain, the following Sunday.

DEATHS

Information to include:

1 Last name of deceased
2 Given name of deceased (also maiden name, if woman)
3 Address of deceased
4 Date of death
5 Age of deceased at time of death
6 Names and relationship of survivors
7 Time and place of funeral services
8 Time and place of interment
9 State whether services are private or open to friends and relatives
10 If flowers are not wanted, say "Please omit flowers."

Some newspapers either discourage or refuse to accept the "omit flowers" notice. (The New York Times *does not.) In this case, you may have to be satisfied with a sentence such as "Memorial contributions to* ——— *preferred." For an illuminating, amusing, and hor-*

rifying account of how florists and funeral directors have engineered this censorship, see Chapter 8 of The American Way of Death *by Jessica Mitford.*

Example:

Smith, Jane (nee Sullivan) of 000 West 89th Street, Manhattan, suddenly on October 15, in her 65th year, beloved wife of John Smith and mother of James, William, and Frederick Smith. Funeral services at Funeral Chapel, 000 West 92nd Street, Wednesday, October 17 at 8 P.M. Interment Woodlawn Cemetery, Thursday at 10:00 A.M. Friends and relatives invited. Please omit flowers.

If the organization to which the deceased belonged is inserting the notice, it should contain the following information:

1 Last name, given name of deceased
2 Name of lodge, society, or organization
3 Time and place of funeral services
4 Names of officers
5 Any other information appropriate to a family notice may be included

Example:

Walsh, John. The officers and members of Tabor Lodge record with deep sorrow the passing of their esteemed Treasurer and benefactor. Members are asked to attend funeral services to be held Wednesday, July 1, 11 A.M. at Park West Chapel, 79th Street and Columbia Ave.

James Brown *Pres.*
Robert Green *Secretary*

MARRIAGES

Information to include:

1 Family name of man
2 Family name of woman
3 Name of parents, relative, or guardian making the announcement

4 Address of parents, relative, or guardian making the announcement
5 Given names of woman
6 Full name of man
7 Address of man
8 Time and place of ceremony

Example:

Johnson-Miller Mr. and Mrs. Andrew J. Miller of 000 Central Park West announce the marriage of their daughter, Jane Elizabeth, to Edward D. Johnson, at the Calvary Baptist Church, West 57th Street, Thursday, June 1.

When the announcement is made prior to the ceremony, some phrase such as "will be married" or "will take place" and the date should be included.

Example:

Johnson-Miller Mr. and Mrs. Andrew J. Miller of 000 Central Park West announce that their daughter, Jane Elizabeth, will be married to Edward D. Johnson at the Calvary Baptist Church, West 57th Street, Thursday, June 1.

When the announcement is made by a divorced or surviving parent, or by a relative or guardian, this should be indicated in the manner shown under "Engagements."

GREETINGS

Information to include:

1 Family name of advertiser
2 Full name of advertiser
3 Address of advertiser

Example:

Black Mr. and Mrs. Joseph D. Black of 000 Riverside Drive wish their friends and relatives a happy and prosperous New Year.

IN MEMORIAM

Information to include:

1 Last name of deceased
2 Full name of deceased
3 Date of death
4 Name or relationship of person making the announcement

Example:

Smith In memory of Arthur Montgomery Smith, who departed this life October 14, 1926.

There is nothing rigid about this form. Many people prefer to record their remembrances in other ways. Here are three actual examples with fictitious names:

Connors Elaine. Cherished birthday memories of our beloved sister.

JOE and MARGARET

Horvath Lee. In loving memory of our beloved mother.

JIM, MILDRED, and NONNIE

Jackson Marvin Norton. November 23, 1965. It will always be lonely without you. Thank you again for the wonderful gifts of the spirit. A man of your greatness will never die.

A beloved friend

APARTMENTS FOR RENT

(See information about discrimination on page 252.) If you have an apartment to rent, include in your classified ad all the information that you think will attract the interest of likely prospects. The following list of features is quite extensive, and while you may not think it necessary to include every point mentioned, it's a good idea to put in as many as possible. Remember that trying to save a line or two in order to reduce the cost of the advertisement can be foolish economy, for you may leave out an important feature that would attract an otherwise indifferent prospect.

Information to include:

1 Street address, section of city, or name of town
2 Number of rooms and baths
3 Size and layout of rooms
4 Exposures
5 If furnished, a brief description of furnishings
6 Improvements and conveniences:

Newly decorated	Cross ventilation
Closet space	Refrigeration
Fireplace	Roof garden
Shower	Etc.

7 Service:

Doorman	Maid
Elevator	Full hotel
Telephone Switchboard	Etc.

8 Convenience to transit lines
9 Rent
10 Length of lease
11 Concessions
12 Date of occupancy
13 When apartment may be seen
14 Name of advertiser, address, apartment number, and telephone number

NOTE: In suburban apartment advertisements, add the following information:

a. Distance from transit facilities, schools, churches, etc.

b. Running time from main downtown transportation terminals or other central points in the city.

The following advertisements are for average apartments. By using descriptive phrases, the advertisers have made them appear unusually attractive.

GREENWICH VILLAGE Call XY 0-0000 AM or AB 1-1111 3 to 5 PM, for the most gracious 4½ room apt on a high floor with a lovely view. 2 bedrooms, spacious dining area, windowed kitchen and bath, large living room, 2 baths. Fine building with 24 hour doorman service. Only $300. 1111 E. 1st St.

The word "gracious" and the mention of "lovely view" have strong sales appeal.

69th St., East IMMED. OCCUP.
LARGE PRIVATE TERRACE
2 bedrms (separated) 2 baths, din rm breakfast rm, totally equipped kitch. including dishwasher, ample large closets. New luxury centrally air cond. bldg. 24 hr drman AB 7-7777

This advertisement begins with a strong attraction—a large terrace.

E 19th St. Betw Ave C & D. 6 rms, 3 bedrms, upper 2 fam, excel shop'g. Transit, pvt entr, adults-teens $140 AB 3-3333

The owner of this apartment wisely indicated proximity to transportation, and the private entrance.

1st Ave, 22nd St. Splendiferous floor thru, 55 feet, Roman bath, new paint, wall-to-wall carpet, fully equipped. Suit 2/3 persons. $238 AB 6-6666

The prospective renter gets the impression of a truly luxurious apartment when he sees "splendiferous" and "Roman bath."

14 St, 350 E.
2 Spectacular Skyline Views Great corner apt, 2½ rms, 19th fl, 4-yr old luxury bldg. Full of windows & light. Spacious living room, sleeping alcove. Sep kitchen, windowed bath. Contemporary w/Oriental antiques $210 Call CC 3-4567 aft 6 PM & wkend

Who can resist the appeal of an apartment with an excellent view? This one boasts of two.

HOUSES FOR SALE OR RENT

(See information about discrimination on page 252.) If you plan to advertise your house, do some careful planning before writing classified. A good classified can mean thousands of extra dollars in your pocket or, what may be even more important, a quick sale.

Here's an example of what I mean. Not long ago, a family in Piscataway Township, N. J., wanted to move to a larger house. They listed their home with five brokers, who for three months ran the following types of ads in the papers:

> PISCATAWAY Lake Nelson. Cozy 6-room ranch with fireplace, garage, tile bath, oil hot-water heat. Convenient to Rutgers campus, stadium, golf courses and primary school. $18,000.

> PISCATAWAY TOWNSHIP. Lake Nelson
>
> North side. 1st time offered. Ranch, living room, formal dining, eat-in-kitchen, family room with fireplace, 2 bedrooms, tiled bath, attached garage, oil burner hot water radiant heat, trees, established neighborhood ½ block from Randolphville School. Lake privileges. $17,900.

Now, there's nothing wrong with either of these ads. They give a fairly good description of the house, and in general, they're on a par with the hundreds of thousands of other real-estate classifieds that run in papers throughout the country.

However, no suitable buyers appeared. Then the wife took matters into her own hands, and wrote this advertisement:

> PISCATAWAY Lake Nelson north side.
>
> We'll miss our house. We've been comfortable in it, but 2 bedrooms are not enough for us, so we must move. If you like to be cozy by a fire while you admire autumn woods through wide windows, protected from the street; if you like a shady yard in summer; a clear view of winter sunsets and quiet enough to hear frogs in spring, but want city utilities and conveniences, you might like to buy our house. We hope so. We don't want it empty and alone at Christmas. The price is flexible.

Six people replied the next day, and the house was sold to one of them.

The last advertisement was successful because the inventive wife put herself into it—she wrote about what was important to her—and of course, it was important to potential buyers. Interestingly, she gave only the slightest bit of factual information about the house, namely, that it had two bedrooms. This was enough to snag the interest of anybody looking for a house of approximately that size; once the reader knew the house was large enough for him, it was almost impossible to avoid being intrigued by the rest of the ad.

Within that framework, then, what are the essentials of a good advertisement? Turning again to the *New York Times'* list, here are the kinds of information on which to base your classified. At the very least, consider which of these elements would be likely to interest a prospective buyer; then try to build your advertisement on them. Consider these points:

FOR HOUSES

1 Street address, section of city or name of town
2 Old or modern
3 Style and construction
4 Description of exterior: roof, copper leaders and gutters, screens, awnings, storm sash, size of plot or dimensions of property, lawn, gardens, trees, garage, etc.
5 Number of rooms
6 Description of interior: size of rooms and layout, number of baths, decorations, open fireplaces, floors, closets, sun porch, lighting fixtures, heating plant.
7 If furnished, description of furnishings: piano, radio, stove, refrigerator, dishes, etc.
8 Rental or selling price and terms.
9 Name of advertiser, address, and telephone number.
10 If a suburban house, consider including this information:
   a. Distance from stores, transportation, schools, etc.
   b. Running time from main railroad and bus terminals.

Examples:

Centreville Christmas in Conn.? Not for us. We've been transferred. Must leave comfortable home with 4 bdrms, 3 ceramic baths, liv rm w/frpl. Pvt area on waterfront. Beach and docking. Mins from RR and Tpke. We will miss our cool scrnd porch and open terrace next summer. Plantings & mature trees give pvcy. Many extras. For quick sale priced in low $50s. 888-777-6666 or your broker.

The question will immediately attract the attention of the reader. And note the human touch about the porch and terrace.

MIDDLETON Comfortable Home

FOR A HAPPY CHILDHOOD!

Cozy fireplace for winter night stories, family rm for TV & games, trees for climbing, lake for skating, playmates. This handsome 4 bedrm, 2½ bath Co. on a winding lane is for living "happily ever after." High $50s.

Some people (myself included) may feel that this classified is a bit too cute. Nevertheless, I found myself reading it closely, and getting a poetic image of how nice it would be to read stories to my own children by that fireplace.

FOR COUNTRY HOMES AND FARMS

1 Section of country: state, country, or name of town.
2 Size
3 Kind of farm
4 Describe house
5 Description of land: topography (hilly, rolling, flat, etc.), amount of tillage, amount of woodland and kinds of trees, orchard (state fruit), stream or brook on property.
6 Buildings, equipment, and stock: barns, stables, silo, chicken coops, amount of livestock and details, farming tools and equipment
7 Hunting, fishing, other recreational facilities
8 Distance from village, town, railroad, stores, schools, churches, main road; types of roads
9 Distance from important central city
10 Price and terms
11 Name of advertiser and address

Examples:

NEW ENGLAND VILLAGE COLONIAL

Circa 1790! Completely renovated & modernized. 14 rooms, 4 fireplaces, 1½ baths, sunporch. 2 good barns, outbldgs. Lovely grounds enclosed by stone wall. 45 acres, mostly woodland. Timber & sugar orchard, family fruit. $19,500. Near Rte. 17 Middleville. 333-444-5555

This is a good, simple, functional ad. Notice that it describes not only the buildings, but the stone wall—always a desirable feature.

EAST LITTLETON: moving, must sell, best offer, large Colonial house with 2 tenant houses. 16 acres, corner Rte. 216 and Smith Rd. 2000 ft. road front. An executive-type home.

This is just about the minimum you might put into an ad.

PECONIC BAY

Ideal summer home directly on water; 80 mi from N Y; 2 miles from village; exclusive private beach; splendid fishing and boating. House in center of property with water frontage of 387 feet and depth of 400 ft; Old English studio type with entire ground floor one immense room with alcoves for dining, library and music rooms; 2 large fireplaces downstairs, one upstairs; spacious porch on front and side, large kitchen, 4 bedrooms and 2 bathrooms upstairs, extra lavatory downstairs; furnished or unfurnished. Will sell for $50,000. A Smith, 123 Main St., Peconic Bay, N. Y. 999-123-4567.

This is probably a relatively small home: only one real room downstairs with "alcoves." But doesn't it sound majestic? Partly, this is because the advertiser has emphasized the extensive waterfront.

LOTS AND ACREAGE

(See information about discrimination on page 252.)

Information to include:

1 Street location, section of city or name of town
2 Exact location of lot (if in city, describe neighborhood)
3 Dimension of lot
4 Use best suited for

5 Improvements: gas, electricity, sewers, paved streets, sidewalks and curbs, restrictions, etc.
6 Distance from transit lines, business center, station, schools, etc.; distance from city or other central point
7 Price and terms
8 Name of advertiser, address, and telephone number

Examples:

NEWBROOK: 8 wooded hillside acres, 800 ft. front. Route 55, small stream. Beautiful vista. $4900. 666-777-8888

SMITHTOWN, wooded location, approx 3½ acres, rolling terrain, part lake, water piping. Box 8351

COLLINGFORD 119 × 100′ plot ready to build w/plans, survey, ctr hall Col home. 4 bdrms, 2½ bths, rec rm, 2 car gar. 111-222-3333

ROOM AND BOARD

(See information about discrimination on page 252.)
In the city:
Information to include:

1 Street, address, or section of city
2 Description of room
    a. Large or small
    b. Double or single
    c. Furnishings
    d. Number of persons that can be accommodated
    e. Exposure
    f. Number of windows
3 Improvements and conveniences
4 State type of cooking; "French cuisine," "southern cooking," "Kosher cooking"
5 Type of house
    a. State whether private or apartment house
    b. If private family state this, or say "no other boarders"
6 Transit facilities

7 Tenants desired: ("Gentlemen," "Lady," "business person," "couple," etc.)
8 References
9 Rates
10 Name and telephone number of advertiser (include address if not given at beginning of advertisement)

Examples:

Large sunny room, private home, excellent Amer. food for elderly lady. 222-4321

Two rooms, new furniture; for business couple. Large apt. near subway. $100 a month; ref. required. 111 Smith St.

Not much light, but, oh, my! If you want a room that makes you feel like a French nobleman, with Oriental rugs, 18th cent. furn., in beautiful private home near major public transport., you'll want to see this. Spacious enough for two to live very happily—at less than $75 monthly. Call 234-5678.

IN THE COUNTRY

1 Town, county, or section
2 Type of house (private, farm, boarding house, hotel)
3 Length of time established
4 Accommodations
   a. Single, double suites
   b. Private or semiprivate bath
   c. Running water
   d. Number of guests accommodated
5 Type of country, altitude
6 Sports available

a. Summer		b. Winter
Golf	Fishing	Skiing
Tennis	Riding	Skating
Swimming	Hiking	Hiking
Boating		Tobogganing
		Hunting

7 Distance from beach, golf course, transit, etc.

8 Other attractions
   a. Shady lawns
   b. Large porches, sun parlor, garden
   c. Size of grounds (number of acres)
9 Table
   a. Type of cuisine (French, Southern, etc.)
   b. Fresh vegetables
   c. Own garden
10 Open season
11 Traveling time or distance from major central points
12 Booklet (if one is issued)
13 Name and address of advertiser

When invalids, convalescents, or the aged are accommodated, the following information should also be included:

1 The kinds of patients accepted
2 Whether a registered physician or nurse is in attendance
3 Attention to diet

Examples:

TRAINED NURSE will care for elderly person, private home, own room. No stairs. Southern cooking. Light laundry. $150. South side of Centreville. ABC-1111

UPPER VALLEY REST HOME
Upper Valley, Nev.
An ideal home away from home for convalescent and elderly ladies. Competent staff with registered nurse on duty at all times. Dietary laws and special diets. Reasonable. 999-1234

FOR VACATIONERS

FOR A CHANGE
Enjoy yourself. Informal, modern hideaway for delightful, talented, creative guests. Folk and square dancing, cocktail parties, day camp. Winter sports, skiing nearby. 300 scenic acres are yours to be happy in.

The Pines
Centerville Hills
Tel: 123-456-7890

FUN IN THE SUN

Relax and enjoy the wonderful New Mexico climate . . . ride romantic desert trails . . . golf . . . swim . . . ride gentle horses by gentle moonlight . . . enjoy informal living in a friendly atmosphere with your friendly hosts. And bring your appetite. Write for our brochure and our moderate rates.

Mr. and Mrs. Jim Handy
Cupcake Ranch
Cupcake, New Mexico

WANT ADS

BOATS AND ACCESSORIES

In advertising a boat, remember that you're selling not just a piece of equipment, but a share of pleasure. If you can, try to get some of this feeling into your ad, along with a description of the hardware.

Information to include:

1 Type of boat
2 Dimensions
3 Make of motor, horsepower, speed
4 Cabin space and layout
   a. Galley
   b. Lavatory
5 Woodwork
6 Sleeping accommodations
7 Condition of boat
   a. Motor
   b. Hull
   c. Paint
8 Equipment
   a. Electric light
   b. Furnishings
   c. Kitchen and cooking equipment
   d. Life preservers, running gear, tools, etc.

e. Mooring lines and anchor buffers
f. Radio
g. Tender
9 Price and terms
10 Where and when boat may be seen
11 Name and address, telephone number of advertiser

Examples:

BOUGHT LARGER BOAT

Lovely aux. sloop. Must sell. 28′ × 19′ × 7′5″ × 4′. Built in Denmark 1958. Rugged mahogany and bronze. Berths 3, full galley, head, Palmer 22 HP rebuilt 1965, R.D.F., depth finder, lifeline, etc. Quite fast, very pretty. Painted and ready to launch in the spring at Mason Marina. Call 555-222-1111, or write Jameson, Box 333, Centreville.

BUY NOW, DREAM WINTER AWAY. Perfect family day sailer. 24 ft Fiberglas rainbow 1965. Solid, dry, safe. Huge cockpit for all the kids plus head. Or leave kids home and race (all racing gear and sails included). Worth $3,900; make offer. 111-2345, any time.

AUTOMOBILES

Points to be included:

1 Make of Car
2 Model
3 Year of model
4 Color
5 Horsepower
6 Special features
a. power steering
b. power brakes
c. power windows
d. power seat
e. power antenna
f. air conditioning
g. wire wheels
h. tape recorder

7 Mileage
8 Snow tires
9 General condition
   a. interior b. exterior
10 Price
11 Address, phone number of advertiser

Examples:

BUICK 865 Riviera, power steering, brakes, windows and antenna. Air conditioning, garaged; 5,000 miles. After 6 PM: 234-5678

CHEV. '62 Bel Air V8, 4 dr Sed. Power steer. Aut. trans. R/H Orig owner. No reason. offer refused. 123-4567

FORD 1960 Fairlane 500 2-dr sedan. Excel cond, power brakes & power steering, 8 cyl, no rust. 31,000 miles, orig. owner. Must sell. $670 or best offer. XY 8-5432

HELP WANTED

(See information about discrimination on page 252.)

A. For a commercial (non-domestic) position

Points to be included:

1 Start with a word or phrase describing the position
2 Requirements: age, education, experience
3 Nature of business, details of position, hours, possibilities of advancement, etc.
4 Compensation offered
5 References required
6 Name, address, and phone number, or box number

Examples:

SECRETARY

Delightful opening available for girl who can type at least 60 wpm, shorthand at 80 wpm, work for busy sales promotion account supervisor. Fine working conditions, good starting salary, company benefits, convenient location in midtown. Please call for confidential interview. A.B.C. Co., 222 E. Main St., AB 2-2222

"Delightful" is an unusual word to find in a help wanted ad, but it sets this classified apart from its competitors. It's good, too, because it spells out the employer's requirements and the benefits to the employee.

DICTAPHONE Secretary & Asst. to College Dept. English Editor. College graduate with intelligent interest in publishing essential. Box XYZ

Asst. bookkeeper, experienced, knowledge of typing, midtown location, reply in own handwriting. Box FGH

MAN FOR SHOP OFFICE

Of major distributor of construction equipment in metropolitan area. Prefer man experienced in dispatching trucks, handling service calls, knowledge of cost records & pricing. State age, exp. & salary desired. Box ABC

SHIPPING DEPT. SUPERVISOR

Metropolitan shoe manufacturer. Exc. working conditions and benefits. Send résumé stating salary. Box ABC

SALESMAN or sales engineer, aggressive, to sell commercial refrigeration, air conditioning & associated products. College grad or experience necessary. Need car. Drawing account or percentage plus expenses. Start Jan. 1. Call or write U.S. Air Conditioning Co., 111 E. 111th St., Centreville 623-456-7890

B. For domestic positions

Points to be included:

1 Start with a word or phrase describing the position, such as "Cook," "Lady's Maid," etc.
2 Requirements: age, experience, etc.
3 Number of adults and children, respectively
4 House or apartment
5 Place of employment, whether in city, suburbs, or country
   a. Winter home
   b. Summer home

6 Sleep in or out
7 Other help kept
8 Salary
9 References required
10 Name, address, and telephone number, or box number

Examples:

HOUSEKEEPER Excellent Salary

Small, informal home, attractive suburban community. Light housekeeping duties. Own room, TV; must love children–ages 5, 3 and infant. Older two in nursery school. Thursday & every other Sun. off. Call 234-5678

COMPANION for sick elderly lady. Exp., references. Sleep out. 5 days AB 3-4567

BABY-SITTER. Exchange baby-sitting for rm & board. Own rm/bth 123-4567

MAID. Large rooming house; read & write English. Assist in laundry rm & light maid duties. Union wages. 111 N. 11th St.

SITUATIONS WANTED

If you're looking for a job, a properly worded classified can help you to draw the attention of a likely employer. On the other hand, if you make a poor impression in your advertisement, it's like making a poor impression on an interview: you damage your chances of getting the job.

Selling your abilities in a classified is similar to selling a product. The more attractive you can make yourself, the greater interest you'll engender. A good way to plan any ad, then, is to write down the sort of job you'd like and the kind of company you'd like to work for.

Next, ask yourself, what kind of qualifications would an employer look for in a prospective employee? Make a list of these and then, beside it, list those of your own qualifications which might fit into the employer's requirements.

This information will give you a general idea of the kind of material you should include in your ad. The more specific you can be, the stronger your ad will be. Let's compare two examples that might have been prepared by the same person:

1. HOTEL & RESTAURANT MANAGER

Are you interested in a very capable industrious and experienced man? Please call: 123-4567 bet 6 & 10 PM

2. HOTEL & RESTAURANT MANAGER

20 yrs. exp. lge & small operations. Fluent Eng./Ger. Married. Seek day position. 123-4567 bet 6 & 10 PM

Classified 1 shows little planning, little skill at self-selling. Obviously, any prospective employer looking at the Situations Wanted column is interested in a capable, industrious, and experienced man. So the advertisement tells the employer nothing. When the job-seeker sits down and plans out his ad, however, he comes up with something like Classified 2. The prospective employer immediately sees that the job-seeker is not just "experienced," but that he has two decades of experience. He sees that the man can speak two languages. He sees that the man is married, and therefore assumes that he's likely to be a steady worker. And he sees that the man wants to work certain hours.

Obviously, Classified 2 will work harder for the job-seeker.

Keep the following points in mind when planning your Situations Wanted ad:

1 Type of job wanted
2 No. of years of experience doing similar work
3 What results can you show?
4 Have you related skills which might be valuable?

Examples:

ENGINEER CONSULTANT

Strong background on computer and hardware, electronic systems engineering. Commercial, government experience. Digital testing and circuit analysis, latest high-speed general computers. Box 3456

See how well this job-seeker describes his background.

COST ACCOUNTANT with master's and four years' job order experience seeking position within 30 miles of Centreville. Box 82

Designer-Patternmaker of children's and ladies underwear. Former manufacturer, did $200,000 annual bus. with chains and retail stores. Now employed, wish to work for expanding firm. Box 324

A prospective employer knows that this man can produce.

YALE GRADUATE, 27, writer, needs steady work Wed., Fri., Sat. Must take home $50 weekly. Knows sports and arts well. Box 2345

Here's an ad by a young man who is not too concerned with the type of work he does, but does spell out his needs and his interests.

LOST AND FOUND

Points to be included:

1 Article lost or found
2 Description
3 Location where article was lost or found
4 Date and time of day article was lost
5 Reward, if one is offered
6 Name, address, and telephone number of advertiser

The *New York Times* and many other papers do not accept ads which specify a store or hotel or any other commercial location as the site of the loss. They request that the wording read "between Macy's and Hotel Astor," or "vicinity of Macy's." This is done mainly to protect the commercial organization from legal claims by the advertiser, and to protect the newspaper from claims that might be brought against it by a commercial organization which felt it had been hurt by the ad. For your own protection, it may be a good idea to follow this practice in writing your own ads.

Examples:

PLATINUM earring 3 rows tiny diamonds (20). Lost Sat., 12/4, vic. Biltmore Hotel. Reward. Box 4567

GOLD WEDDING RING. Engraved name Matt. Reward $25 and keep pearl ring lost same time, vic. Public Library, June 5. Great sentimental value, husband now dead. Box 22

POODLE, miniature, hair short black, white stripe chest, lost Feb. 14, 3:00 PM, 73rd-Main Sts. Reward. MA 2-3245

MISSING PERSONS

These ads usually follow a standard format. The *New York Times* gives this example:

Brown–information sought regarding James G. Brown, who disappeared from his home, 00 West 96th Street, New York City, March 20, 1954. Age 55, dark complexion, brown eyes, dark brown hair, height 5′8″, slight build. Wore dark gray suit, tan shoes, blue overcoat, brown hat. Anyone having information as to his whereabouts communicate with John Jones, Attorney, 000 Broadway, Havemeyer 2-0000.

The information included in this type of ad consists of:

1 Last name of missing person
2 Full name of missing person
3 Where he disappeared from
4 When he disappeared
5 Physical description
   a. Age
   b. Complextion
   c. Color of eyes
   d. Color of hair
   e. Height
   f. General build
   g. Noticeable identifying marks
6 Clothing worn when last seen
   a. Suit
   b. Overcoat
   c. Hat
   d. Shoes
7 Name, address, and telephone number

LEGAL ANNOUNCEMENTS

Certain types of classified ads are of a legal rather than a commercial nature. You'll find three of the most common legal announcements below. But, a word of warning is in order.

Consult your lawyer before inserting them. While their formats are pretty generally standardized, a lawyer's advice is essential in order to ensure that your particular case is properly covered by the advertisement.

1. Sale of business

   John B. Jones sold confectionery store at 000 Amsterdam Avenue to Robert E. Smith. Submit all claims before April 1.

2. Husband-wife separation

   My wife, Mary Smith, having left my bed and board, I will no longer be responsible for any debts contracted by her. Roger Smith, 230 West 00 Street.

3. Dissolution of partnership

   The partnership of John Smith–David Blank, Inc., 00 West 00 St., will be dissolved effective July 31, 1964. (signed) John Smith
   David Blank

COMMERCIAL BUILDINGS

The classified-ad principles involved in renting or selling commercial buildings or apartments are similar to those involved in any other kind of property: give as much information as possible to interest prospective buyers or renters. Here's the kind of information that might be included for

FACTORIES

1 Street location, section of city, or name of town
2 State whether building is for sale or lease
3 Number of stories
4 Depth and frontage of building
5 Use best suited for

6 Total floor space
7 Floor loading capacity in pounds
8 Improvements: elevator, live steam, electric power supply, lighting arrangements such as windows, skylights, etc.
9 Fire safeguards: fireproof construction material, sprinkler system, fire escapes
10 Shipping facilities: yards, driveways, loading platforms, railroad siding, distance from terminals, etc.
11 Price and terms, or rental
12 Name of advertiser, address, and telephone number

Examples:

EXCEPTIONAL BUSINESS BUILDING

for lease on long-term basis. 4-story fireproof, 100% central air conditioning. Plot 115 × 102. 40,000 sq. ft., 10,000 sq. ft. each floor. If required, can add two floors, making total of 60,000 sq. ft. Possession any time. All clear floors, good floor load, excellent light. Suitable heavy and light mfg. Five-year-old building. Rental $120,000 per year net. Assessment $750,000, 1966–1967. Mid-Centreville location. James B. Smith, Owner, 111 W. 111th Street. AB 1-2345

A REMARKABLE VALUE

38 St (near 7 Ave). 2,500 sq ft capacity, 225 pounds per sq ft, daylight on all sides, suitable light manufacturing, fireproof brick building, 12′ ceilings, cement floors, sprinkler system throughout, fire escapes; self-service passenger and freight elevators, live steam available to large consumers, also high-voltage current supply; excellent shipping facilities, loading platforms; near piers, railroad, bridges. $8,000 yearly; month's concession. 5-year lease. Immediate possession. Joe's Realty, 00 W. 42 St., LA 4-4000

STORES

Information to include:

1 Street location, section of city, or name of town
2 Dimensions of store
3 Use best suited for
4 Kind of neighborhood: residential, business, theatrical, etc.

5 Improvements: window space, fixtures, etc.
6 Location on street: corner, middle of block, etc.
7 Distance from transit facilities, main arteries, etc.
8 Terms: rent, lease, etc.
9 Date available for occupancy
10 Name of advertiser, address, and telephone number

Example:

CENTERVILLE
Fabulous

Near Woolworths and other big chains; 25 ft. glass frontage (3100 sq. ft. sales space plus 2,000 ft. storage); heart of town, 500,000 people and focal point of 15 bus routes and trains; more than $15 million sales in this area last year! Available now, completely fixtured and air-conditioned at very attractive rental.

James C. Johnson
32 Centerville St.
Centerville
AL 5-5555

APARTMENT HOUSES

Information to include:

1 Street location, section of city, or name of town
2 Number of stories
3 Depth and frontage
4 Number of apartments and layout
5 If building includes stores, give details
6 Improvements: passenger and service elevators, heating equipment, refrigeration, incinerator, plumbing, etc.
7 Condition
8 Per cent rented
9 Average gross rental
10 Price and terms: mortgages, annual amortization, cash required
11 Name of advertiser, address, and telephone number

Example:

CENTERVILLE
111 Avenue

6 floors, 100′ × 150′, corner location; 30 apartments, 10 twos, 10 threes, 10 fours; basement garage; main facades of building face south and east; tailor, drug, grocery, and stationery stores; signal control elevator; oil burner; automatic electric hot water heater; hardwood floors, tiled halls, baths; copper plumbing; only 10 years old; in excellent condition; 100% rented; gross rental $60,000, nets 8%. Price $200,000. Cash required only $40,000. Liberal terms.

J. B. SMITH

123 4th St. (111) 222-3456

BUSINESS OPPORTUNITIES

Under this classification we include advertisements relevant to the buying, selling, leasing, and renting of a variety of goods and services, and to the obtaining or investing of capital. This material is based on a booklet, "How to Write a Better 'Business Opportunities' Advertisement," published by the *New York Times.*

CAPITAL WANTED

Include the following information:

1 Whether active partner or inactive investor is wanted
2 Amount of capital and purpose for which it is required
3 Type of business, new or established
4 Annual volume of sales
5 Box number or name and address and/or phone.

Examples:

Established
PLASTIC
GOODS
Manufacturer

Wishes to expand $700,000 a year business. Complete modern plant.

Facilities to triple present volume. Unusual opportunity for active partner or investor with $150,000.

John A. Jones

000 W. 00 St. AB 3-4567

GO-GETTER WANTED

To join nationally known mail-order house doing $300,000 business. Invest $25,000 for one-third interest. Good income. Write giving details of experience, background. Box Y1000

CAPITAL TO INVEST

Include the following information:

1 Nature of business sought
2 Location
3 Amount of capital available
4 Extent of participation
5 Extent of experience
6 Box number, or name and address and/or phone.

Examples:

$50,000 TO INVEST
IN METAL PLANT

Prefer shop in Connecticut with general-purpose working machinery, lathes, milling machines, drill presses, etc., or stamping equipment such as punch presses and shears. Former production manager. Fully capable of active participation in executive capacity. Box X123

COLLEGE GRAD

Man, 31, married, excellent business references, invest services, moderate capital or buy profitable working business anywhere USA. Box 678

BUSINESS CONNECTION

Information to include:

1 Service offered
2 Type and purpose of connection
3 Requirements or qualifications

4 Remuneration
5 Box number or name and address and/or phone

Examples:

SALES-MANUFACTURING-ADMINISTRATION

Young executive (37), capable, complete charge manufacturing concern. Experienced sales, production, administration. Has set up plants. Would make valuable assistant to president, larger concerns. American citizen residing in Canada, willing to relocate. Will accept $15,000 year. Box V567

CONTROLLING interest available in an old, well-established home improvement sales organization with an excellent name and background in the community. Located in Essex County, Conn. Excellent opportunity for an experienced man or merger. Box 9876

RETAIL BUSINESS

Information to include:

1 Type and size of store
2 Location
3 How long established
4 Equipment and inventory
5 Parking facilities
6 Annual volume
7 Reason for selling
8 Sale or rental terms
9 Box number, or name and address and/or phone

Examples:

DRUG STORE

Showing Enormous Net Profit

Outstanding location in downtown city. 40′ × 80′. Doing $600,000 annually, 175-200 Rxs daily. Rent $350–500, long lease. Fountain business $60,000 more than pays rent. $100,000 cash necessary includes $60,000 inventory; owner retiring. Write Box 5678

BEAUTY SHOP, established 20 years in heavily populated section. 8 booths, all equipment, 2-story brick building, six beautiful rooms. High-type clientele. Gross $40,000 a year. Complete price $22,500. Retiring. Call FL 2-0000

DEPARTMENTS AND CONCESSIONS

Information to include:

1 Type
2 Location
3 Equipment and inventory
4 Annual volume
5 Clientele
6 Parking facilities
7 Percentage or rental terms
8 Box number or name and address and/or phone

Examples:

MEN'S haberdashery department for rent in midtown men's fine clothing store, doing $115,000 volume. Steady patronage with heavy transients. Department ready for business, excellent opportunity for full-experienced, style-conscious young man. Call YU 9-0000

NURSERY FURNITURE

Unusual opportunity to buy one of the top nursery furniture stores in Michigan. Well established. Rated tops in field. Quality operation, unlimited opportunity to branch out in red-hot area. Must be ambitious and young. Retiring because of old age. Will consider selling half now, the rest later. Box ABCD.

RETIRING to Florida. You must see this beautiful liquor store to appreciate it. Priced for quick sale. 567-8902

CHOICE LOCATION—GOURMET GROCERY

Established 20 years on West 73rd St. $26,000 including stock and fixtures. Ill health forces sale. Pkg. for eight cars. 567-2222

SNACK bar and beach chair concession at new exclusive beach club,

North Long Beach, nets $12,500. Excellent opportunity for experienced concessionaire. Percentage basis. Box 00.

HOTELS AND ROOMING HOUSES

Information to include:

1 Location
2 Number of rooms, dining facilities
3 How long established
4 Volume of business, gross or net
5 Furnishings and equipment
6 Special features
7 Whether seasonal or all-year
8 Sale or rental terms
9 Box number or name and address and/or phone

Example:

YEAR-ROUND HOTEL
WHITE MTS

A 45-acre vacation resort established 25 years, offering riding, golfing (9-hole course), fishing and swimming on the premises; ½ mile frontage on main highway. 22 guest rooms, all but two with running water. 10 baths. Modern equipped kitchen. Dining room handles 38. Large lobby with twin fireplaces. Nets $15,000 during summer. Winter business varies according to snow conditions. Completely furnished and equipped. $38,000. Box 21.

RESTAURANTS, BARS AND GRILLS

Information to include:

1 Location
2 Parking facilities
3 Cuisine
4 Seating capacity
5 Equipment (description and condition)
6 Volume of business
7 Price, terms
8 Box number and name and address and/or phone

Examples:

MONEY-MAKING
RESTAURANT

Established 1947; French cuisine. $30,000 income reported last year; well known for its fine foods and pleasant surroundings; seats 60. Splendidly equipped, well-stocked; 28′ × 70′ building, modern living quarters. On U.S. Highway, in town. Parking in rear. Low price—$16,000; terms. Owner's incapacitation only reason for sale. B. G. Foreman, 65 Main St., Middleburg

BAR & GRILL, Cocktail Lounge

In city; seats 40, completely equipped, grossing $1,200 weekly; long lease; modern refrigeration equipment. Unusually good location; priced for quick turnover. Call Mr. Green, MU 3-4567

GARAGES AND GASOLINE STATIONS

Information to include:

1 Location in relation to highways and routes
2 Frontage
3 How long established
4 Number of pumps
5 Servicing facilities (equipment)
6 Sale or rental terms
7 Box number or name and address and/or phone

Examples:

TEXACO gas station, new; block front. 10-year lease, 6 bays, auto laundry, wheel alignment, etc. $10,000 cash necessary. 1868 Oak Blvd., between Arcade and Bentley Aves. Inspect and call. Cape Oil Co., BY 3-9876

GARAGE MIDDLEVILLE
CHOICE MIDTOWN SECTION

In business 10 years. Approx. 55,000 sq ft, 3 floors, 2 ramps, 1 elevator. Accommodates 300 cars. Repair facilities. 1 pump. New long-term lease direct from landlord. $40,000, terms. Call RE 6-8763

PROFESSIONAL PRACTICE OR OFFICE

Information to include:

1 Type of practice
2 How long established
3 Location
4 Volume of business
5 Equipment, furnishings
6 Reason for selling
7 Sale or rental terms
8 Box number or name and address and/or phone

Examples:

DENTAL PRACTICE
Exceptional Opportunity
Highly lucrative. In outstanding mid-town location. Doing over $12,000 year on part-time basis. 1964 operated full time, grossed over $20,000. Established 21 years. Rent $60 month. Fully equipped; 2 operating chairs. Will remain 3 months. Retiring. $6,000 cash necessary. Box 4567

OPTOMETRIST practice in Middleville. Illness compels disposal. Grossing $16,000 with unusually high net earnings. Moderate rental in growing business area. $10,000 cash required. Box 3425.

PHYSICIAN'S OFFICE in Manhattan, equipped, including late model 100MA Picker X-ray, Cambridge EKG-stethogram and Jones metabolism machines. Sacrifice. Leaving town. 20-year practice free. $10,000 cash required. BY 6-3000

CAMPS

Information to include:

1 Location
2 Whether girls, boys, or co-ed
3 Accommodations
4 Equipment, facilities
5 Recreational features

6 Camper's fee
7 Price, terms
8 Box number or name and address and/or phone

Examples:

CO-ED CAMP

Reputable camp in Poconos for sale; accommodates 250, plus facilities for parents. Modern, up-to-date buildings, all with plumbing. Attractive lake, elevation 1,600′. Present director will cooperate. Well booked. Fee $560. Price $100,000. Attractive terms. Available to experienced and responsible buyer. Box 348.

BOYS' camp for sale on Lake George; accommodations for 300; equipped; large enrollment; fee $350. Immediate sale, $125,000, terms. Jones, 00 W. 00 St.

TOURIST COURTS AND MOTELS

Information to include:

1 Location
2 Number of units, description
3 Furnishings, equipment, utilities
4 Dining facilities
5 Recreational facilities
6 Volume of business
7 Sale, rental, terms
8 Box number or name and address and/or phone

Examples:

TOURIST HOME & SKI LODGE

Centerville, Vt.; in town, on U.S. Hway; est. 1958; completely furn & eqpd; attractive dwelling. 12 rms, 3½ baths; steam heat, elec; also ski lodge with built-in bunks, bath, shower, extra lavatory & toilet; servant quarters; 3 acres, brook borders; river view; last year gross $20,000; sacrifice for quick sale, $15,000, terms. Box 555

MOTEL, completely modern, 20 rooms plus manager's apartment; excellent earnings record. $40,000 year; mild climate in beautiful

Ozarks. Attractive stone buildings. Beautifully landscaped, spacious grounds. Completely furnished, all utilities, including restaurant. $25,-000, terms. Box 960

PATENTS:

Information to include:

1 Kind of patent
2 Uses
3 Features
4 Preference for outright sale or royalty
5 Box number or name and address and/or phone

Examples:

SELL outright patent or manufacturing rights to safety manicuring clipper; also combination safety razor and stropping holder. Low manufacturing cost. Tremendous market. Suggested selling price $5. Martin Essex, Middletown.

AMAZING SWISS
INVENTION

Offered to American producer with factory equipped to turn out small brass parts and plastic molds for new sealed electric connection. Royalty basis. Only reputable firms will be considered.

BOX 5600

BUSINESS SERVICES

Information to include:

1 Type of service
2 Special features
3 Price of rates
4 Box number or name and address and/or phone

Examples:

USE PICTURE POSTCARDS
To Sell Your Merchandise
5000 PICTURE POSTCARDS $12.50M

4000 PICTURE POSTCARDS $13.50M
3000 PICTURE POSTCARDS $14.00M
2000 PICTURE POSTCARDS $17.00M
MADE FROM YOUR PHOTOGRAPH
FREE! YOUR AD ON BACK OF CARD!
Cardmakers
6767 Main Street
Middleville

REDUCE

Your art costs. Major out-of-town art and production studio seeks contract art work. Low overhead. Former N.Y. designers, artists and illustrators. Pick up and delivery daily. Write Mason Associates, 00 Main Street, Middletown.

OFFSET—SHORT RUNS

50 copies 8½ × 11, $1.80; 100 copies 8½ × 11, $2.20; add'l 100's 60¢. Min. order $3.00. Price list avail. Media Printing, 321 Main St. 432-4567.

APPENDIX: TABLE OF SALUTATIONS AND ADDRESSES

U. S. GOVERNMENT OFFICIALS

PERSON	ADDRESS	SALUTATION
The President	The President The White House Washington, D. C. 20500	Dear Mr. President or Dear Mr. (last name)
The Vice President	The Vice President United States Senate Washington, D. C. 20510	Dear Mr. (last name)
Chief Justice of the U. S.	The Chief Justice The Supreme Court Washington, D. C. 20543	Dear Mr. (last name)
Associate Justice of the U. S. Supreme Court	Mr. Justice (last name) The Supreme Court Washington, D. C. 20543	Dear Mr. (last name)
Speaker of the House of Representatives	Mr. (full name) Speaker of the House of Representatives Washington, D. C. 20515	Dear Mr. (last name)

PERSON	ADDRESS	SALUTATION
Cabinet Officer	Mr. (full name) Secretary of the Interior Washington, D. C. 20240	Dear Mr., Miss, or Mrs. (last name)
Under (or Assistant or Deputy) Secretary of a Department	Mr. (full name) Under (or Assistant or Deputy) Secretary of [Department] Washington, D. C. (Zip Code)	Dear Mr., Miss, or Mrs. (last name)
Director of an Office, or Chief of a Division or Bureau	Mr. (full name) Chief, Bureau of [name of Bureau or Division] Washington, D. C. (Zip Code)	Dear Mr., Miss, or Mrs. (last name)
U. S. Senator	Mr. (full name) United States Senate Washington, D. C. 20510	Dear Mr., Miss, or Mrs. (last name)
U. S. Representative	Mr. (full name) House of Representatives Washington, D. C. 20515	Dear Mr., Miss, or Mrs. (last name)
Resident Commissioner	Mr. (full name) Resident Commissioner of [area] Washington, D. C. (Zip Code)	Dear Mr., Miss, or Mrs. (last name)
Presidential Secretary	Mr. (full name) Secretary to the President The White House Washington, D. C. 20500	Dear Mr., Miss, or Mrs. (last name)

Presidential Secretary with Military Rank	General (full name) Secretary to the President The White House Washington, D. C. 20500	Dear General (last name)
Assistant Presidential Secretary	Mr. (full name) Assistant Secretary to the President The White House Washington, D. C. 20500	Dear Mr., Miss, or Mrs. (last name)
All Other U. S. Government Officials	Mr. (full name) Title Washington, D. C. (Zip Code)	Dear Mr., Miss, or Mrs. (last name)

LOCAL AND STATE OFFICIALS

State Governor	Mr. (full name) Governor of (state) (capital city, state, Zip Code)	Dear Mr., Miss, or Mrs. (last name) or Dear Governor (last name)
Lt. Governor	Mr. (full name) Lt. Governor of (state) (capital city, state, Zip Code)	Dear Mr. (last name)
All Other Nonjudicial Officials	Mr. (full name) Title Address	Dear Mr. (last name)

COURT OFFICIALS

State Supreme Court Chief Justice	Mr. (full name) Chief Justice of the Supreme Court of (state)	Dear Judge (last name) or Dear Mr. Chief Justice:

PERSON	ADDRESS	SALUTATION
State Supreme Court Chief Justice (*cont'd*)	(capital city, state, Zip Code) or The Honorable (full name) Chief Justice of the Supreme Court of (state) (capital city, state, Zip Code)	
Presiding Justice	Mr. (full name) Presiding Justice, Appellate Division Supreme Court, (city, state, Zip Code)	Dear Mr. (or Madame) Justice:
Court Judge	Mr. (full name) Judge of the United States District Court for the Southern District of (state) (city, state, Zip Code)	Dear Judge (last name)
Clerks of Courts	Mr. (Full name) Clerk of the (name of court) (city, state, Zip Code)	Dear Mr., Miss, or Mrs. (last name)

U. S. DIPLOMATIC OFFICIALS

U. S. Ambassadors	Mr. (full name) American Ambassador (city, country) or The Honorable (full name) American Ambassador (city, country)	Dear Mr. or Madame (last name) or Dear Mr. or Madame Ambassador

U. S. Ministers	Mr. (full name) American Minister (city, country)	Dear Mr., or Madame (last name) or Dear Mr. or Madame Minister
U. S. Chargé d'Affaires ad Interim	Mr. (full name) American Chargé d'Affaires ad Interim (city, country)	Dear Mr. or Madame (last name)
U. S. Consul General, Consul, or Vice-Consul	Mr. (full name) American Consul General or American Consul or American Vice-Consul (city, country)	Dear Mr. or Madame (last name)
High Commissioner	Mr. (full name) United States High Commissioner to (country) (city, country)	Dear Mr. or Madame (last name)
U. S. Delegate to the United Nations	Mr. (full name) or The Honorable (full name) Chief of the United States Mission to the United Nations New York, N. Y. 10017	Dear Mr. or Madame (last name) or Dear Mr. or Madame Ambassador

FOREIGN OFFICIALS

Because foreign officials are likely to cherish protocol a bit more than their U. S. counterparts, it may be wise to stick to the more traditional forms of address.

PERSON	ADDRESS	SALUTATION
Foreign Ambassador in the U. S.	His Excellency (full name) Ambassador of (country) Washington, D. C. (zip code) (Note: Use the name of the country from which the ambassador comes in all cases except that of Great Britain. All of Great Britain's ministers in the U. S. should be addressed as British Minister, British Ambassador, etc.)	Dear Mr. or Madame Ambassador
Foreign Minister in the U. S.	The Honorable (full name) Minister of (country) Washington, D. C. (Zip Code)	Dear Mr. or Madame Minister
Diplomatic Official with a Personal Title	His Excellency, Count (full name) Ambassador of (country) Washington, D. C. (Zip Code)	Dear Mr. or Madame Ambassador
Secretary General of the United Nations	Mr. (full name) Secretary General of the United Nations New York, N. Y. 10017	Dear Mr. or Madame (last name)
President of a Republic	His Excellency (full name) President of the Republic of (country) (capital city, country)	Dear Mr. President

Prime Minister of Great Britain	The Right Honorable (full name), M.P. Prime Minister London, England	Dear Mr. (last name)
Prime Minister of Canada	The Right Honorable (full name), C.M.G. Prime Minister of the Dominion of Canada Ottawa, Canada	Dear Mr. (last name)

U. S. ARMY AND U. S. MARINE CORPS OFFICERS

When addressing a letter to an officer in the Regular Army, put a comma after his name, followed by USA. If he's retired, put a comma after his name followed by USA (Ret.).

When addressing a letter to an officer in the United States Army Reserve, after his name, put in a comma, followed by USAR. Note that Army usage calls for no periods after the initials.

If he's retired, put a comma after his name, followed by (Ret.).

If he's in the Reserves and retired, put a comma after his name, followed by USAR-(Ret.).

If he's in the Marine Corps, use USMCR to indicate that he's in the Reserves.

If he's retired, use USMCR (Ret.).

General, Lt. General, Major General, Brigadier General	General (full name) (address)	Dear General (last name)
Colonel, Lt. Colonel	Colonel (full name) (address)	Dear Colonel (last name)
Major	Major (full name) (address)	Dear Major (last name)
Captain	Captain (full name) (address)	Dear Captain (last name)
First Lieutenant Second Lieutenant	Lieutenant (full name) (address)	Dear Lieutenant (last name)
Chaplain	Chaplain (full name) (Rank), USA (or USAR) (address)	Dear Chaplain

U. S. NAVY OFFICERS

When addressing a letter to an officer in the Regular Navy, put a comma after his name, followed by USN.

If he's retired from the Regular Navy, put a comma after his name followed by USN (Ret.).

If he's in the Navy Reserve, put a comma after his name followed by USNR.

If he's retired from the Navy Reserve, put a comma after his name followed by USNR (Ret.).

PERSON	ADDRESS	SALUTATION
Fleet Admiral	Fleet Admiral (full name) (address)	Dear Admiral (last name)
Vice Admiral	Vice Admiral (full name) (address)	Dear Admiral (last name)
Rear Admiral	Commodore (full name) (address)	Dear Commodore (last name)
Captain	Captain (full name) (address)	Dear Captain (last name)
Commander	Commander (full name) (address)	Dear Commander (last name)
Lieutenant Commander	Lieutenant Commander (full name) (address)	Dear Mr. (last name)
Lieutenant	Lieutenant (full name) (address)	Dear Mr. (last name)
Lieutenant, Jr. Grade	Lieutenant, J.G. (full name) (address)	Dear Mr. (last name)
Ensign	Ensign (full name) (address)	Dear Mr. (last name)
Chaplain	Captain (full name) (Ch.C.) (address)	Dear Chaplain (last name)

CATHOLIC CLERGY

The Pope	His Holiness The Pope Vatican City Italy	Your Holiness
Cardinal	His Eminence (first name) Cardinal (last name) Archbishop of (name of area) (address)	Dear Cardinal (last name)
Archbishop	The Most Reverend (full name) Archbishop of (area) (address)	Dear Archbishop
Bishop	The Most Reverend (full name) Bishop of (area) (address)	Dear Bishop
Abbot	The Right Reverend (full name) Abbot of (abbey) (address)	Dear Father Abbot
Canon	The Very Reverend Canon (full name) Canon of (name of church) (address)	Dear Canon (last name)
Monsignor	The Right (or Very)* Reverend Msgr. (full name) (address)	Dear Monsignor (last name)
Brother	Brother (full name) (address)	Dear Brother (last name)

* Depends upon rank or other titles. See *Official Catholic Directory* in case of doubt.

PERSON	ADDRESS	SALUTATION
Superior of a Brotherhood and Priest	The Very Reverend (full name) (title) (address)	Dear Father Superior
Priest	The Reverend (full name) (address)	Dear Father (last name)
Sister Superior	The Reverend Sister Superior (address)	Dear Sister Superior
Sister	Sister Mary Pia (address)	Dear Sister
Mother Superior of Sisterhood	The Reverend Mother Superior (name of convent) (address)	Dear Reverend Mother
Member of Community	Mother (full name) (name of convent) (address)	Dear Mother (last name)

PROTESTANT CLERGY

PERSON	ADDRESS	SALUTATION
Anglican Archbishop	To His Grace The Lord Archbishop of (area) (address)	Dear Archbishop
Presiding Bishop of the Protestant Episcopal Church in the U. S.	The Most Reverend (full name) Presiding Bishop of the Protestant Episcopal Church in America (address)	Dear Bishop

Methodist Bishop	The Reverend Bishop (last name) Methodist Bishop (address)	Dear Bishop
Protestant Episcopal Bishop	The Right Reverend (full name) Bishop of (area) (address)	Dear Bishop
Protestant Archdeacon	The Venerable (full name) The Archdeacon of (area) Diocese of (area) (address)	Dear Archdeacon
Dean	The Very Reverend (full name) Dean of (cathedral or seminary) (address)	Dear Dean (last name)
Protestant Minister or Priest	The Reverend (full name) (address)	Dear Mr. (last name) Note: If he possesses a doctoral degree, e.g., Ph.D., D.D., etc., he may be addressed Dear Dr. (last name)

JEWISH CLERGY

Rabbi	Rabbi (full name) (address)	Dear Rabbi (last name) If he possesses a doctoral degree, e.g., Ph.D., D.D., etc., he may be addressed Dear Dr. (last name)

COLLEGE OFFICIALS

PERSON	ADDRESS	SALUTATION
College or University President	Mr. (or Dr., if he has a doctoral degree) (full name) President (college or university) (address)	Dear Mr. (or Dr.) (last name)
College or University Chancellor	Mr. (or Dr. if he has a doctoral degree) (full name) Chancellor (college or university) (address)	Dear Mr. (or Dr.) (last name)
Professor	Mr. (or Dr., if he has a doctoral degree) (full name) (college or university) (address)	Dear Mr. (or Dr.) (last name)
Dean or Assistant Dean	Mr. (or Dr., if he has a doctoral degree) (full name) Dean (school or department) (college or university) (address)	Dear Mr. (or Dr. or Dean) (last name)

INDEX